YouTube® Channels
FOR
DUMMIES®
A Wiley Brand

by Rob Ciampa and Theresa Moore,
with John Carucci, Stan Muller,
and Adam Wescott

FOR
DUMMIES®
A Wiley Brand

YouTube® Channels For Dummies®

Published by: **John Wiley & Sons, Inc.,** 111 River Street, Hoboken, NJ 07030-5774, www.wiley.com

Copyright © 2015 by John Wiley & Sons, Inc., Hoboken, New Jersey

Published simultaneously in Canada

No part of this publication may be reproduced, stored in a retrieval system or transmitted in any form or by any means, electronic, mechanical, photocopying, recording, scanning or otherwise, except as permitted under Sections 107 or 108 of the 1976 United States Copyright Act, without the prior written permission of the Publisher. Requests to the Publisher for permission should be addressed to the Permissions Department, John Wiley & Sons, Inc., 111 River Street, Hoboken, NJ 07030, (201) 748-6011, fax (201) 748-6008, or online at http://www.wiley.com/go/permissions.

Trademarks: Wiley, For Dummies, the Dummies Man logo, Dummies.com, Making Everything Easier, and related trade dress are trademarks or registered trademarks of John Wiley & Sons, Inc. and may not be used without written permission. YouTube is a registered trademark of Google, Inc. All other trademarks are the property of their respective owners. John Wiley & Sons, Inc. is not associated with any product or vendor mentioned in this book.

LIMIT OF LIABILITY/DISCLAIMER OF WARRANTY: THE PUBLISHER AND THE AUTHOR MAKE NO REPRESENTATIONS OR WARRANTIES WITH RESPECT TO THE ACCURACY OR COMPLETENESS OF THE CONTENTS OF THIS WORK AND SPECIFICALLY DISCLAIM ALL WARRANTIES, INCLUDING WITHOUT LIMITATION WARRANTIES OF FITNESS FOR A PARTICULAR PURPOSE. NO WARRANTY MAY BE CREATED OR EXTENDED BY SALES OR PROMOTIONAL MATERIALS. THE ADVICE AND STRATEGIES CONTAINED HEREIN MAY NOT BE SUITABLE FOR EVERY SITUATION. THIS WORK IS SOLD WITH THE UNDERSTANDING THAT THE PUBLISHER IS NOT ENGAGED IN RENDERING LEGAL, ACCOUNTING, OR OTHER PROFESSIONAL SERVICES. IF PROFESSIONAL ASSISTANCE IS REQUIRED, THE SERVICES OF A COMPETENT PROFESSIONAL PERSON SHOULD BE SOUGHT. NEITHER THE PUBLISHER NOR THE AUTHOR SHALL BE LIABLE FOR DAMAGES ARISING HEREFROM. THE FACT THAT AN ORGANIZATION OR WEBSITE IS REFERRED TO IN THIS WORK AS A CITATION AND/OR A POTENTIAL SOURCE OF FURTHER INFORMATION DOES NOT MEAN THAT THE AUTHOR OR THE PUBLISHER ENDORSES THE INFORMATION THE ORGANIZATION OR WEBSITE MAY PROVIDE OR RECOMMENDATIONS IT MAY MAKE. FURTHER, READERS SHOULD BE AWARE THAT INTERNET WEBSITES LISTED IN THIS WORK MAY HAVE CHANGED OR DISAPPEARED BETWEEN WHEN THIS WORK WAS WRITTEN AND WHEN IT IS READ.

For general information on our other products and services, please contact our Customer Care Department within the U.S. at 877-762-2974, outside the U.S. at 317-572-3993, or fax 317-572-4002. For technical support, please visit www.wiley.com/techsupport.

Wiley publishes in a variety of print and electronic formats and by print-on-demand. Some material included with standard print versions of this book may not be included in e-books or in print-on-demand. If this book refers to media such as a CD or DVD that is not included in the version you purchased, you may download this material at http://booksupport.wiley.com. For more information about Wiley products, visit www.wiley.com.

Library of Congress Control Number: 2014948511

ISBN: 978-1-118-95817-9; 978-1-118-95818-6 (ebk); 978-1-118-95906-0 (ebk)

Manufactured in the United States of America

C10003294_081418

Contents at a Glance

Table of Contents

Introduction

Maybe you're looking to become a YouTube sensation with your next video or you simply want to share your insights or your particular expertise with the world. Perhaps you'd even like to use YouTube and video to help your business, which could be a local coffee shop or a Fortune 500 company. No matter how you plan to make use of your video-making skills, YouTube has made sharing the results of those skills easy. And with the tips and techniques included within the pages of *YouTube Channels For Dummies,* you'll be ready to take full advantage of YouTube's user-friendly platform when creating your very own YouTube channel.

To get a better sense of how YouTube has changed the entertainment playing field, cast your mind back to ten or so years before the turn of the millennium — if you can remember back that far. Despite an explosion of ever better and ever cheaper video equipment for consumers, sharing a video still meant gathering family and friends around your giant 25-inch, tube-laden television screen so that everyone could watch your latest video masterpiece. Back in those days, someone who wasn't in the room watching along was clean out of luck.

YouTube changed all that. It globalized the viewing experience, reinventing how people show videos by making it possible to share with audiences considerably larger than that bunch of friends and family gathered around the TV set eating popcorn. Any viewer who wanted to see any video anywhere in the world only had to type www.youtube.com into their favorite browser, search for the video they wanted to see, and click the Play button — and there it was.

As easy as it is for a viewer to take full advantage of YouTube, it's almost as easy for a contributor to become part of the YouTube mix. After setting up an account, it's a snap to start uploading video. And, if the video you're uploading takes off, you could become famous and even earn a good chunk of change from your YouTube exploits.

Notice that we said "if the video you're uploading takes off." That can be a very big *if.* Not just any video will do. The truth of the matter is that the low-quality, badly shot videos that were still popular a few years ago no longer cut the mustard. Viewers expect higher quality these days, which is why you need to step up your game and produce the best possible content. This book can help show you the way.

About This Book

In some ways, reading a book to find out all about YouTube channels seems a bit odd. Isn't YouTube the place that specializes in videos designed to teach you about any topic on earth? Why not just stick with the YouTube videos that are all about YouTube?

First off, it's a bit self-referential and incestuous to get all your information about YouTube channels from YouTube videos. Second, that video purporting to tell you how to strike it rich on YouTube may have been shot and edited by the neighbor kid down the street who has never made a dime from YouTube and who may never move out of Mom and Dad's basement. In other words, just as you shouldn't believe everything you read on the Internet, you shouldn't believe everything you see on YouTube. Sometimes it pays to listen to the true experts (like us) who have a track record in advising folks how to put their best foot forward on YouTube.

We also know that there are only so many hours in a day and that everyone's schedules seem to be getting more and more hectic each day. That's why we've written a book that doesn't beat around the bush — in other words, it gets straight to the point so that you can get in and get out with the information you need. In that sense, *YouTube Channels For Dummies* is the exact opposite of all those wordy instructional manuals that spell out a hundred ways to do something but never get around to telling you the best way. No matter if you're looking to set up a channel, create an effective header, or figure out ways to maximize your monetization potential, we show you the quickest, most effective way to get the job done.

Foolish Assumptions

Whether you're an experienced videographer or you just bought your first camcorder, you should treat YouTube with an open mind. Just because it's easy to make a video and upload it to YouTube doesn't mean that you won't hit the occasional bump in the road, so don't fool yourself into thinking you don't need help from time to time.

That goes for pretty much everyone, from pros make a living producing video to ambitious students looking to showcase edgy movie shorts to absolute beginners looking to upload their first video. Regardless of whether you identify with one of these situations or you have a truly unique one, you'll find content in these pages just for you. See whether you can see yourself in one of these categories:

- ✔ **Newbies:** You shoot lots of videos but have never uploaded one to YouTube. But then the feeling overtook you to upload your best ones and share them with the world. No problem: This book can answer some of your most basic questions.

   You want your movies to look really cool so that you can post them on YouTube and all your other favorite social media haunts, and if you use this book to answer your most basic questions, trust us — your movies will be awesome.

   This book doesn't require your fluency in technospeak. Instead, it's written using a down-to-earth tone. Through clearly written explanations, lists, illustrations, and tips, you'll find out how to best use your equipment, set up video shoots, and navigate the YouTube upload process.

- ✔ **Students:** If making movies is what you do and you're interested in sharing your work, this book can get you started by helping you set up your own YouTube channel as your stage. Since you already understand the fundamentals of making a movie, you can concentrate on the creation and maintenance of your channel. Before long, you'll be uploading videos, building a following, and transforming yourself into the next Steven Spielberg.

- ✔ **Videographers:** You're already comfortable with making movies, you know all about effective editing practices, and you're ready to share your professional work with the world. You'll find tons of info in this book to help set up your channel and grow your audience so that you can transform your video page into a moneymaking endeavor. Ripe with tips, this guide puts you in the easy chair, filling in the blanks with the best ways to showcase your videos and effectively monetize your content.

- ✔ **Business professionals:** YouTube is great for business because it can help drive awareness and increase sales. These days, consumers turn to YouTube to learn more about the products or services they're considering. YouTube creators have become trusted advisors for viewers and more frequently collaborate with many of the world's most famous brands to give buyers (or potential buyers) all the information they need to enhance their product choices.

- ✔ **Entrepreneurs:** You may already have a moderate following on YouTube, whereas others are new to the game. Regardless of your level of success, you share the same goal, and that's to use YouTube as a business tool. Whether you're looking for the best ways to earn money with your channel or looking at the bigger picture for promoting your business or service, this book has much to offer for finding the most effective strategy.

How This Book Is Organized

YouTube Channels For Dummies is divided into five sections, with each section detailing the various phases of setting up and mastering your channel. Each reader will no doubt prefer a particular area. Some may relish the section that pertains to making a home on YouTube, for example, whereas others may skip ahead to the section on growing and knowing your audience or the cool ways you can build a following. Think of it as a smorgasbord of information.

Part I: Getting Started with YouTube Channels

This section provides a swift overview of YouTube and how to set up your channel. Whether you're a beginner looking to share videos with a global audience, a working video professional looking to take advantage of monetization, a business owner looking to close the distance, or anyone in between, this group of chapters covers all you need to know to get started.

Part II: Making Good Videos and Not Making Bad Videos

Regardless of the device or camera used, the language of cinema remains the most important aspect of making good videos — and not making bad ones. The chapters in this part cover fundamental moviemaking for YouTube channels, from using the right tools to putting all the pieces together in postproduction.

Part III: Growing and Knowing Your Audience

After understanding how to build your channel and fill it with great content, it's time to concentrate on building your audience. The chapters in this part can help you find your way to building a healthy following.

Part IV: YouTube Channels Are Serious Business

This part covers what you need to get started with the business side of YouTube. Whether you're looking to raise brand awareness or considering collaboration with your fellow YouTubers, the chapters in this part can help you get the job done.

Part V: The Part of Tens

The *For Dummies* version of a top ten list found in this part of the book provides insight into the common, and the not so common, aspects of mastering your YouTube channel. More specifically, you'll find out all about the steps you can take to improve your YouTube search results so that viewers are better able to track down your masterpiece. You'll also find out ten things everyone should know about copyright so that you can keep the lawyers off your back.

Icons Used in This Book

What's a *For Dummies* book without icons pointing you in the direction of truly helpful information that's sure to help you along your way? In this section, we briefly describe each icon used in this book.

This icon points out helpful suggestions and useful nuggets of information.

This icon marks a generally interesting and useful fact — something you might want to remember for later use.

When you see this icon, you know that there's techie stuff nearby. If you're not feeling techie, feel free to skip it.

The Warning icon highlights lurking danger. With this icon, we're telling you to pay attention and proceed with caution.

Beyond the Book

This book isn't the end of your experience with YouTube channels — it's just the beginning. We provide online content to make this book more flexible and better able to meet your needs. Look for these cool additions online:

- ✔ **Cheat Sheet:** You remember using crib notes in school to make a better mark on a test, don't you? You do? Well, our cheat sheet is sort of like that. It provides you with some special notes about some YouTube-related tasks that not every other person knows. You can find the cheat sheet for this book at www.dummies.com/cheatsheet/youtubechannels.

- ✔ **Dummies.com online articles:** A lot of readers were skipping past the parts pages in *For Dummies* books, so the publisher decided to remedy that problem. You now have a truly good reason to read the parts pages — online content. Every parts page has an article associated with it that provides additional interesting information that wouldn't fit in this book. You can find the articles for this book at www.dummies.com/extras/youtubechannels.

- ✔ **Bonus Chapters:** We had so much to say about YouTube channels that in the end we weren't able to fit everything within the confines of these pages. Check out the Extras page at www.dummies.com/extras/youtubechannels for bonus chapters on YouTube channel income opportunities ("Quitting Your Day Job") and MCNs, otherwise known as multichannel networks ("Multichannel Networks and Other Opportunities").

- ✔ **Updates:** If this book has any updates after printing, they will be posted at www.dummies.com/extras/youtubechannels.

Part I
Getting Started With YouTube Channels

For great online content, check out http://www.dummies.com.

In this part . . .

- ✔ Find out how to set up a home on YouTube.
- ✔ Master all the YouTube basics.
- ✔ See what's involved in building your own YouTube channel.

Chapter 1

Making a Home on YouTube

In This Chapter

▶ Understanding the importance of being on YouTube

▶ Becoming a viral video star

▶ Making your channel unique

▶ Producing video for fun and profit

*Y*ouTube is the new business and entertainment frontier, which means there's as much excitement and creativity associated with creating and managing a YouTube channel these days as had been the case during the early days of television, when the sky seemed the limit. YouTube — like television before it — is caught up in the same adventure that comes from defining its target audience as well as finding out what audiences are willing to watch.

For television, the adventurous nature of their early endeavors could be traced to the fact that TV was so new that audiences really didn't know what they wanted. For YouTube, working in today's market, it's much more about meeting the diverse interests and needs of an audience that attracts more than a billion people from all over the planet.

Anyone that wants to show off their video prowess or share their vision with the world can hang a virtual shingle on YouTube by starting their own channel. Of course, when television began, we humans had more toes than the TV had channels. These days, you can multiply those stubby digits by 100 million to count the number of YouTube channels. That makes running a successful YouTube channel seem a bit more daunting.

Having more than 500 million channels can make getting noticed on your channel feel like searching for a virtual needle in an online haystack. Yet, regardless of the steep increase in competition, the intention has always been the same — getting people to watch your channel. But it's not all bad news — you also have an advantage over your counterpart in the 1940s. Back then, it took a great deal of capital to get started on television. Today? Not so much. In fact, if you just want a platform for presenting some of your video work, YouTube can make that possible without you having to fork over one thin dime.

Knowing that YouTube is free should reduce some of your worries — at least from a financial perspective. Couple that with the size and diversity of the YouTube audience — and the endless number of topics that interest them — it's easy to believe that you have a fair chance of success for your channel. That's true, up to a point — the point being that, if you want your channel to thrive, you need to provide your viewers with compelling content.

Saying that your channel needs to host solid content that people actually want to see seems as glaringly obvious as saying a hamburger joint must make a good burger in order to survive. But content merely makes up the first part of the equation; the rest depends on how you bring viewers to that content — YouTube is free, video production certainly is not. Unless you want to shell out money from your own pocket, you need to generate some funds to produce content for your channel. In the world of YouTube, one major way to generate such funds is through advertising revenue — and it should come as no surprise that the more viewers you can attract, the greater your potential to generate advertising revenue. How much depends on your needs and ambitions, but increased revenue can lead to better production values, which brings it all back to more revenue.

But before you start worrying about all that money you're going to make, let's take a look at what it takes to get started on a YouTube channel for you or your business.

The YouTube Phenomenon – Why You Need To Be on YouTube

Like snowflakes on a winter day, or episodes of *Law and Order,* there are more topics that viewers can appreciate on YouTube than any human can count. And since you already love making videos and most likely exhibit some expertise or viewpoint to share with the world, then YouTube may be your best creative outlet.

On the downside, you're not the only one hoping to get noticed on YouTube. Many others with the very same intention are looking to build an audience for their YouTube channels, too. ("How many?" you ask. The number exceeds the number of those pre-approved credit card applications that plague your mailbox, so we're talking lots.)

Your journey on YouTube begins with knowing your strengths. Some users relish documenting the quirks of their existence to the gentle amusement of others. Others have some type of expertise to share. Then you have performers who regard the video hosting site as their personal stage — the list could go on and on. Even businesses realize it's a great place to inform consumers about their products or provide a great level of customer service. Regardless of your passion, a potential audience is waiting for you.

Audience, audience, audience

Have you ever noticed the repetitive way people describe what's the most important thing about a piece of real estate? Yes, we know it's all about location, so much so that realtors, among others, feel compelled to say it three times, as though saying it once doesn't get the point across.

Maybe that need for the special emphasis that comes with repetition is justified, because when it comes to success on your YouTube channel, we're of the opinion that saying the word "audience" just once doesn't do justice to its importance. Paying homage to our real estate buddies, we can agree that success for your YouTube channel depends on . . . (drum roll, please) audience, audience, audience!

So, what's a YouTube audience actually like? You'll find people from all walks of life, and you'll soon discover that they can spend a great deal of time meandering through YouTube's seemingly endless virtual walls, sometimes just entertaining themselves, sometimes educating themselves, sometimes engaging quite passionately with what they see, sometimes letting it all just wash over them. Given the amount of time folks spend on the site, there's a good chance that someone ends up seeing your video. Not a great chance, of course, given the fact that there is so much content on the site and only so many viewers to watch that content, but still a good chance.

So, how do you move from "good" chance to "great chance"? First and foremost, your success depends on the strength of your content. Right behind strong content, though, you'll find that you need to be a virtual wrangler, capable of bringing people who may not know anything about you to your channel. In order to do that, you need to know what excites your viewers, what they're looking for in video content, and how they consume what they like. With that information in hand, you can fine-tune your content to better serve your (current or potential) audience.

Gathering information on the viewing habits of your audience is a crucial first step in determining what they want to see and how long they're willing to do it. YouTube makes it easy to gather lots of information on your viewers — YouTube Analytics, covered in Chapter 11 is a big help here — but sometimes consulting friends and family about their viewing preferences is a good place to start.

Incorporating YouTube into your business and marketing plans

Just like cool sheets on a summer evening, YouTube goes perfectly with social media when it comes to your business and marketing needs. Why not? You already know that your presence on Facebook, LinkedIn, or Twitter keeps you connected with all the right people. Guess what? YouTube can help raise your social media profile as well. (See Figure 1-1.)

By integrating your video content with social media, you can drive interested parties to your channel; your channel, in turn, can point them back to your social media platforms and your contact information. This synergy helps build a strong following, because you can inform potential customers about your business through multiple avenues.

Video is the perfect partner when it comes to showing products, demonstrations, providing tutorials, or other features designed to increase awareness of your brand. And YouTube is the perfect partner to host your videos.

When coming up with a plan to incorporate your YouTube-based video content into your business and marketing plans, here are some areas to consider:

- ✔ **Have effective titles:** Your video should have clear and succinct titles. They should get to the point about your product or service, so that people can easily find your video.

- ✔ **Add more metadata:** Having a strong title is a good place to start, but it doesn't end there. You should also have a detailed description of the video, as shown in Figure 1-2, and use as many keywords as are appropriate for the content. The more information that's included with each video makes it easy for viewers to find exactly what you have to offer in a Google search.

- ✔ **Include your contact info on the video:** Always add your business or personal information to the video and its description fields, such as your phone number, email address, and social media sites.

Figure 1-1: Using social media can let people not on YouTube know there's something for them to check out.

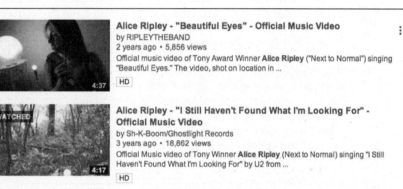

Figure 1-2: All the necessary details are included in the description for this music video.

Becoming a star!

Are you ready for your close up? Or maybe framing one is your thing. It doesn't matter, because YouTube gives you a platform right up there with radio, film, and television as yet another means of achieving stardom. By doing so, YouTube has created a dedicated community that offers one more way for the world to notice you.

The thought of stardom often leans toward actors and musicians — and the creators behind them. Many have found great success after being discovered on YouTube. (Can you say "Justin Bieber"?) The rock band Journey found its current lead singer on YouTube. Aerosmith guitarist Joe Perry also found a singer for his other band, The Joe Perry Project.

Actors have also found work by showcasing their clip reel, performances, and auditions. YouTube has even made some stars of its own — personalities offering everything from rap parodies to lip-synching to video game analysis and commentary have made a name for themselves on YouTube. Epic Rap Battles in History, to take one example, has been seen by hundreds of millions of viewers. (See Figure 1-3.)

So, proof positive that YouTube can provide a stage big enough to start, and perhaps sustain, a career.

Going viral

If you're a millennial or someone who remembers the world before the turn of the century, the phrase "going viral" could have two different meanings. So, in addition to meaning the spread of a virus, which is a bad thing, the term refers to the rapid spread of a video, and that's a great thing.

When an uploaded video goes viral in the good sense, it becomes a sensation that users share and share and share — in the process gathering more numbers of viewers than there are grains of sand in an hourglass. Having your video go viral is like releasing a hit record or having your book make the New York Times best seller list, except that you're unlikely to get anywhere near as rich from going viral even if you get a couple of million hits.

Figure 1-3:
Epic Rap
Battles in
History.

Planning on a video going viral is like planning on winning the lottery. It *could* happen, but you shouldn't bet on it. If you are seriously interested in earning some ad revenue from your video content, work on creating a range of compelling content for your channel, rather than hoping on that one-shot, grand slam home run.

While there's no way of telling if a video will go viral, there are some traits that successful ones share. While we will discuss ways to improve the odds of your video going viral throughout the book, here are some factors that can make a video a runaway success:

- **Spontaneity:** There's a real in-the-moment feel to a viral video that captures a random and decisive moment that you could never repeat. The popular Sneezing Panda and its 200 million clicks comes to mind.

- **Be light hearted:** People love stuff that's silly and that makes them laugh and think — or even consider trying something, much like the Coke and Mentos video collection that have drawn hundreds of millions of views.

- **Get it out on social media:** Yeah, you can rely on chance that someone stumbles across your video, but that's sort of passive, like waiting by the phone for someone to "find you" for the job. A better tack would be for you to let social media know about your latest masterpiece. Just a few tweets here, a Facebook post there, and then maybe an announcement on Reddit could instantly start turning the wheels of virality.

Wasting lots and lots of time

One person's waste of time is another's quest for information, or someone's need to laugh, or learn about something, so YouTube viewers simply spend a lot of time watching videos.

That's a good thing, and a win-win situation all around. The audience gets its dose of entertainment, education, and exploration. And your channel benefits because as viewership increases so does the potential for someone to find you, and when that someone finds your channel and you happen to have set it up for receiving advertising revenue (the YouTube term here is *monetization*), you can earn some money.

Here are some numbers provided by YouTube that indicate how much (potential) time-wasting is really going on:

- More than 1 billion unique users visit YouTube each month.

- Over 6 billion hours of video are watched each month on YouTube — almost an hour for every person on Earth.

- According to Nielsen, YouTube reaches more US adults ages 18 to 34 than any cable network.

Seeing What Makes a YouTube Channel Unique

Four walls do not make a home — but it does provide a good start. How you adorn those walls and furnish those halls is what makes it uniquely yours — uniquely your home, in other words. Well, your YouTube channel is not much different.

When you first create a YouTube channel, it's nothing more than an empty template on a page. Over time, you add videos, make playlists, and create a header with graphics, logo, and other information. Obviously, your video content plays a big part in what make your channel special, but so does the channel's look and feel. Everything from the layout and font color to the type of content and its subscribers helps set one channel apart from the others.

Though this book takes pride in describing effective ways to create and maintain your YouTube channel for the next couple of hundred pages, let's look at some basics first:

✔ **Have people find your channel.** If a tree falls in the forest and nobody hears it fall, does it make a sound? Who knows? More appropriately, if you create a YouTube channel and nobody visits it, it's a safe bet to say that all your good work has come to nothing.

Viewers have to know that your channel exists before they can visit. The main way you have of letting people know you exist is by making sure your content shows up high in the search results of both Google and YouTube itself. (Don't forget that YouTube is the second-most-popular search engine, just behind Google.) To get those high rankings, you have upper-left to associate tons of search-engine-friendly keywords with each of your videos — doing that will bring viewers searching for content in contact with *your* content, rather than someone else's content. It's also important that viewers watch, like, comment on, and share your video — yet more indications to the search engines that your content and channel are important. For good measure, use social media to prep your audience for content that's coming down the pike — just like a movie studio creates a buzz for a big summer blockbuster by teasing you with previews and trailers weeks before release.

Users often take advantage of the Browse Channels feature, which they can access by clicking the drop-down menu to the right of the YouTube TV icon in the upper-left corner of the home screen. (See Figure 1-4 for a view of that drop-down menu.) The more appealing your channel looks at first glance, the more likely a viewer will stop to spend some time exploring your offerings.

✔ **Connect with your viewers.** You definitely want to build a community of followers, and for that to happen, you need to actively communicate with them. That means everything from having them subscribe to your channel, engaging with them in your channel's Comments section, and exposing them to your social media. You can do all this directly on your channel page.

✔ **Provide them with a clear description of your channel.** When viewers know what your channel has to offer, and if it appeals to their interests, they're more likely to visit often, and maybe even subscribe to it. But you need to get the word out.

Angling for subscriptions

Viewers who like your content will come back and watch more, but viewers who love your content will want to subscribe. Why not? When you keep reaching for the same magazine whenever you see it, eventually you just subscribe to it so it regularly comes to your door. YouTube offers repeat viewers of your channel the same option. Basically all they have to do is click the Subscribe button, as shown in Figure 1-5, on your channel's home page.

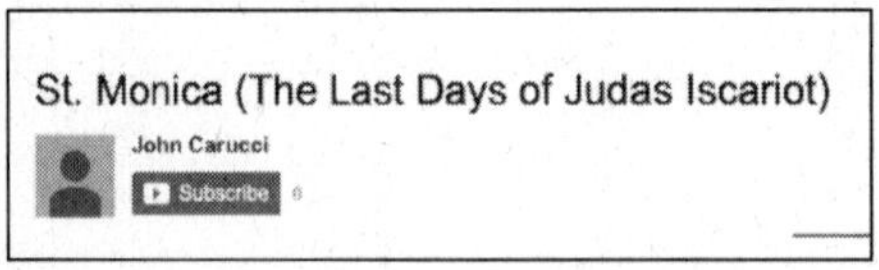

Figure 1-5:
The Subscribe button lets viewers become subscribers with a single click.

St. Monica (The Last Days of Judas Iscariot)

John Carucci

▶ Subscribe 0

After viewers subscribe to your channel, you have to make it worth their while to view it, or they'll unsubscribe faster than you can say Jack Nicholson. Here's what "making it worth their while" entails:

✔ **Stay in touch subscribers.** According to YouTube, viewers subscribe to millions of channels every day, so it's important to stay in touch if you want to stay uppermost in their minds. Suggest that viewers follow you on social media so that you can let them know when new content is available. This strategy helps your audience grow as you amass a devoted fan base.

✔ **Actively upload videos.** It's difficult to imagine a television station maintaining viewers if it doesn't add new programs. Even if it were all *Seinfeld* all the time, chances are good that viewers would eventually drift off to something else. Well, the same concept applies for your YouTube channel. If you don't upload new video content, you'll lose the interest of your subscriber base. The takeaway here? Always provide new content.

> ✔ **Pay close attention to tagging.** Tagging is where you categorize your video after uploading it to YouTube. When a video is properly identified, it increases the possibility of someone else finding it, and that extends to future subscribers.

Establishing your brand

Whether it's a consumer or a viewer, a brand makes your product or service immediately identifiable. Imagine that the Coca-Cola logo looked different every time you saw it, or maybe the apple on your PowerBook wasn't the same apple you saw one embossed on your iPhone. This lack of consistency could shatter your confidence in the product; you may start wondering if what you had was a cheap knock-off of the real thing, rather than the genuine article.

Branding is designed to restore confidence in the product — that familiar logo makes us relax, knowing that we are sure to get the real thing. When it comes to your YouTube channel, branding becomes the identifiable element that lets viewers know who you are and what you're all about, thus creating a similar feeling of confidence. Just like consumers flock to brands they identify with, your audience will do the same with your brand.

Branding takes on many forms on YouTube:

> ✔ **Intro clip:** Before each video runs on your channel, you can insert a three-second clip that acts as a label for your content. The torch-carrying lady wrapped in a flag for Columbia Pictures and the roaring MGM lion are good examples of a branding element. Your job, if you choose to accept it, is to come up with an intro of your own that is equally compelling.
>
> ✔ **Channel header:** This element is the banner on top of your main page, and at first it's as empty as a blank page. (See Figure 1-6.) You'll definitely want to click that Add Channel Art button to add a compelling picture or another graphic along with the name of your channel. The channel header can also include your contact info and specify how often you intend to upload new videos.
>
> ✔ **Logo:** Companies spend millions on branding when they have to come up with a new logo, because they have to track down and replace every single instance of the old logo. We're guessing that's not your problem — you just have to come up with your own logo, perhaps using a simple image and your name. If you feel graphically challenged, you can find places on the web to create one inexpensively. Or just have an artistic friend design a logo for you.

✔ **Playlists:** If you have enough videos on your channel, you can create a running order of them. This playlist can provide an overview of your content or a specific sub-topic of your videos. You can name every playlist, and even re-arrange them.

✔ **Trailer:** In a YouTube context, a trailer is a video that can automatically play when visitors come to your channel. You can use the video most representative of your content as a kind of advertisement for your offerings, or you could make a short video that shows viewers what your channel is all about and how they can benefit from watching your videos.

Figure 1-6:
Empty
header
waiting to
be filled with
an image
that repre-
sents your
content.

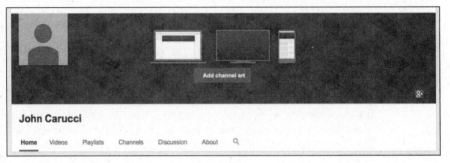

Managing Channels for Fun and/or Profit

Everybody has a reason for making a video, and YouTube doesn't discriminate as to why you do it. Whether you were influenced a little too much by the silly, everyday situations depicted on television series like *America's Funniest Home Videos,* or you want to show off your post-film-school prowess, or you're looking to educate the masses with a series of how-to videos — there's a place for you on YouTube, and (you hope!) an audience that's willing to follow your exploits.

In addition to the pleasure that comes from a job well done, there's also (potentially) a business side to running a YouTube channel. If you post videos that draw a lot of views, it's worth your time for you to *monetize* your channel — generate some income from ad revenue, in other words. But that's not the only business purpose YouTube channels can help with: They can serve as a great showcase for your particular skills or services, or act as a delivery system for product descriptions, tutorials, and testimonials associated with whatever your business is selling.

Creating content

Whether you grab a 10-second video of a gathering of friends, have something meaningful to say on your video blog, or plan a highly structured production with sets and actors, you're creating content.

Almost every topic under the sun is represented on YouTube. That diversity in topics is matched by an equally broad range of production levels. Some videos are quite sophisticated, displaying amazing production values, but many are fairly average. And a great deal are just poorly done and end up getting shown in film classes as examples of what not to do.

Better production values increase your ability to grab viewers' attention — maybe enough for them to watch the entire video and maybe enough for them to even consider watching whatever else you have to offer. The Holy Grail, of course, is having them feel so enthusiastic about what they see that they then share it with others.

But great video quality doesn't happen accidentally; rather it's done consciously, from conception to upload. Though the topic is more thoroughly represented throughout this book, here are some key suggestions to always keep in mind.

- ✔ **Plan before you film.** Great videos begin in pre-production. That means having an idea of the shooting location and working with some sort of script (or at least a storyboard of the kind of shots you want for the video).

  Great planning leads to great production.

- ✔ **Know your audience.** When you're just getting started, you try to make solid videos with good descriptions and hope that your audience finds you. After you have attracted a following, it's still important to understand who they are and whether your content is right for them. For example, if you start an entertainment blog that talks about up-and-coming hip-hop artists, you should use language that's consistent with a younger demographic. Don't overlook the importance of being highly aware of your potential audience.

- ✔ **Keep viewers entertained.** Regardless of the subject matter, it's important for viewers to enjoy the experience so that you hold their attention. Remember that hooking a viewer's attention starts with the first ten seconds of the video (Why? Because viewers may leave before the good stuff and continues until it's over).

- ✔ **Let them learn something.** People generally click on a video link in search of information. If they find it quickly and they were entertained, chances are good that they will love you.

Building an audience

After you create great content, you have to find people to watch it. After all, isn't that the entire purpose of sharing your video with the world? Whether it starts with ten people who run across your student film, or a million people viewing your talking puppy video, building your audience is essential.

YouTube is no different from other media when it comes to emphasizing the importance of building an audience. For example, you may have the catchiest song of all time, but if no one has ever heard it or even knows it exists, then that song cannot by any stretch of the imagination be called a success. The same is true for your videos — you need to work at getting as many people as possible to watch them.

Successfully building your audience depends on understanding their needs and making sure you can deliver on what your channel promises. Catering to your audience — whether it consists of one person or ten million — centers on understanding them and satisfying their appetite. (For more on building your audience, check out Chapter 10.)

Building a business

In addition to letting you upload your videos to satisfy the fun side of your personality, YouTube can work wonders for your business side. You can easily set your account to monetize video content, as mentioned in the next section; as long as enough viewers click on your video, you can earn some extra money. If you've got something to sell or a service to offer, you can also leverage YouTube for some pretty cool and powerful advertising. As you'll see in Chapter 13, it's simple enough for anyone to do it.

Monetization

You can earn money with your YouTube channel every time someone clicks on your video. The more people who view your content, the more money you can potentially make, and YouTube makes it easy to do so. All it takes is an account in good standing, an understanding of the guidelines, and your guarantee to upload only original content to get approval from YouTube.

Now that users have found the potential to make money on YouTube, it's become like the California gold rush of 1849. Motivated entrepreneurs are setting up shop in the hope of striking it big with their YouTube channels.

As you might expect, not everybody will strike it rich. In fact, very few will strike it rich. Nevertheless, it is possible to earn a goodly amount, especially if you take advantage of the multiple ways you can make money through your YouTube channel, including views of your video (an ad plays at the beginning) or clicks on a banner or other display ad on your channel's page. Just keep in mind that slow and steady wins the race — making money takes time, or at least it will take time until you build a massive following. (For more on monetization, check out Chapter 14.)

Chapter 2

The Basics of YouTube

*I*n the simplest sense, YouTube is a website designed for sharing video. Before YouTube's founding in 2005, posting and sharing a video online was difficult: The bandwidth and storage needed to stream video were expensive, and many copyright risks were involved in letting people upload whatever they wanted. Because YouTube was willing to absorb the costs and ignore the risks, it provided the infrastructure for users to upload and view as much video as they wanted, for free. This proposition turned out to be a popular one.

Google acquired YouTube in 2006, and YouTube's growth continued. As of 2014, users watch more than 6 billion hours of video per month, and more than 300 hours of video are uploaded every minute.

Let us say that last part again: 300 hours of video are uploaded to YouTube *every minute*.

Given that amount of content, you, as an individual, could never watch everything that's available on YouTube. For every minute of video you watch, you're 300 hours behind. For every work of genius, such as "Cat in a Shark Costume Chases a Duck While Riding a Roomba," YouTube has literally tens of thousands of poorly shot, poorly edited videos of family vacations, dance recitals, and bad jokes that could possibly be of interest only to the uploader. This chapter serves as your (essential) guide to finding the good parts while skipping the bad. (Hey, it's a tough job, but somebody had to do it, and that somebody was us.) We help you navigate the YouTube interface, establish an account, and start looking ahead to planning a channel. If you're new to YouTube or you need to dig a bit deeper as a user, this is the chapter for you.

What You'll Find on YouTube

You'll find, in a word, videos on YouTube. You'll find, in several words, just about anything on YouTube. We would say that you'll find anything you can imagine, but even we never would have imagined that anyone would make a 10-hour loop of the Nyan Cat meme video, and we definitely wouldn't have imagined that it would have been viewed over 39 million times. The best way to describe what's on YouTube may be to start with the categories YouTube lists on its home page.

Managing your identity

Your entire YouTube experience is driven by whether YouTube knows who you are. It doesn't use any magic to figure that out. Instead, YouTube simply determines whether you're logged in or logged out. When you log in, YouTube can make video recommendations based on your viewing behavior. In other words, after YouTube knows what you like, it does its best to bring more of that great video content to you.

YouTube and its parent Google are in the advertising business and are not promoting online video for the betterment of mankind. (Though some channels on YouTube actually help achieve that goal.) By understanding your viewing behavior when you're logged in, YouTube and Google are able to serve better and more relevant ads to you. That's good for them, for the advertiser, and for the viewer. Sure, most people don't like ads, but YouTube is truly trying to do a better job of targeting ads. (Chapter 13 covers this topic in more detail.)

As you can see in this chapter and throughout the book, you need to be logged in to do most of the important things on YouTube. Sure, you can watch videos without being logged in, but you'll miss a good part of the experience. You need a Google account to log in, and we show you how to set up one of those a little later in this chapter. You also have the option of creating a YouTube channel that goes with your Google account.

You don't need a YouTube channel to log in to YouTube, just a Google account. Having a channel though, as you'll soon find out, will help you organize your YouTube viewing without having to create any videos.

Navigating the home page

The home page of YouTube (www.youtube.com) is a fickle beast. It was once the fount of discovery for YouTube users. If you were looking for new content, the home page was the place to be. Over the years, though, YouTube changed the home page experience. Many changes have been tied to the company's desire to know its users. Users who are logged in with accounts and who have a history of using YouTube see videos that might appeal to them based on past usage. New users and those not logged in see the things that are currently most popular on the site.

The logged-in experience

As long as you're logged in to YouTube when you watch videos, the site is busily keeping track of everything you see and trying to form an idea about what kind of videos you like. This information dynamically drives the home page you see, and YouTube tries to show you videos that it thinks you'll like. Your home page will come to be dominated by material that is similar to material you've watched in the past.

Here's a quick tour of what you're likely to see when you log on to www.youtube.com after you create an account. (Again, we tell you more about creating an account later in this chapter.) Take a look at Figure 2-1 to see how a YouTube home page looks when you log in, and then read the descriptions in the following list:

Along the top

- ✔ **The YouTube button:** Though it looks exactly like the YouTube logo, this button actually does something in addition to looking pretty; clicking it always brings you back to the YouTube home page.

- ✔ **The Guide icon:** This button, consisting of three horizontal bars with a small down arrow, sits next to the YouTube button. Clicking it brings up a guide of channels and topics that may be of interest to the viewer.

- ✔ **The Search box:** This is where you search for videos. Enter keywords to find videos that may match what you're looking for.

- ✔ **The Upload button:** When you're ready to upload a video, you get started by using this button. (Read more about the Upload button in Chapter 9.)

- ✔ **The Notifications bell:** As a YouTube channel manager, you can be notified when activity happens on your channel, including comments, video sharing, and more.

Channel icon

YouTube button   Search box

Guide icon

Notification bell

Upload button

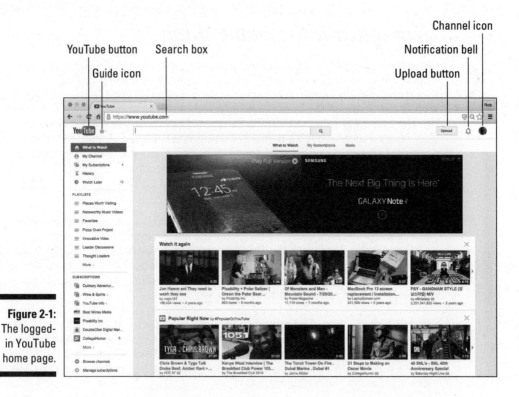

Figure 2-1:
The logged-
in YouTube
home page.

✔ **Channel icon:** A round image button shows either the channel icon you come up with or an image associated with your Google ID when you're logged in. Use this to get to Creator Studio, which is your YouTube "mission control center," or to configure your YouTube account settings. You'll learn about both of those features in Chapter 3.

You can log into YouTube through your Google account, but we recommend having an associated YouTube channel to get all the benefits of your YouTube experience, such as creating playlists. (For more on playlists, see Chapter 3.)

Down the left side

The menu functions running down the left side of the screen complement the functionality of the ones that run across the top and focus more on content. You can toggle what's shown on the left side by clicking the Guide icon.

✔ **What to Watch:** This option is selected by default when you arrive at the YouTube home page. When this section is selected, the main window of the site shows you lists of channels and videos that YouTube assumes you'll like:

- **My Channel:** Clicking this link brings up the home page of your YouTube channel and shows you how other viewers see it. My Channel includes channel art, video trailers, sections, and channels you recommend. To handle all the behind-the-scenes management, you use Creator Studio, which you learn about in Chapter 3.

- **My Subscriptions:** This is where you manage the channels you're subscribed to. Subscriptions are a good way to keep track of the channels you like on YouTube, but the subscription model has changed a lot in the past couple of years. We talk about subscriptions in detail in Chapter 10.

- **History:** Click here to review your YouTube history, which can be extensive. You can track which channels you've visited and which videos you've watched, and even see your comment history, all in one place.

  You'll end up seeing a lot of videos on YouTube and there's going to be a point where you'll want to go back to see what you've viewed or to watch a particular video again. The History section is a great way to keep track of what you've watched and analyze your viewing.

- **Watch Later:** This link leads to a list of videos you've flagged for later viewing using the creatively named Watch Later button in the YouTube player window.

✔ **Playlists:** Playlists are a great way to organize videos you've discovered on YouTube. This section highlights some of your playlists and has a clickable link to your Playlist Management page. There, you can create and edit playlists for your own consumption, or you can use them to organize the videos on your channel, as discussed in detail in Chapter 3.

✔ **Subscriptions:** This section highlights some of your subscriptions and has a clickable link to your Subscription Management page. You learned earlier that subscriptions are a good way to keep track of the channels you like on YouTube.

✔ **Browse Channels:** This link takes you to a page where YouTube makes suggestions of channels that may interest you based on your prior viewing habits. It recommends channels in many of the categories we look into in the "Logged-out experience", later in this chapter.

- **Manage Subscriptions:** Click to go to the Subscription Management page, where you can control how your subscriptions are organized and how you're notified about activity on the channels to which you subscribe.

✔ You've now seen more than a few references to subscriptions in the Guide. Subscriptions and subscription management are a big deal on YouTube because they serve to support a strong connection between a viewer and a channel.

Advertisement

✔ **Banner ad:** Last but not least, the largest element on the YouTube landing page is a banner ad — sometimes with and sometimes without its own, embedded video. The ad is probably not what you came to YouTube to see, but ad revenue keeps the lights on and the video flowing.

✔ If you'd rather not look at the big banner ad, you can usually close the ad by clicking the Close Ad button in one of the banner's corners.

The logged-out experience

When you arrive at YouTube before you've taken the trouble to create an account, you see the pure, innocent YouTube of the viewer with no viewing history. Treasure this moment, this innocence, this pure instant of seeing the site as it is. You'll soon be a jaded viewer, with a viewing history filled with reminders of the hours spent watching One Direction videos. Have a look at Figure 2-2 to see what YouTube looks like to the user who is logged out.

Why does YouTube have ads?

It's always flattering when people listen to you and seem to be interested in knowing exactly who you are. You might think that YouTube is a great listener, just because it takes a great interest in the kinds of videos you're watching, but that's not because YouTube has suddenly decided that you two are going to be Best Friends Forever. The truth is that YouTube's *product* — the way it makes money — is *not* streaming video. In fact, the streaming video part costs the company quite a bit of money because it's expensive for it to host the GoPro videos you made of your dog's bath.

So if YouTube isn't making money hosting and serving videos, how is it making money?

Here's the dirty secret: *It's making money selling advertisements!* That means *you* are YouTube's product. It's selling your attention to advertisers, and that's why YouTube wants so badly to know you. It wants to be able to tell its ad-buying customers exactly who is watching their ads.

Though all this information may seem to be much like a dystopian police state, it turns out that it's something that can work in your favor when you launch a channel with an eye toward making money from your content. We get to the details on grabbing your share of YouTube ad revenue in Chapter 14.

Figure 2-2:
The logged-
out YouTube
home page.

On the left side of the screen, you see a list of links to the Best of YouTube channels. These *verticals,* as they're called, are the primary content divisions on YouTube. Verticals are sort of like the sections of a newspaper. Like a newspaper, YouTube is organized into sections so that you can find the type of content you want to watch. You can subscribe to any of these verticals like it's a normal user channel.

The programming on YouTube is divided into verticals. (Anywhere else, these content divisions would be called *genres.*) Verticals are all a combination of YouTube native content (content produced by regular YouTube users) and content produced by traditional media companies like CNN and The Onion. One amazing aspect of YouTube is that individuals can still manage to have a voice just as loud as the major media players (which is one fundamental point of this book).

It's time to see what the verticals have to offer:

- ✔ **Popular on YouTube:** This one is very much what it sounds like — a channel filled with what's currently popular now on YouTube across diverse categories, from news to music videos and everywhere in-between. It's also a great way to keep up with what's hot in contemporary culture.

- **Music:** Music is a big deal on YouTube. Twenty-two of the 100 most-subscribed channels are music channels. Though MTV once showed music videos, that niche is now filled by YouTube, and much of that traffic is dominated by VEVO, which offers music videos from big-name entertainment conglomerates such as Universal Music Group and Sony Music Entertainment.

- **Sports:** Sports videos are also extremely popular on YouTube. The Sports vertical is an interesting blend of mainstream sports video from sources like ESPN, the NFL, and other major sports leagues, to parkour and extreme sports videos shot with the extremely popular GoPro camera line.

- **Gaming:** This vertical is one of the most mysterious. It has, of course, the content you'd expect, including promotional videos from game publishers, reviews and news from established video game voices like IGN, reviews from YouTube users, and content from some of the largest multi-channel networks, such as Machinima. (You'll learn more about multi-channel networks, also known as MCNs, in Bonus Chapter 2.) The Gaming vertical is also the home of the Let's Play genre, one of the most popular on YouTube. Creators such as PewDiePie and Sky Does Minecraft garner millions of viewers posting videos of themselves play-ing popular video games and commenting on the gameplay as they play. These videos are hugely popular, and Minecraft demonstrations especially have a huge audience of young people on YouTube.

- **Education:** In the Education vertical, you'll find a wide range of educa-tional videos. Universities and education foundations are very active, but it also has many YouTube natives, like the Khan Academy, CGP Grey, Minute Physics, Crash Course, and SciShow. Language learning is another immensely popular subsection of the Education vertical.

- **Movies:** This one is home to YouTube's movie rental business. You can rent Hollywood releases for streaming here, but we've never heard of anyone doing that. Some free movies are available and are worth checking out.

- **TV Shows:** In the TV Shows section, viewers can rent — you guessed it — streaming television shows.

- **News:** The News vertical consists of channels that cover a wide range of beats, including national news, world news, science, sports, entertain-ment, and so on.

- **Live:** You can catch live events from gaming to music to sports and much more.

✔ **Spotlight:** This is somewhat different from "Popular on YouTube" in that it itemizes what's new and emerging. Because it covers a collection of topics, you may find yourself spending more time in this section than you originally planned.

✔ **Browse channels:** Consists of a summary look at channels across different categories and interest groups.

You can get a look at the home page without all the baggage of your past video views at any time. That way, you'll be sure to see (unfiltered) what's trending on the site. Just put your browser in a private browsing mode, such as Chrome's incognito browsing, and you'll see the YouTube home page with new eyes. You'll see which videos are hot on the site without any of the context of your past browsing.

In Apple's Safari browser and Mozilla Firefox, incognito browsing is called *private browsing*. In Internet Explorer, it's called *InPrivate browsing*.

Watching a video

The reason that most people visit YouTube is to watch videos. That should probably be one of the first things you do when you arrive. After familiarizing yourself with the home page, try clicking on a video. You're taken to a Watch page, which should look a lot like the one shown in Figure 2-3.

The Watch page is, first and foremost, for viewing videos, but it has a number of other functions as well. You'll want to be familiar with a number of elements on this page:

✔ **Video Player:** Front and center is the video player, which you'll use to watch the video.

✔ **Video Info:** Tucked beneath the video player you'll see the video info, including the video's title, view count, and a description field with information about the video.

✔ **Comments:** Everybody has an opinion, right? What's true about the world outside is equally true in the world of YouTube. Here's where viewers can comment on and discuss the video, and where the uploader occasionally joins in the discussion.

✔ **Suggestions:** Along the right side of the screen are the suggested videos, which are YouTube's best guesses about what you might want to watch next, based on the video you're watching and your overall watch history.

The Counter

Display controls

Figure 2-3:
The Watch
page.

Mute/Volume button

Settings

Play/Pause button

Closed Captions

Watch Later

That's the birds-eye view. The next few sections take a closer look at some of these features in a bit more detail.

The YouTube *algorithm,* the mysterious piece of code that is responsible for guessing what you want to watch next, is uncannily effective a lot of the time. The suggested videos have the ability to suck you into what is known as the YouTube spiral, in which you can potentially lose hours of your life clicking on video after video and eventually end up watching infomercials from the mid-1980s with no clear idea how you got there.

The player

The most noticeable item on the Watch page is the video player. As with most video players, the YouTube version has a number of controls ranging along the along the bottom. Here's an overview of what each control does:

- ✔ **The Scrubber:** This bar runs the length of the video player and allows the viewer to jump around in the video. Click on the white circle and drag it to the right to "scrub" forward in the video.

- ✔ **The Play/Pause button:** This button stops and starts the video stream.

- ✔ **The Mute/Volume control:** When you roll over the speaker symbol, the Volume bar appears. Click the speaker to mute the audio. Use the volume slider to adjust the volume.

- ✔ **The Counter:** This is the timer for the video. It shows you how much viewing time has elapsed as well as the total length of the video.

- ✔ **Watch Later:** This button looks like a clock, and it simply adds the current video to the Watch Later playlist. The idea here is that, with this playlist keeping track of what you want to watch, you can easily wait for that perfect moment to watch the desired video(s).

- ✔ **Closed Captions:** This button, marked CC, toggles the captions. Not every video has good captions. (For more on captions — good, bad, and indifferent — check out Chapter 9.)

- ✔ **Settings:** You have to click the little Gear icon to access the Settings menu, but that's not too hard to do. For most videos, the available settings include toggling annotations on and off (we cover annotations in Chapter 10), changing the video speed, and setting the resolution of the video. We're big fans of watching the videos at normal speed and at the highest available resolution.

- ✔ **Display Controls:** You can change the size of the default player to show across the width of the browser (Theater mode) or take over the entire display (Full screen).

    Most videos do not default to 1080p or 720p HD. The default playback is often 480p or lower, which doesn't look that great. If you want to watch videos in high definition, you have to become familiar with the Settings menu. Keep in mind that your Internet connection needs to be fast enough to stream HD video to avoid interruption.

The video info section

Directly below the video player, you'll find a bunch of information about the video that we usually call the *video info*. You can see a lot of data about each video there, as you can see in Figure 2-4.

Figure 2-4:
The video
info section.

Here's a list of the most important information to pay attention to in the video info:

- **Title:** In large type just below the video player is the title of the video. (We talk more about titles — more effective titles, to be specific — in Chapter 9. For now, think "catchy and relevant.")

- **Channel information:** Just below the title you'll find the channel name and a logo known as the channel icon.

- **Subscription status and control:** In Chapter 10, you discover that subscriptions are important to channel managers and viewers because subscriptions provide a better level of engagement among the two. The Subscribe button, which is to the right of the channel icon, appears in red with a subscriber count number if the viewer is *not* subscribed. Simply clicking the button enables the subscription, and the button turns gray while adding a secondary subscription setting button that looks like a gear. Click this secondary button to control how you want to receive updates from the channel. To unsubscribe to a channel, all you need to do is click the gray Unsubscribed button.

✔ **Like or Dislike:** The Thumbs Up and Thumbs Down buttons allow you a quick, simple way to let your feelings about a video be known. Just to be clear, punch the Thumbs Up button if you like the video; punch the Thumbs Down if you don't.

✔ **Add to:** Over time, you'll want to keep track and organize the video you're viewing. If you're using YouTube videos to help you with a kitchen renovation, you may want to keep all the videos about cabinet installation in one place. That place is the playlist, and you learn about it in Chapter 3 and Chapter 9. You can save a list of all the videos you want to watch later or videos that are your favorites.

✔ **Share:** Next up is the Share link. When you click the Share link, you're shown a few different ways that you can share the video and get the world to look at it. (You can see the various Share settings in Figure 2-5.) Don't forget that YouTube is also a social media platform that's quite capable of letting you easily share to Facebook, LinkedIn, reddit, and other sites. YouTube also lets you share video on a website with simple HTML embed code, and if that's not your style, you can simply email a video link to your friends.

Figure 2-5:
Sharing
videos.

- ✔ **More:** This catch-all button lets you see more information on the video if the channel manager offers it up. This info includes statistics about the video and a transcript. You can also report this video to YouTube if you see something inappropriate in its content. This last piece should be used only sparingly — Chapter 10 covers the details.

- ✔ **Description:** The video description field should provide all sorts of helpful information about the video and a way for viewers to get additional information, which may include links to make a purchase or support your candidate, for example. Only part of the description is shown, so a viewer can click the Show More bar under the description summary to see the rest of the information. Chapter 9 shows you how to best organize the description field.

- ✔ **Comments:** Comments about the video are placed just below the description section. Regular YouTubers know that comments can be highly informative and occasionally pretty bad. Remember that YouTube is a social media platform and with it comes the good, the bad, and the ugly — especially in the Comments section. As a channel manager, you definitely want comments, but keep in mind that you can filter out inappropriate ones or ban specific users who only cause trouble. (We tell you more on comments management in Chapter 10.)

Working with a YouTube Account

There are a number of reasons you'd want to open a YouTube account. Though the logged-out experience is interesting, you need an account to subscribe to channels, create playlists, comment on videos, and generally become part of the YouTube community. Not to mention, you need an account to launch your channel where you will upload videos, run ads on those videos, and generate some revenue.

Be aware that signing up for a YouTube account means signing up for a Google account. Google owns YouTube, and recently, Google has been busy unifying its products under a single login, allowing you to use one username and password to log in to its complementary services like Gmail, Google Drive, Calendar, and Maps in addition to your new YouTube account. You'll also create an account for Google's almost universally unpopular social network, Google+. This Google+ integration has been a big deal at Google in the past couple of years, and Google+ has slowly infiltrated many of Google's most popular offerings. This has caused some unhappiness among longtime YouTubers, but for the new user, it shouldn't be too much of a burden.

Getting an account

One of the first things you notice when you arrive on the YouTube home page is the Sign In button in the upper-right corner of the screen. Google and YouTube want you logged in so it can monitor your viewing habits and provide more focused video recommendations and — ultimately — relevant advertising. If you already have a Google account and you want to use that account to house your channel, you can. If you're creating a new channel, it may make sense to create a new Google account to go with it.

You're going to be using this channel as your business and, as someone once said, "You should never mix business and pleasure." Though not always 100 percent true — many people have jobs they truly enjoy — this statement definitely applies in this case. If you take all the principles in this book to heart, and have a bit of luck, your channel could become very popular. You'll then be in the unenviable position of running your new online video business in your personal email account, and you'll be stuck with the job of sifting through the guilt-inducing emails from your mother, the advertisement for the big sale at the store where you bought a gift for your ex once (like 12 years ago), and, of course, stuff that might actually be important. Rather than deal with that hassle, just go ahead and start a new account. It's free.

Follow these steps to get a Google account you can use on YouTube:

1. **Click the blue Sign In button.**

   Doing so takes you to the Google login screen, shown in Figure 2-6, where you can log in or create a new account.

   Last time we checked, the big blue Sign In button was in the upper-right corner of the screen, but be aware that YouTube, like all other websites, tends to redesign things and move buttons around from time to time.

   If you already have a Google account, you may already be logged in. If you're creating a new account to go with a new channel, it may help to use a private browsing mode in your web browser to avoid confusing Google.

2. **Click the Create an Account link below the Username and Password fields.**

   Doing so takes you to the Create Your Google Account page.

3. **Fill in the necessary information.**

   The fields shown in Figure 2-7 are much what you'd expect, but here's a description of each item anyway:

   - *Name:* This is the name that will be associated with your account. You can use your real name here, or a made-up name that has something to do with your account. Just be aware that the name will function as the public face of your channel, so sophomoric attempts at humor are probably not the way to go. Note that creating a new account here automatically creates a new (linked) Google+ account.

- *Your current address:* We like Gmail, so create a new Gmail address when setting a new account rather than using your current email address. It will make all your YouTube work easier. Below this field is a link that offers the option to create a new Gmail account.

- *Password:* You've probably done the Create a Password and Confirm Your Password song-and-dance a thousand times before, so we won't offer any advice other than to recommend that you follow the sound password tips that Google offers during this process.

- *Birthday:* No ifs, ands, or buts — you need to choose a birthday. You may not wish to show your real age, what with YouTube largely being a young person's game, but we're also not going to encourage you to lie.

If you're going to be a smart aleck and decide to give the age of your channel rather than your own age, make the age at least 18. Some content on YouTube has age restrictions, and giving your channel a birthday that makes it less than 18 years old can come back to bite you.

- *Gender:* Gender is truly up to you. It's a sensitive subject these days, so we're not going to joke about it here. Personally, when we're creating business accounts, we usually choose Other, because we think of the channels as an inanimate object.

- *Mobile phone:* A mobile phone number is required for identity confirmation and account recovery processes. (You use account recovery when you've forgotten your password.)

- *Prove you're not a robot:* Prove that you're a human by typing in the alphanumeric code that's shown in the image. Google does what it can to prevent computer programs (known as *robots* or '*bots*) from setting up accounts.

- *Set your location:* Google's terms and conditions for YouTube are dictated by country. When we think of the Internet, we don't necessarily consider borders, but it's especially important for video rights.

- *Agree to Google's terms and services agreement:* This is the requisite "fine print." We'll leave it to you and your legal representation to decide whether you're comfortable with it.

- *Email:* If you've chosen to set up new Gmail email address, you'll be asked to provide an alternative email, also for security and recovery. If you're using your current email, then this field won't appear.

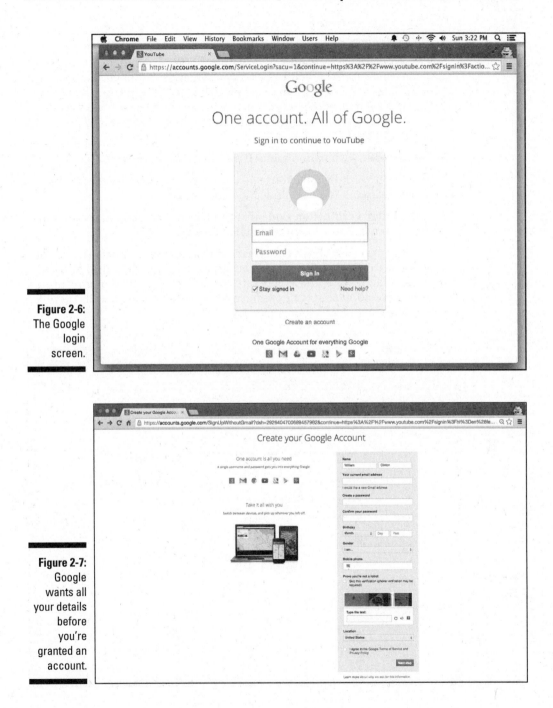

Figure 2-6:
The Google
login
screen.

Figure 2-7:
Google
wants all
your details
before
you're
granted an
account.

4. Click Next Step.

If Google doesn't recognize your phone number or your current or alternative email address, you'll need to verify your account via text message or a voice call. You're given the choice on a page like the one shown in Figure 2-8. If it does recognize you, it will ask you to set up a Google+ profile. If that's the case, you don't need to verify and you may proceed directly to Step 7.

5. Choose your verification method and then click Continue.

Whichever method you choose — Voice Call or Text Message (SMS) — Google manages to get a verification code sent your way.

6. In the Enter Verification Code text field, enter the code that was sent to you (see Figure 2-9) and then click Continue.

The next screen requires that you create a Google+ account. This is not optional. Google has had trouble attracting users to its social network, Google+, and this is how it generates user interest — by requiring users of its more popular services to have a Google+ account as well. There's no getting out of it, so don't even try.

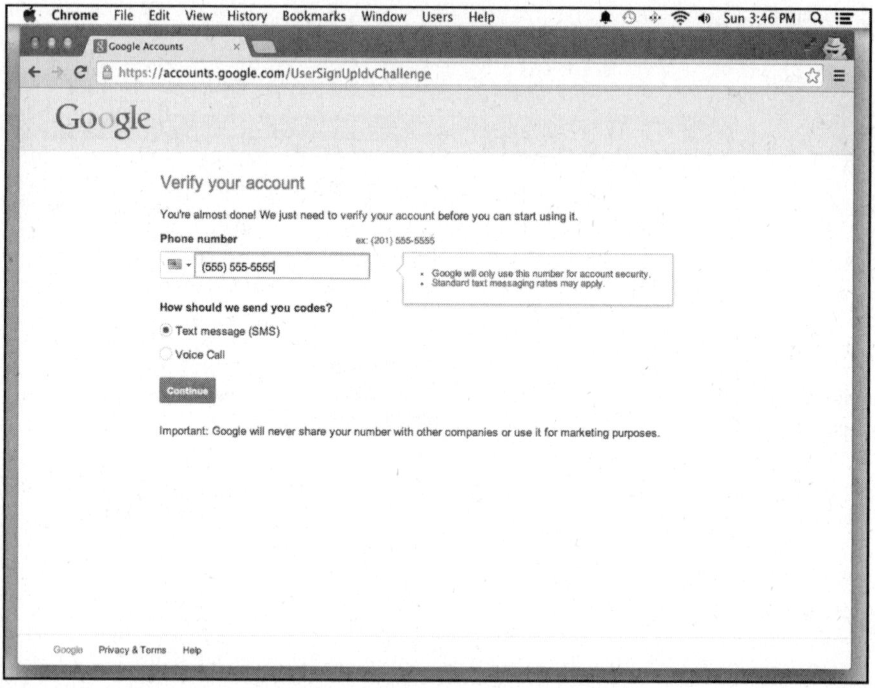

Figure 2-8:
Verify your account by text message or phone call.

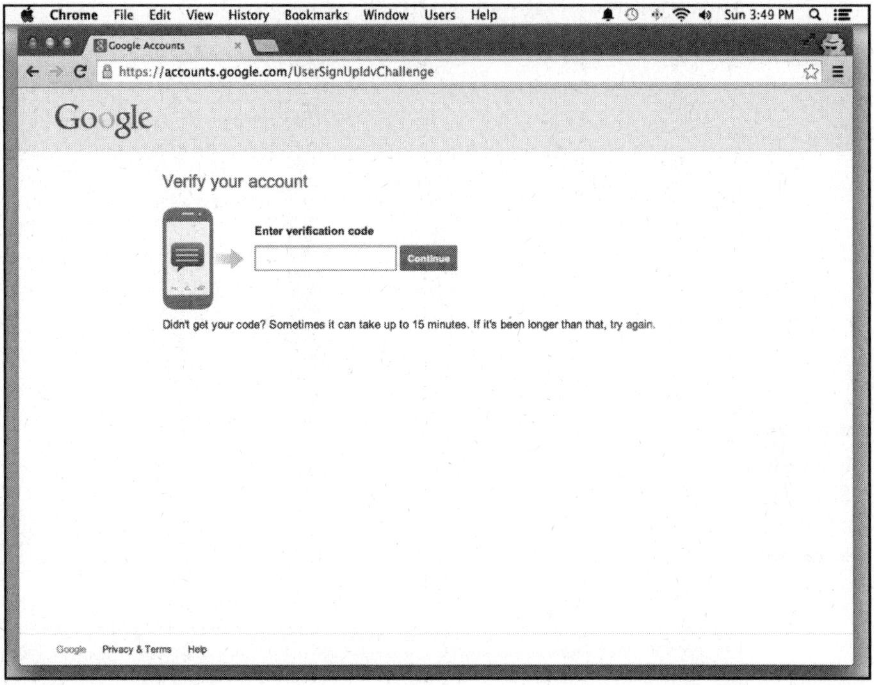

Figure 2-9:
Enter your
verification
code.

7. **Click Next Step to optionally create a public Google+ profile, as shown in Figure 2-10.**

   Google displays a lovely Welcome screen, addressed to you personally. You can add an account picture by clicking the Add a Photo link. Note that you don't need to create a public profile, but YouTube management is bit easier if you do. Click the Create Your Profile button if you want a Google+ profile; otherwise, click the No Thanks button.

8. **After admiring Google's warm and human touch (Figure 2-11), click the Back to YouTube button to wend your way back to YouTube.**

Logging on to your YouTube account

If you have completed all the steps to set up your YouTube account, including clicking that Back to YouTube button to close out the process, you should be logged in to the YouTube site automatically. If that doesn't happen,

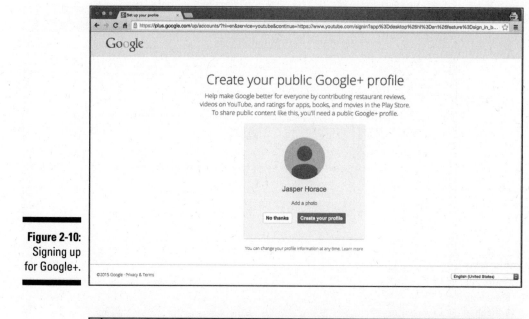

Figure 2-10:
Signing up
for Google+.

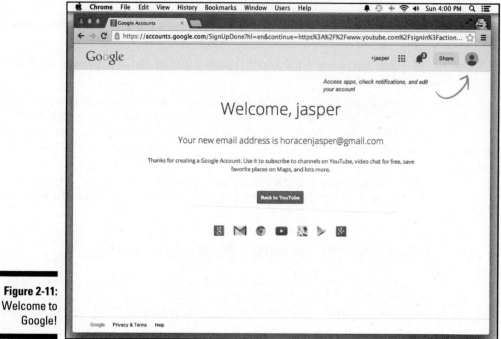

Figure 2-11:
Welcome to
Google!

the first thing you get to do is log in with the account you created using these steps:

1. **Click the Sign In button at the top of the YouTube main screen.**

   You're taken once again to the Google Sign In screen (refer to Figure 2-4) and prompted to enter your account details.

2. **Sign in with the email address and password that you used when creating your account.**

   You're in! You'll see a blue banner across the top that says "You are now registered with YouTube!"

At this point, you're logged into YouTube, but don't yet have your channel set up. We'll cover that in the next section.

Creating a YouTube Channel

Building a channel is what you came here to do, and now it's time to get to it. You can do the work to establish your channel after you've logged in to YouTube with a Google account. After that's done, follow these steps to get your channel off the ground:

1. **Log in to YouTube, and click your channel icon in the top right to bring up the Creator Studio and YouTube Settings pull-down menu.**

2. **Click the Gear icon.**

   You're taken straight to the Account Settings Overview screen.

   In most Google products, this Gear icon means "settings."

   You should now be looking at a simple overview of your account information, similar to the one shown in Figure 2-12.

3. **To create your channel, click the Create a channel link next to your email address.**

   Doing so opens the Use YouTube As dialog box, shown in Figure 2-13, which prompts you to choose a channel name.

4. **Decide on a channel name.**

   Your choices are to go with the name associated with your Google+ account for your channel — click the OK button in the Use YouTube As dialog box to do that — or to choose a custom name. Most readers of this book are hoping to make a business of their YouTube channel, so you'll probably want to choose a custom name.

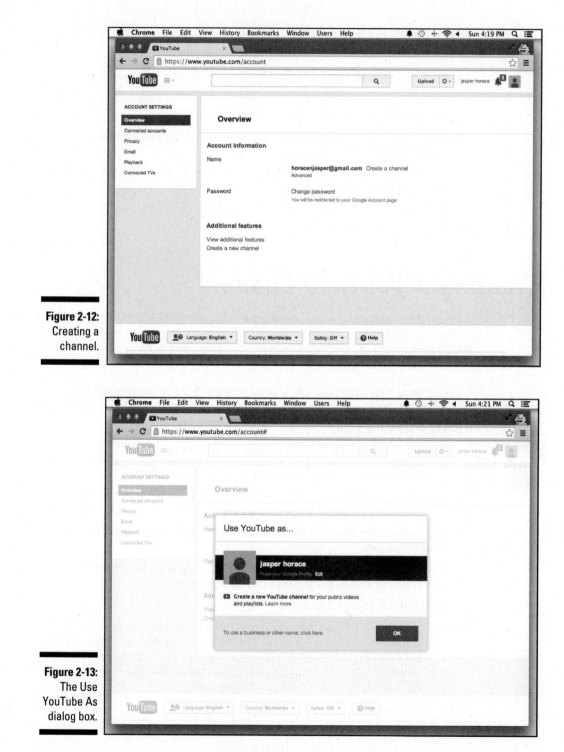

Figure 2-12:
Creating a channel.

Figure 2-13:
The Use YouTube As dialog box.

5. **(Optional) To choose a custom name, click the link labeled To Use a Business or Other Name, Click Here.**

   Sometimes it's okay to use your real name for your channel. If your content will be personality based (a vlog based around you, for example), this can work just fine. See the nearby sidebar, "Choosing a channel name," for more insight on picking a good channel name.

6. **(Optional) Enter your custom channel name into the Create a New Channel dialog box, as shown in Figure 2-14.**

7. **Choose a category for your channel from the drop-down menu below the channel name.**

   Your (rather limited) choices here are pretty much what you'd expect:

   - Product or Brand

   - Company, Institution, or Organization

   - Arts, Entertainment, or Sports

   - Other

Figure 2-14: Choose your channel name, and make it a good one.

Choosing a channel name

Take a reflective pause before you choose a username or channel name or other identifying criteria you want as your public face for the whole YouTube world. An overhasty decision here could end up being one that you regret later. Many a creator has made the mistake of beginning to upload videos to what they thought would remain a low-key, personal channel, only to have that channel take off in popularity, at which point they begin to feel trapped in a channel named after their cat. (Okay, just to be clear, this wouldn't be a problem if the channel is actually about your cat). The Google+ integration actually makes changing the channel name on the fly pretty easy and painless, even after the fact. The channel URL, however, is a different story, and you'll learn about that later in this chapter.

Keep the following advice in mind when making your reflections:

Don't rush into anything. You should think hard about this decision. Though it seems like a light one, it really can impact the success of your channel in the long run if you choose a bad name.

✔ **Try to relate the name to your content**. Are you creating a channel about video games? Try to work a gaming term into your title. If you plan to create fitness-related content, try to integrate workout or sports terms.

✔ **Avoid profanity, vulgarity, and inside jokes.** Though you may find it hilarious to name your channel Dadfarts, a name like that will necessarily limit your market. It's hard to predict what path your videos might take on their way out into the world, and a sophomoric name (or a downright obscene one) might deter your viewers from sharing your video. ***Note:*** *You want people to share your videos!*

✔ **Make the name catchy.** Your channel name needs to be memorable. People love puns, rhyming, and alliteration, but don't try to integrate all three. That might be a little much.

✔ **Make it easy to spell.** People need to be able to find your channel, and choosing a word that's difficult to spell can prevent people from finding you. Do *not* see this as a felicitous opportunity to create a recondite channel name thronged with abstruse vocabulary that will confuse and confound your potential viewers.

✔ **Make it easy for people to talk about.** When you think you've hit on the perfect name, try reading it aloud a few times and make sure you can pronounce it. You want to have a channel name that people can talk about and make themselves understood. The best test for this is to call a friend on the phone and direct her to your channel. If you can tell your friend the channel name and she can get there without your having to spell it, you've got a usable name on your hands.

✔ **Make sure the name is available and that you won't be confused with another business on YouTube or elsewhere.** You should search the web in general and YouTube specifically to make sure your brilliant channel name isn't already in use elsewhere. You should also ensure that the URL you prefer is available. YouTube's allocation of URLs is not automatic, and you choose your custom URL in a later step. So, even if your channel name is available, your custom URL may not be available. Check this in advance, or else it can turn into a real problem.

After you've chosen a channel name and a category, YouTube notes that you're also creating *another* Google+ account, this one in the name of your channel.

You can assign verticals or genres to each video individually when you upload it. For more about that process, check out Chapter 9.

8. **Agree to the terms and conditions for Google+ accounts by selecting the check box.**

    You'll also get a new Google+ page by default. You don't have to do anything with this, but it's a good place to share some of your YouTube and social media activity if you have a following there.

9. **Click the Done button.**

You are now the proud owner of a channel with no content and a boring default layout. (Check out Figure 2-15 to see what we mean.) You'll notice in the upper-right corner that the name has changed from your Google account name to your brand-spanking-new channel name. But all that is covered in Chapter 3. You have even *more* account setup tasks to complete.

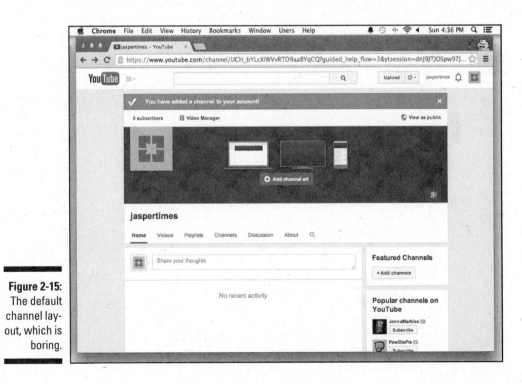

Figure 2-15: The default channel layout, which is boring.

Verifying Your YouTube Channel

Before you get around to beautifying your channel and making it your own, you need to verify your channel to prove that you're a real human being and not some kind of Internet robot who has created this channel for nefarious purposes. Several steps are involved in verifying your account:

1. **Log in to YouTube and click your channel icon in the top right to bring up the Creator Studio and YouTube Settings pull-down menu.**

2. **Click the Gear icon.**

3. Doing so takes you to the Account Settings Overview page.

   Click the View Additional Features link (refer to Figure 2-12).

   A long list of features appears, but you're interested in the Verify feature — you need to verify again before you can move on.

4. **Click the Verify button.**

   The Account Verification page appears, spelling out that account verification is a two-step process. The first step of the verification asks for your country location and asks you to specify how you want to receive a verification code, as shown in Figure 2-16.

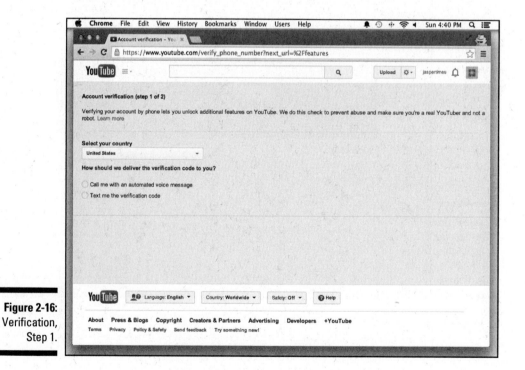

Figure 2-16:
Verification,
Step 1.

5. **Specify your country location, choose a verification method, and then click Next.**

   You can receive a verification code by text message or voice call. Since you needed a mobile number to sign up for your basic Google account, you'll probably choose Text Message, but if you want the pleasure of listening to an automated phone system, you can opt for the voice call. Just pick an option and click Next, which takes you to Step 2, as shown in Figure 2-17. Whichever delivery method you choose, you'll soon receive a numeric code.

6. **Enter your verification code and then click Submit.**

   You move on to a screen with a satisfying check mark that informs you that you're verified.

7. **Click Continue.**

   You are now verified! You're returned to the Additional Features page, where this whole verification thing began.

This simple verification unlocks a number of features within your YouTube account, many of which now have green dots next to them on the Additional Features page. We list only a few of the new abilities you've just unlocked for your channel:

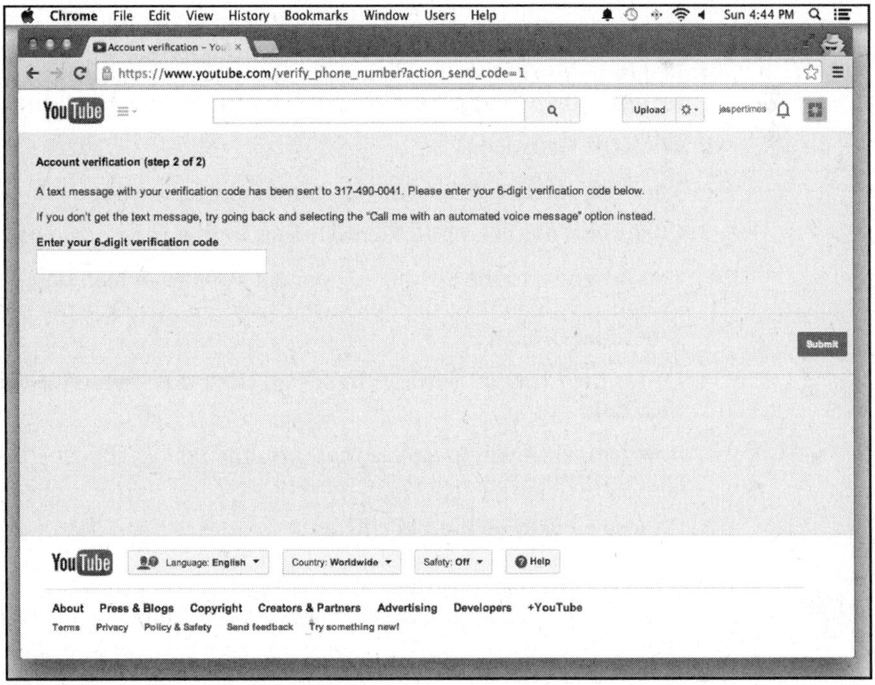

Figure 2-17: Verification, Step 2.

✔ **Longer videos:** You can now upload videos more than 15 minutes long.

✔ **External annotations:** Links to outside websites can now be placed in your videos. (For more on how to do this, check out Chapter 10.)

✔ **Custom thumbnails:** You can now upload custom images to act as the thumbnail for your video. (Chapter 9 also has more on custom thumbnails.)

✔ **Unlisted and private videos:** Ever wanted to grant limited access to your videos to a chosen few? Now you can. (More on this neat feature in — you guessed it — Chapter 9.)

Setting Up a Custom Channel URL

By default, YouTube assigns your channel an ugly, random, and completely unmemorable URL. (URL, short for *Uniform Resource Locator*, is a fancy name for a web address.) You'd do well to replace this ugly URL with one that supports your branding and helps viewers remember your channel. Just note that, to update the URL, your channel must be in good standing. In some cases, YouTube may make you wait for 30 days to create a new channel name. (Not sure what "in good standing" means? Check out Chapter 9.)

Anyway, here's how you get the customizing process started:

1. **Log in to YouTube and click your channel icon in the top right to bring up the Creator Studio and YouTube Settings pulldown menu.**

2. **Click the Gear icon.**

   You're taken straight to the Account Settings Overview screen.

3. **Click the Advanced link located right below your new channel name**.

   You progress to the advanced channel settings, which you can see in Figure 2-18. In the Channel Settings section, you see the randomly generated URL.

4. **Under the Channel Settings heading, click the Create Custom URL link.**

   Doing so takes you to a page that prompts you to choose a new, custom channel URL, as shown in Figure 2-19.

5. **Choose a custom channel URL.**

You get only one chance at this, so get it right. If you screw it up and choose a channel URL you hate, you need to delete your channel and start over.

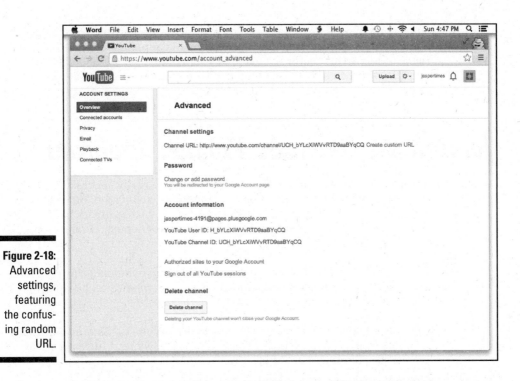

Since you followed the advice earlier in this chapter and checked to make sure your URL was available before you chose your channel name (right? right?), you can just enter the name of your channel and you'll be all set up with a nice, clean URL that matches your channel — something like `http://www.youtube.com/user/mychannelname`.

Joining the YouTube Partner Program

It's possible to make money on YouTube. If you're really successful, producing content for YouTube could be your full-time, exciting job. But don't run to the bank yet, because you're going to need to create a great channel, fill it with wickedly good content, build a passionate community of fans — and join the YouTube Partner Program.

The YouTube Partner Program is a formalized way of helping content creators (which usually goes hand-in-hand with channel owners because they're often one and the same) make money several ways:

- ✔ **Advertising:** You can allow Google and YouTube to place ads against your content and receive a share of the ad revenue. You learn all the details about this in Chapter 14.

- ✔ **Subscriptions:** You can offer paid subscriptions with viewers paying a monthly or yearly fee for access. This is not for everyone, and you're going to need some unique content. Viewers on YouTube usually don't like to pay.

- ✔ **Sales:** You can use your content to help sell your product and actually provide special links where viewer can go buy your stuff. This is done through a special clickable overlay?, called a Merch annotation. Though there are several types of annotations (see Chapter 10 for all the details), this one is available only to partners.

Though the monetary aspect of the YouTube Partner Program is the primary driver for most creators, YouTube also provides some support for content generation though places like YouTube Spaces, special studios built just for YouTube creators and advertisers around the world. Check it out at `https://www.youtube.com/yt/space`.

Our recommendation is to not rush into the partner program right away. Focus on your channel, content, and community, which you learn about in detail in this book. With all that in place, you can check out Chapter 14 to get the revenue engine humming.

Chapter 3

Building Your Channel from the Ground Up

. . . .

. . . .

A YouTube channel is where the creator can track activity, maintain account settings, and — most importantly for a creator like you — upload videos. The ability to find your way around your channel and understand the different features that YouTube offers is essential to building your audience, and — drumroll, please — obtaining revenue.

Navigating Your Channel

A YouTube channel has two primary purposes. For most users, YouTube is for watching videos. When you log in to your YouTube account, you're met with a page offering a lot of videos for you to watch. You'll also see a large ad — no surprise there — as well as suggestions from YouTube for what you should watch. There are sections for some of the channels you subscribe to, and some guesses at stuff you might like. A lot of the logged-in experience is covered in Chapter 2, but it's time to dig a little deeper and look at what you can do with your channel.

YouTube's initial page view defaults to the familiar What to Watch tab, but along the left side you'll find the keys to the castle, so to speak — links that lead to all the important channel controls.

The My Channel link

The value of making your channel look really good can't be overestimated. Though your videos are ultimately the most important tool you have for attracting viewers and subscribers, the look of your channel is a big deal, too. YouTube wants viewers to spend more time watching content. What better way to do this than by giving content creators like you the tools to make an awesome YouTube channel experience.

When you're logged in on YouTube, clicking the My Channel link in the top left-hand corner brings you straight to your channel in Edit mode, as shown in Figure 3-1. Note the following elements:

✔ **The header bar:** This element runs across the top of your My Channel page, and gives you access to some pretty important information.

- *Subscribers:* Since your channel may be new, you probably have zero subscribers — the link on the header that reads `0 subscribers` is at the top to point that out. Hopefully, that number won't be 0 for long.

  When you click the Subscribers link, you see a list of your subscribers, where you can see who is subscribed to your channel and review the information that they share publicly.

- *Video Manager:* Clicking the Video Manager link leads you — no surprise here — straight to the Video Manager, which is the most useful place to manage the settings for your individual video uploads. You can read more about the Video Manager in Chapter 9.

✔ **Channel art:** The large, gray box with all the gray triangles as background is the default channel art for your channel. It has a picture of a computer, a TV, and a phone, and a large Add Channel Art button. Adding channel art is something you'll want to do as soon as you can. (Before you do though, check out the later section "Customizing and Branding Your Channel.") You can also add links to websites, links to social networks, and an email contact button to this area, all of which you can do later in this chapter.

✔ **Channel icon:** Overlaying your channel art on the left side is the *channel icon.* The default channel icon is a light blue square with a nondescript dark blue icon in the middle. This element is an important one because it acts as your channel's identifying mark on YouTube and Google+; it appears next to your channel's name all over both sites; it shows up in subscription lists; and it appears next to every comment you make. If your channel art is the face of your My Channel page, this icon is your face everywhere else on YouTube. Channel icons are typically a brand logo or a picture of the channel's content creator.

Channel icon   Header bar   Channel art

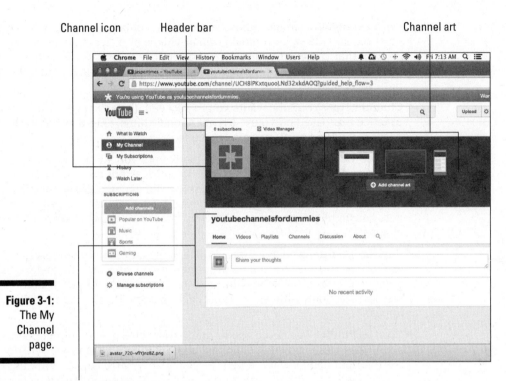

Figure 3-1:
The My
Channel
page.

About This Channel

When you roll the mouse pointer over the different areas of the My Channel page, a small, gray box with a pencil icon in it appears. This is the Edit button. When you get around to customizing your channel later in this chapter, the Edit button is what you'll use to access the controls for each of these elements.

Figure 3-1 shows the basics of the My Channel page, but you can add more. Here's a list of the kinds of things that you can display there:

- ✓ **Channel trailer:** You can add a channel trailer for unsubscribed viewers. (Think "trailer" as in "movie trailer," not "trailer" as in "trailer park.") This is a perfect opportunity to show your audience what your channel is all about, what content you cover, what days you publish and anything else you think might help viewers subscribe to your channel and watch tons of your content.

- ✓ **Sections:** These are groups of videos that help viewers explore your content. Create sections to make it easy for your viewers to browse and find content that interests them. Think of them like bookshelves that gather content of similar types. Sections can contain a playlist, your most recent videos, your most popular videos or other collections of content that you want your viewers to see. The default section on a new channel is Uploads — that's just the list of your most recently published videos.

✔ **Channel Tips:** YouTube wants you to succeed; they even give you best practice tips based on your current channel status. Find these at the top of the right-hand section when logged in.

✔ **Related Channels:** This area will be blank until you add in channels that are related to your channel. This is optional, but also a very good opportunity to highlight any partnerships you may have formed with other YouTube creators. You can highlight your partners and your partners can highlight your channel to help share audience between related channels.

✔ **Popular Channels on YouTube:** YouTube recommends channels that are related to your channel for your viewers on your My Channel page. If you don't want YouTube showing other channels, you can disable this feature. Simply hover over this section and a Disable button will appear.

✔ **View as Public:** Whenever you've made some changes to your channel, you'll want to see how your channel is going to look to your viewers. In the top right-hand corner, note the small planet Earth labeled View as Public. Click this link to view your channel like a normal YouTube user would see it. To go back to Edit mode, click the Done button in the blue bar on top.

Create sections with multiple playlists in addition to just shelves with individual videos. This will help your Playlist tab appear more organized, making it easier for viewers to find more content quickly. Be sure to have a strong thumbnail image for every video in a section and every playlist.

The Channel tabs

Just like a web browser, YouTube channels also have tabs. Tabs are helpful for viewers looking to navigate your channel quickly and efficiently. Each tab has a different functionality intended to help the viewing experience.

✔ **Home:** A viewer sees this tab by default when they click on your channel from a YouTube search or if they manually type in your channel address in their web browser. Your Channel Trailer and Sections all appear here on the Home tab.

✔ **Videos:** The Videos tab contains exactly what you'd expect — all public videos on the channel. The default view is Newest Videos First — the videos that were added to the channel most recently. The viewer can always sort by Oldest Videos First or Most Popular as well.

✔ **Playlists:** The Playlist tab is where all your channel's public playlists can be found. As a creator, you can fill up playlists with your own content. You can also curate content from other YouTube channels for your playlists.

Playlists also come up in YouTube search results, so be sure to always use descriptive thumbnails for your videos, as well as compelling playlist descriptions. Playlists are a great way to extend your viewers' session time on your channel. (Session time directly supports your channel ranking and discoverability on YouTube search.)

✔ **Channels:** If you have partnerships, this tab is the place to add all of those channels that you associate with. If you are a brand that owns many channels, you'll want to make sure all of your channels are listed here for easy discoverability and reference for the viewers. This is a quick way to get interested viewers to consume more related content.

✔ **Discussion:** Viewers are sure to comment on your channel and videos if you are creating engaging content. You can follow along with all the channel comments here on this tab. When logged in, you can remove inappropriate comments or report spam comments directly.

✔ **About:** This tab acts as your opportunity to tell your viewers all about yourself and/or your business. You can include an email address for viewers to contact you outside of YouTube. You can also include any relevant social network sites that you might be active on. Your viewers can come here to see some quick stats on your channel, such as your total view count, number of subscribers, and the date you created your YouTube channel.

The My Subscriptions link

The My Subscriptions link on the left of the My Channel page (refer to Figure 3-1) takes you to a new page displaying a list of channels you're subscribed to. If your channel is new, this is listing is probably empty. As you subscribe to channels that you like (which you will, even as a creator), this page becomes a bit more populated — and a bit more complex. After you've subscribed to some channels, you can look at the information in a couple of different views. You'll use the various links at the top of the My Subscriptions area (see Figure 3-2) to switch between views.

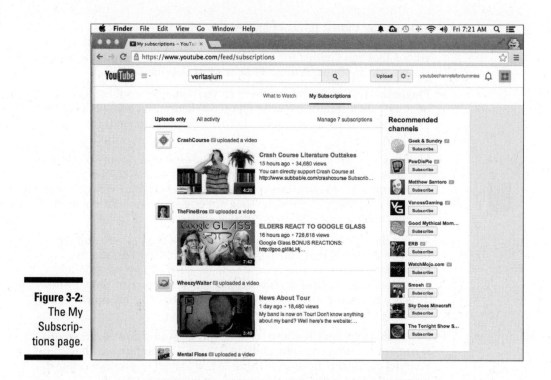

Figure 3-2:
The My
Subscrip-
tions page.

Here are some brief descriptions of what each link does for you:

- **Uploads Only:** This link organizes the channels you are subscribed to in a list of videos. You'll see a list of uploaded videos, showing the most recent first. All your subscriptions are in one long list, so if you have a lot of subscriptions, this can be an overwhelming way to look at things.

- **All Activity:** This view of your subscription feed can be even more overwhelming. As its name implies, it shows all of the activity on the channels you follow — their uploads, their comments, their announcements, and changes to their playlists all show up here if you've chosen to see all that activity. (Note that you can control what you see from each channel you subscribe to using the Manage Subscriptions page — see the next bullet item.)

- **Manage Subscriptions:** This link leads to a page where you can do some detailed management of the channels you subscribe to and control what sort of content you see from that channel. This is also its own section in the main menu on the left, so we cover it in more detail later in this chapter.

The History link

Clicking the History link takes you to a new page listing every video you've ever watched. This page can be deeply embarrassing to visit, because it can reveal to you just how many makeup tutorials and Let's Play videos you've watched in the last week. But whereas this section can lead to feelings of shame and regret for time wasted, it can also be an interesting insight into your viewing habits. Luckily, it is only for you. As the section helpfully points out at its top, "Only you can see your history." (Figure 3-3 shows a Watch History Listing example).

Your watch history is what YouTube's algorithms pay attention to when populating the suggested videos on the front page of your account.

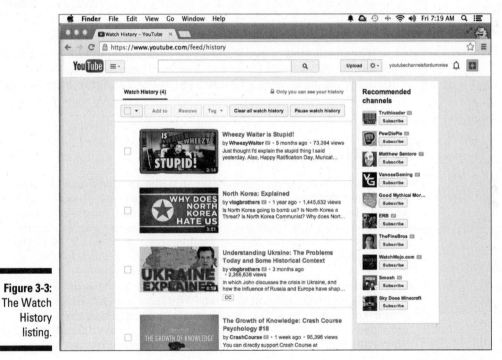

Figure 3-3: The Watch History listing.

Unlike with real-world history — the stuff recorded in encyclopedias and history books — you do have some control over this list. A few controls here let you "rewrite history," as described in this list:

✔ **Clear All Watch History:** This is the nuclear option. If you're ready to undo everything you've ever watched and start over with a clean slate, this button does just what it says and deletes all the information from your watch history.

✔ **Pause Watch History:** This button puts your memory on hold, and allows you to watch videos without them being added either to your history or your video recommendations from YouTube. If you know that you're about to binge-watch a bunch of children's videos and you don't want to be recommended videos like these, this is the option to select. Of course, this strategy works only if you pause before you watch the videos. Otherwise, you'll be in there clearing your watch history before you know it.

✔ **Search History:** This allows you to review all the YouTube searches you have conducted. This is helpful when you forget to save a video and you want to reconstruct the search history. These are clickable links that allow you to be taken right back to the YouTube search results for that query.

The Watch Later link

The Watch Later link opens to a new page that allows you to collect videos in a private playlist to watch later. Your channel subscribers won't be able to see this playlist unless you make it public. After you have watched the content, you can quickly remove it from the list. If you use a streaming device attached to your TV, this can be your TV line-up for the evening. You can easily add videos to Watch Later link as described in the following list.

✔ **Add Videos:** Click this button to add the selected videos to the Watch Later playlist. You can add videos by YouTube Search, URL or by using Your YouTube Videos. Playlists are useful for organizing the videos you like or want to watch later. For example, you can collect all the One Direction videos you've watched into one pop powerhouse playlist.

✔ **Remove Watched:** This is where you can clean up the playlist quickly. If looking through your Watch Later playlist is becoming tedious because of the number of videos listed, you can weed things out by simply clicking the Remove Watched button.

✔ **Play All:** This allows you to play all the videos in the Watch Later playlist.

The Purchases link

The Purchases link allows you to view all of the purchases you have made through Google Play or YouTube. You can watch any movies you have purchased yet again at any time from this link.

The Playlist Section link

The Playlist section on the left side of your My Channel page is where you can see all the recent playlists you have either created on your channel or have recently watched. This section is more for your consumption of YouTube content; this is not one of the creator tools for Playlists. You can click on any one of your playlists from here to easily access the creator tools to modify the playlist.

The Subscriptions Sections link

This section on the left side of the My Channel page lists several of the channels you subscribe to; the number of new videos you have yet to view from this channel will be listed just after the channel icon and name. You have the option to sort these by relevance (the default setting — this highlights those channels from your subscriptions section you view frequently), by new activity, or in alphabetical order. This section is intended for you to utilize as a viewer of your own content collections, not a creator looking to manage your subscribers. You can learn more about your channel subscribers in Chapter 10.

The Browse Channels link

This option on the left side of your My Channel page takes you to a new page where YouTube suggests channels from the top 1 percent most popular channels on YouTube that week. Some of the recommendations are based on your recent viewing history.

The Manage Subscriptions link

This link has a clear and descriptive title — use it to go to a new page where you can manage the various YouTube channels you as a viewer have subscribed to. (Figure 3-4 shows an example of a Manage Subscriptions page.)

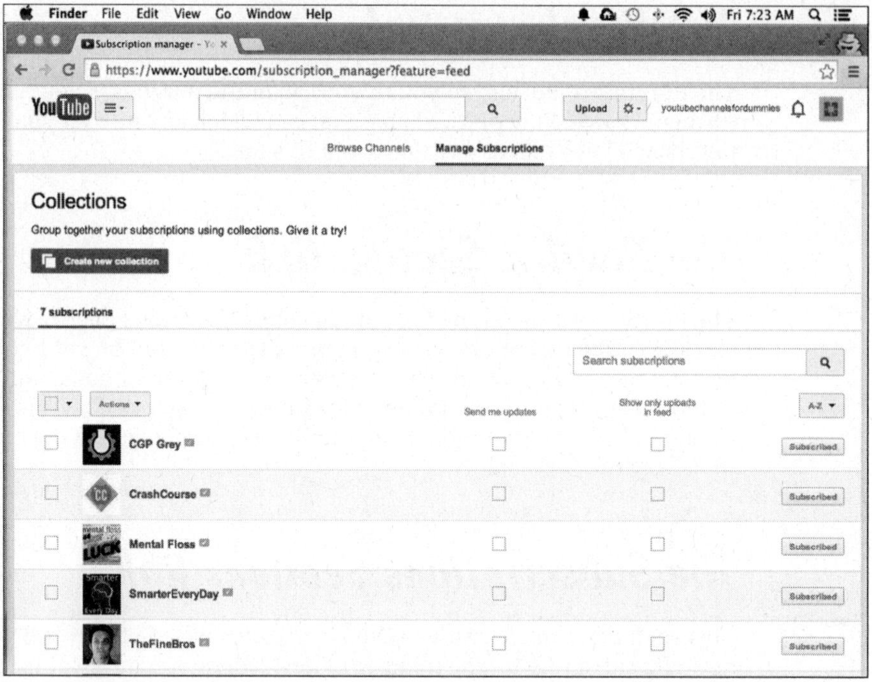

Figure 3-4:
The Manage
Subscrip-
tions page.

To do all this managing, you'll make (frequent) use of this page's extensive set of links, as described in this list:

- **Collections:** You can organize your subscriptions into custom groups called *collections*. For example, if a creator you follow has more than one channel, you can organize those channels into a collection that allows you to keep up with everything that person is doing across a number of channels. The possibilities are nearly endless, allowing you to organize by genre or almost any criteria you can imagine.

  - *The check box:* This button at the top of the subscription list allows you to select all or none of the videos in your list. This is handy when you want to take action on several of your channels at a time.

  - *Actions:* Clicking the Actions button reveals a number of choices, each of which has a check box on the individual channel level of the list. This Actions button is mainly for performing actions on more than one channel at a time. You could, for example, check the Send Me Updates option, which will send you email notifications when a new video has been released; checking Unsubscribe lets you unsubscribe from multiple channels at the same time. These actions can be taken on the individual subscriptions as well.

✔ **Individual Subscriptions:** Each channel you subscribe to has a line in the subscription list. The most important options are in the check boxes on each subscription's line:

- *Send Me Updates:* Do you want to receive an email every time one of the channels you subscribe to uploads a video? Most subscribers don't, so you can leave this box unchecked. If you have a lot of subscriptions, this option can pretty quickly overwhelm your inbox, so use this option with caution. The upside is that you can set it for each channel, so if you have a few channels that you really care about, this feature can be useful.

- *Show Only Uploads in Feed:* When this check box is selected, you see only new video uploads from that creator in your subscription feed. By default you aren't notified in your subscription feed when this creator comments on videos, favorites videos, or takes any number of actions.

Keeping an eye on more than video uploads might be a good idea in some cases, especially as you're learning about building your audience. For example, seeing how often a channel you admire is commenting on videos and interacting with other creators can give you some insight into how successful creators behave on YouTube. You might learn something about how to interact with your own potential audience.

Customizing and Branding Your Channel

Clicking the My Channel link in the menu along the left side of the YouTube Channel screen takes you straight to the My Channel page, which is where you're going to do the bulk of the customization of your channel. This is a pretty important series of decisions you're about to make, so pay attention to what you're doing. Lots of viewers make decisions about the quality of a channel based on a glance at the My Channel page. If there's one stereotype that pretty much holds true for YouTube viewers, it's that they're highly distractible. A professional-looking front page that holds a viewer's interest indicates to potential viewers that you've put a lot of thought, time, and effort into creating your channel. So get to it!

Creating channel art

The channel art section is in the large gray box at the top of the My Channel page when viewing on a computer. (It will look differently on other devices like mobile phones and TVs, but a computer is the only device you can use to change your channel art, so start there.) By default, it has a few items in it, and you're going to change pretty much all those items. Before getting into the steps of creating your channel art, though, you should keep some important guidelines in mind. YouTube is available on a lot of different devices. Your audience may be watching on a TV, a computer, or a mobile device. Given that fact, YouTube has gone to a lot of effort to create a system that allows your channel to look good across all kinds of delivery platforms. It has come up with some guidelines for artwork that you would be wise to follow. If you pay attention to the size of the graphics needed, you should have no trouble with your channel looking good, no matter how your audience is looking at it.

TIP

Channel art is most effective when it is representative of the channel's content. For example, if your channel is about the hottest new shoes, your channel art should include images of shoes.

REMEMBER

Before you get around to adding the channel art, you need to *create* your channel art. This process requires some kind of image creation software. We recommend software like Adobe Photoshop to create custom channel art, but it's an expensive option. If you're investing in the Adobe ecosystem for editing, Photoshop is probably a good option for you. If you're more interested in free tools, something like GIMP, an open source photo editor (available for download at www.gimp.org) might be more up your alley.

YouTube has created a template (see Figure 3-5) that makes the creation of channel art that works across platforms much simpler to create. The template calls for a 2560 x 1440 pixel image that is no larger than 2MB, and provides you with guidance on how to place text and logos to allow the image to work pretty much everywhere.

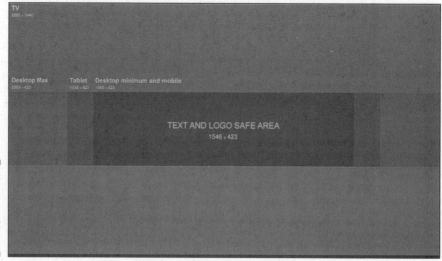

Figure 3-5:
The YouTube Channel Art template.

When creating art destined for use in the YouTube channel art template, it is important to adhere to the advice it provides. You need to be sure that your text lands in the sections of the template that will not be covered up by your channel icon or channel links after you upload this image. If you edge too close to the top-left-hand corner, you'll have a hard time maintaining the continuity of the image across devices and operating systems. Your text and logos might be cut off or unreadable on some devices, and that will contribute to viewers dismissing your channel and moving on to something else. Channel art is an opportunity to make a first impression, and the cold truth is that bad channel art can drive away viewers. Be sure to check how your channel art looks on several different devices.

If you find all this talk of pixels and formats confusing, it might be a good idea to consult with someone who has some graphic design experience. Even tracking down a graphic design student to help you tailor an image to the YouTube specifications can be helpful. If you don't feel comfortable doing the art yourself, and finding help isn't possible, YouTube does provide some stock options, which aren't great, but are a far better choice than the place-holder pattern of gray diamonds. If you do ask someone for help with your channel art, it's important to remember that creative professionals like to be paid for their work. Just because your friend is a graphic designer, or your nephew is an art student doesn't mean they want to work for you for free. Even if you don't pay them the market rate, paying them *something* is the decent thing to do.

Managing channel art

After you've created the art for your channel (or received art from the nice person you convinced to help you), it's time to add that art to your channel. YouTube has made this a pretty straightforward process; here are the steps:

1. **Back in your My Channel page, click the Add Channel Art button.**

   You shouldn't have any trouble spotting this button. It's the blue button that says Add Channel Art in the center of the placeholder banner.

   If you've already set your channel art and want to change it, the Add Channel Art button is no longer an option. In this case, roll the mouse pointer over the banner, and a small box with the familiar pencil icon appears. Click this icon to edit your channel art and open the Artwork dialog box.

2. **In the dialog box that appears (see Figure 3-6), choose from one of the following options to add new channel art:**

   • *Upload Photos:* This is the default option for adding photos to your channel. If you've created your own artwork as spelled out in the previous section, more likely than not your artwork is somewhere on your computer. To upload that artwork, click the Select a Photo from Your Computer button, use the dialog box that appears to navigate to the file's location, and then select it. Alternatively, you can just drag and drop the file onto this window, and it should start the upload.

- *Your Photos:* Selecting this option allows you to choose a photo from your Google+ photo album. Since you've probably just created this account, it's unlikely that you'll have photos in any Google+ albums — the Your Photos option probably won't be the option you choose. You can safely ignore this.

- *Gallery:* If you haven't created your own channel art, the gallery section shown in Figure 3-7 provides you with some stock images that YouTube furnishes for your free use. Though none of them is great-looking, and they're unlikely to be excellent branding choices for your channel, they're miles better than leaving the default placeholder image as your channels banner.

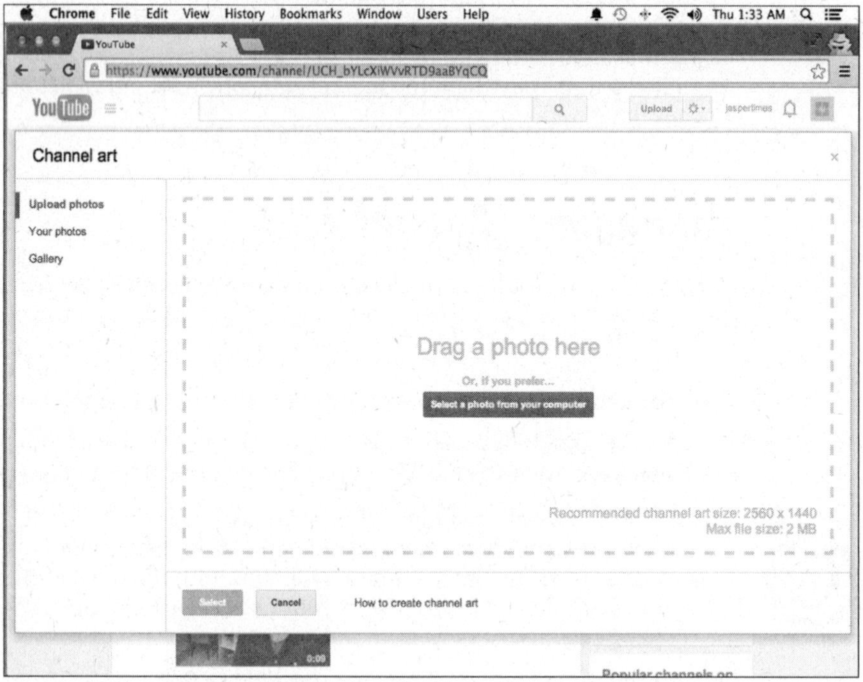

Figure 3-6:
The Upload
Photos
dialog box.

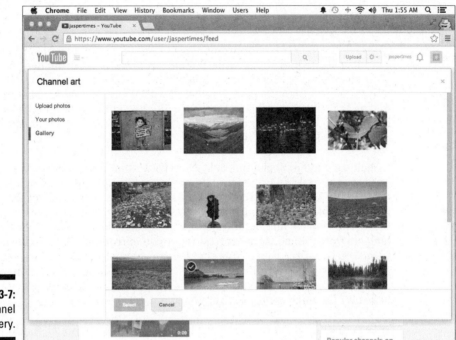

Figure 3-7:
The Channel
Art gallery.

As you complete each step in the process of branding your channel, it's a good idea to click on the View As Public icon on the top right above your banner art. (The icon has the shape of a globe.) Clicking here lets you look at your channel as the public would see it, without all the controls you see as the owner of the channel. This is the best way to understand how the changes you're making will affect the look of your channel.

3. **(Optional) Crop your photo.**

After you select a photo, you'll see a preview with a cropping mask laid over it. If you decide that you want to crop your photo, you can move this cropping mask around to select the portion of the photo you want to use. (Note the Device Preview button that lets you preview what the image will look like on different devices.)

4. **After the size and placement of the image are to your satisfaction, click Select, and your channel art is in place!**

Creating the channel icon

The channel icon is an important aspect of your overall channel art and branding strategy. Though your channel art is the most prominent face of your channel page, the channel icon will be the face of your channel everywhere else. It's also the icon associated with your Google+ account, which means that this icon will appear pretty much anytime your channel is listed on YouTube, and it will appear next to all of the comments you make on the site. So, creating an icon that works is important.

Creating a good icon can be tricky. You want something that is simple and easily recognizable — one that allows viewers to quickly recognize your content as *your* content, in other words. As usual, if you can't pull all that off, at least don't use an icon that will drive away viewers. Don't use an offensive or obscene image, and definitely avoid foul language. Not only will that stuff alienate potential subscribers, it will get you in trouble with the powers-that-be at YouTube. Keeping things simple is probably the best bet, and even a simple-colored background with the first letter or initials of your channel goes a long way toward adding a degree of professionalism. If you can add a little bit of themed art to that simple layout, all the better.

When creating an icon that's going to work with your channel, follow a couple of basic guidelines:

- ✔ **Image size:** Your icon will appear on the site at 98 x 98 pixels most of the time, but you should create your icon as an 800 x 800 pixel square and upload that size. Let the site scale the image down for you, because it results in the best possible image quality for your icon.

- ✔ **File format:** YouTube recommends that you upload your files as JPG, GIF (no animated GIFs are allowed), BMP, or PNG. All these formats should be available in your image editor, so choose the one that works best for you.

Uploading the channel icon

The default channel icon is the blue box overlaying the left side of your banner art. It's marginally okay, but nothing to write home about, so you'll definitely want to replace it. When you have your icon all designed and ready, follow these easy steps to add the icon to your channel:

1. **Roll the mouse pointer over the large icon placeholder at the top of your page to make the familiar Pencil icon appear.**

   Technically, the Pencil icon is referred to as the Edit Channel Icon button.

2. Click the Edit Channel Icon button.

Doing so brings up a dialog box informing you that your channel icon is also the icon for your Google+ page and that you need to go to your Google+ account to make the change.

3. Click the Edit on Google+ button.

This button brings you immediately to the Upload page on Google+.

4. Select a photo using the Google+ dialog box that appears.

As with most things related to YouTube and Google, you have a number of options for selecting a photo. Those options (displayed as a set of links along the top of the dialog box, as shown in Figure 3-8) are described in this list:

- *Upload:* This option is the one you're most likely to use. In the best-case scenario, you've created an awesome custom icon that truly encapsulates and embodies the spirit of your channel. You can drag and drop a photo onto the dialog box or click the Select a Photo from Your Computer button and navigate to the location where the icon is stored on your computer.

- *Albums:* If you select this option, you see a list of your Google+ photo albums. If you don't have any, which is likely, you won't use this option.

- *Photos of You:* This area is also likely to be empty if your Google+ account is brand-new since this section will only be populated with photos that you tagged on Google+ as showing yourself.

- *Web Camera:* This option allows you to take a picture using your computer's built-in web camera (assuming it has one) and using that image as the icon.

We don't recommend using a casual selfie as your icon if you are just starting out. A nicely designed logo looks more professional than a selfie. An exception is if your channel is a personality-based vlog.

5. After making your selection, click the Set As Profile Photo button.

You'll be prompted to post this change as a status update on Google+.

6. Skip the Status Update step, close the Google+ page, and return to your YouTube page.

Your new icon should be in place. If the icon isn't showing up yet, you may need to refresh the browser window. The icon update can take up to 24 hours in some cases.

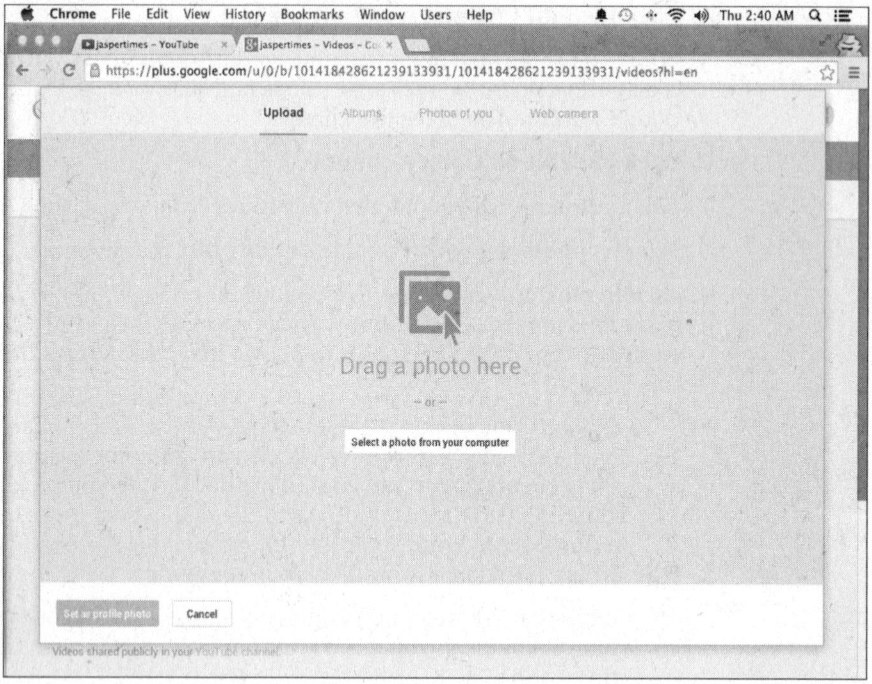

Figure 3-8:
The Google+
dialog box
for adding
an icon
to your
channel.

Managing your links

The last part of the channel art setup involves placing *link overlays* — the custom links pointing to your website or social media pages on your channel art. By default, your channel art has a link to your Google+ page in the bottom-right corner of the banner. You can add links to many social networks, merchandise providers, and even iTunes. You can also add a link to an email address or even your personal website. Adding links is, like many of the tasks in this chapter, accomplished in a few simple steps:

1. **Roll the mouse pointer over the channel art banner and click the Edit button (the Pencil icon) when it appears.**

   Doing so takes you to a dialog box for adding and/or editing your links, as shown in Figure 3-9.

2. **Enter an email address in the Email for Business Inquiries field.**

   Okay, the vast majority of email you'll receive in this context will be spam, but you never know. A legitimate offer may pop up. Stranger things have happened.

3. **In the Custom Links section, click the Add button to begin adding your custom links to your website and social media pages.**

   The dialog box that appears lets you overlay a link on your artwork. YouTube allows users to associate one external website with their channel, which means that you can send your viewers to an external site where they can get more information about you and your channel or maybe even buy merchandise.

4. **Use the drop-down menus in the Social Links section to add your social media links.**

   You can also overlay links to many other social media sites and some e-commerce sites, including Twitter, Tumblr, and Facebook, and even sites like iTunes, Google Play, and Café Press, where you can sell stuff to your audience.

5. **Specify your statistics preferences in the Statistics section.**

   Selecting the Show Views check box does just that — it displays the number of views your channel has logged. Neither is the Show Date Joined option much of a mystery. Selecting this check box reveals to the world when you started your channel. (Personally, we'd leave the Show

Date Joined check box deselected, just because we think you'd prefer to keep the date you joined under wraps. There's no need to tip off the audience that you're new at this.) Any of these "show" options make the selected information public and allow your audience (as well as your competitors) access to this data.

Managing Uploads

Arguably, the most important part of building your channel is adding video content. That is, after all, why YouTube was created. We'll talk more about the nuts and bolts uploading a video in Chapter 9, but we wanted to close out this chapter by at least giving you the big picture.

Before you upload anything to YouTube, it's a good idea to familiarize yourself with the kinds of things that you can't upload to the site. There are several types of content that YouTube doesn't allow, and uploading content that violates these guidelines can get you in trouble. You can even lose your account. YouTube reserves the right to remove any video at any time, but these types of videos are explicitly banned and will get you in trouble with the YouTube authorities:

- ✔ **Pornography:** YouTube doesn't tolerate pornography or any sort of sexually explicit content. YouTube also points out that the company will report any videos of child exploitation to law enforcement if they are uploaded to the site.

- ✔ **Illegal behavior:** YouTube removes videos that show drug abuse, underage drinking or smoking, animal abuse, bomb making, and a host of other illegal behaviors that people might want to document and share.

- ✔ **Gratuitous violence:** Videos that show people being attacked, hurt, or humiliated are also banned from the site.

- ✔ **Hate speech:** Videos that demean a group based on race, ethnic origin, disability, gender, age, or sexual orientation will be removed if flagged by the community.

- ✔ **Threats or harassment:** YouTube is also not a place for stalking, harassing, or predatory behavior. Content of this type will be removed.

- ✔ **Spam:** Videos with misleading titles, descriptions, thumbnails, or other metadata will be removed. Misleading means that the title does not match the content of the video. A good example for a misleading title might be "Katy Perry at my house," when the video is actually about a cat riding a skateboard. It is also unacceptable to post spam comments on videos — for example asking people to subscribe to your channel or to visit your website if it has nothing to do with the video you're commenting on. This will typically lead to the comment being flagged as spam, and this will make it invisible to other users.

✔ **Copyrighted material:** You should only upload content that you own or have the appropriate licensing rights to use. Though the other community guidelines are important to the smooth functioning of the YouTube community, the copyright restriction is hugely important to YouTube as a business. (See Chapter 16 for more information on copyright.)

Part II
Making Good Videos and Not Making Bad Videos

For more on making great videos, check out www.dummies.com/extras/youtubechannels.

In this part . . .

✔ See how you can make your videos the best they can be.

✔ Plan your video shoot.

✔ Edit your masterpiece.

✔ Jump through all the hoops to upload your video.

Chapter 4

What Makes a Good Video a Good Video?

*N*ot that long ago, video was a far cruder, much simpler medium. At home, people had more fingers than television channels, and for those making their own movies, consumer-level video came in two varieties: bad and worse. Maybe that's a bit unfair, but the quality lagged far behind commercial productions.

Clunky cameras that captured low-resolution video were no match for the broadcast-quality content found on television. And the quality of television was inferior to the look of a feature film. Not sure about that last one? Just watch a music video from the early days of MTV, circa 1982.

Since that time, technology has evolved to the point where you can now watch hundreds of channels and where most anyone who wants to has the ability to make a broadcast-quality movie that can be seen by potentially a global audience. Consumer-level camcorders not only come close to broadcast quality but can also even rival it. That means your YouTube video can look truly professional. Of course, *can* is the operative word here.

Clearly, technological advancements have allowed online video to change the rules of consumer-level moviemaking. Yet, because of the relative adolescence of online video, there's some confusion about what makes a good video. Understandably, that criterion depends on the particular genre of video. For example, a music video has a different set of standards than an instructional video on techniques for giving your date a goodnight kiss. And that differs significantly from the standards you'd apply to a video showing your cat chasing a red dot. Though diverse in content, there are still some fundamentals that every video should adhere to.

But what fundamentals are we talking about here? What makes a good video, in other words? Given the nature of human taste, coming up with clear criteria for defining a good video may be a fool's errand, so it might be better to concentrate on avoiding those factors that make a video nearly unwatchable. As a video producer, that makes your job relatively easy. Just eliminate the negatives — such as shaky camera work, distorted audio, or bad exposure — while providing entertaining content.

It sounds easy, but you're right to suspect that it may be a little more complex than that, due in part to some false conceptions that folks still hold about online video. Some people still believe that an online video, or one destined for YouTube in this case, doesn't require the same quality as any other production destined for broadcast. That's simply no longer true. The way things have shaken out, more and more viewers are watching content online rather than on broadcast TV, and they are demanding better and better quality. This demand means that, with more people watching video on sharing sites like YouTube, the bar continues to rise when it comes to production value and content.

We talk a bit more about fundamentals later in this chapter, but right now we want to take a look at the *most fundamental* fundamental out there — your choice for capturing video.

Picking the Right Camera for Your Needs

Once upon a time, a video camera was that bulky device you bought to capture moving images on video tape. Over the years, the cameras got smaller and tape formats evolved from analog to DV and from HD to 4K, with corresponding increases in the ease-of-use and quality categories. Not only that, but the prices dropped precipitously, which means that you can now buy a decent camera at an affordable price.

The only difference now is that there's a wider — some might even say "bewilderingly wide" — selection of cameras. The following list describes the major categories:

✔ **Dedicated camcorder:** Once it was the only way to capture video, but now the trusty dedicated camcorder has been relegated to simply being one option among many. Benefits include a time-honored design for comfortable shooting, dedicated features and controls specific to moviemaking, and a wide zoom range on a single built-in lens, as shown on the Panasonic HD camcorder in Figure 4-1. It's also designed to accept a variety of accessories — an on-camera light, say, or an external microphone or a handheld rig. On the downside, camcorders lack the ability to capture a wide-angle view. Most can cover a long telephoto range but can barely fit all the subjects in a room into the frame. Another dilemma is its monomaniacal devotion to a single task — making movies. That means some users may pass on a camcorder simply because they can't use it to send a text or make a call.

Figure 4-1: This Panasonic HD camcorder is far more compact than its predecessors, yet bigger than most cameras that capture video these days.

✔ **Digital SLR:** The digital single-lens reflex camera (or digital SLR, for short) rightly dominates the still-photography market, but it turns out that many models provide the ability to capture pretty good HD video. That's a great thing because the image sensor (when compared to conventional camcorders) is significantly larger, and therefore captures better quality. The camera can take advantage of all lenses that fit its mount, so you can capture movies using a wide range of lenses, from extreme telephoto to ultrawide-angle. In addition, you can make a movie out of still frames and add an audio track and maybe some music. Many accessories are available, from mounting rigs to external microphones to LED lighting. On the downside, the camera controls and the way the camera fits in the hand favor still photography over moviemaking, and the accessories can be expensive.

✔ **GoPro:** This mini marvel is rugged, waterproof, and relatively inexpensive, and it's mountable on just about anything to capture amazing quality, from a unique perspective on a skydiving helmet to the rider's view on a BMX bike, as shown in Figure 4-2. Some models can even capture 4K video, the new standard for ultra-high-definition television. On the downside, the GoPro is limited to capturing an ultrawide-angle view.

Figure 4-2: Mounted directly on the bike with a handlebar mount, the GoPro provides a view that wasn't possible just a few years ago.

✔ **Smartphone:** Just a few short years ago, considering a cellphone as a means of capturing a serious video would earn you an eye roll because the results were often dismal. Not anymore, because serious works have been captured on a phone, including the Oscar-winning documentary *Waiting for Sugarman.* On the downside, you have little control in adjusting the audio or video quality. You also have limited choices for accessories.

✔ **Webcam:** A webcam is inexpensive to purchase, on the off chance that you don't already have one built into your computer. That makes it perfect for situations where you sit down in front of the computer. Just plop yourself down, check the lighting, and start talking. Since most can now capture in HD, you're good to go. The downside is that you need to stay put or else you might position yourself out of the frame. The audio can sound "thin" if you're not using an external microphone. And worse than that, if the lighting is too harsh, you can look *really* bad.

Purchasing a top-quality model and instantly expecting to make great movies isn't much different from thinking you can purchase a Gibson Les Paul and become a great guitarist without knowing how to strum a single chord.

Both guitar playing and videography depend on understanding technique. Gone are the days of haphazardly handholding the camera while randomly shooting a movie on the fly. It will not only lack cohesion but can also make the audience feel like they're having a seizure. As much as we like talking, thinking, and writing about cool cameras, we want to stress the fact that technique is crucial. That's why we focus much more on technique in this chapter than on fancy hardware.

Knowing What Makes a Good Video

An immediate side effect of watching bad video is that you no longer want to watch it. But that still begs the question of what makes a YouTube video truly good. Sometimes, that answer is a little harder to figure out. The more obvious indicators of a good YouTube video are that it's informative, depicts compelling situations, and, of course, makes people laugh. All these factors certainly contribute to the success of a YouTube video, but you have more pertinent issues to consider that deal with the technical aspects of making these videos enjoyable.

Keeping the camera steady provides a good start, as does making sure the lighting effectively represents the scene and that the audio is clear and pristine for the viewer to understand. It's also important to have a mix of shot types to keep things visually interesting — in an interview, for example, cut between the subject and a scene of what the subject is discussing. Though these attributes are somewhat "below the radar" when people are enjoying the video, they lie nonetheless at the core of an enjoyable experience.

Here are a few of the components that make a good video:

- ✔ **Good lighting:** "Let there be light" remains one of the oldest phrases ever. And for good reason. Without light of any kind, people clearly wouldn't be able to see anything — though good video depends on more than just seeing the subject. Good lighting — as opposed to merely adequate lighting — needs to bathe the subject in a flattering way, as shown in Figure 4-3. It doesn't matter if you're using a sophisticated light kit or ambient illumination or depending on the sun, as long as the final product looks good.

- ✔ **Top-quality audio:** The better a video sounds, the better it looks. Less-than-stellar visual elements can easily be accepted when the sound is clear. But the opposite statement rarely applies.

Figure 4-3:
The peppers come to life as the sun bathes this outdoor market in late afternoon light.

✔ **Steady camera:** Using a tripod (shown in Figure 4-4) or another means of stabilization clearly makes it easier to maintain a steady shot, but if you're stuck without a tripod, at least try to keep your handheld camera as steady as possible so that you can avoid that annoying herky-jerky motion.

✔ **Shot structure:** If you're editing video, you should strive for a nice selection of shot types and angles in order to keep your viewers engaged. Think about it: Nobody wants to see the same exact shot and angle for 10 minutes.

Figure 4-4:
Neither tripods nor cameras need to be big now, as proven with this GoPro mounted on a Gorillapod.

Mastering the Genres in Your YouTube Videos

YouTube videos cover a wide range of subject matter that appeals to a wide range of viewers. Though each requires its own, special finesse to make it effective, all share the same need for quality.

The following few sections take a look at the different types of video and the special needs for each type.

Mastering music videos

Music as a subject pervades the YouTube landscape in many forms. These include everything from the official video for the song from a recording artist to live concert performances to high school musicals and musicians seeking viral exposure. When it comes to musicians creating that "breakout" video, consider the South Korean pop star Psy. He became an international sensation with his "Gangnam Style" video. To date, that song has been viewed more than 2 billion times and counting. Of course, music videos, official or otherwise, represent a large share of YouTube's content, so you'll have to be creative to stand out.

With any type of music comes copyright concerns, either about the song or the band performing it. See Chapter 16 for more details on copyright.

So when it comes to making your music-based video, here are a couple of suggestions to consider:

 ✔ **Get the audio right.** If the music doesn't sound good, the picture won't look good. That statement applies to just about any video, but when the subject is music, it takes on an even greater purpose.

 ✔ **Keep it visually interesting.** Conventional wisdom suggests that some situations require compelling visuals, like in an MTV-style music video, whereas in other situations, the performances are more straightforward and may work well with merely a limited number of camera angles. Just be sure that the visuals work with the music — just because you've got a great tune doesn't mean that you should skimp on the camera work. Remember that it's an audiovisual experience, so take advantage of it, as shown in Figure 4-5.

Figure 4-5:
Still frame
from the
"Beautiful
Eyes"
video, by
Alice Ripley
(video
produced
by John
Carucci).

Figure 4-5: Still frame from the "Beautiful Eyes" video, by Alice Ripley (video produced by John Carucci).

If you're making a music video, here are a few tips to follow:

- ✔ **Listen to the song.** And do it over and over. That's the only way you can get a true feel for the most effective way to visually depict it.

- ✔ **Create a concept.** After listening to the song, you should have a better sense of writing an effective script. Just don't let your vision exceed your capabilities. You can run out of time, exhaust your budget, or maybe embark on something you're not ready to accomplish.

- ✔ **Find your locations.** You have to shoot your video someplace, so why not find the best place possible? Uncovering the best spots to shoot the video, obtaining the necessary permissions, and observing the light and flow are all tasks you'll want to do well in advance. For the music video shown in Figure 4-6, the area was scouted for proper lighting and setting.

- ✔ **Communicate with the artist.** A music video is a collaboration between the artist and you. That's why it's a good idea to make sure everyone is on the same page regarding concept and ideas. If a disagreement crops up during production, you could find yourself majorly frustrated.

Producing your very own vlog

Ever hear of a *portmanteau* word? It's when two different words are combined to form a new one that best describes the situation. Think about *Brangelina,* the couple known separately as Brad Pitt and Angelina Jolie, or *staycation,* the stay-at-home vacation, though it's generally more home than vacation. In the video world, the portmanteau word of choice is *vlog,* the strange blend of consonants that brings together the words *video* and *blog*.

Figure 4-6:
Still frame
from a
shoot in
California's
Muir
Woods.

Before the turn of the millennium, one might take the odd word *vlog* to mean something completely different. But these days everyone knows about the vlog. The vlog has in fact become a staple on YouTube. Some vlogs are quite funny, and others truly informative, yet way too many are simply not worth watching.

That's because vlogs are either poorly produced, or they lack focus in their subject matter, or they suffer from a combination of both. Like most other staples, the bar has been raised on what's now acceptable.

Here are some suggestions to maximize your potential when it comes to your vlog:

✔ **Use a good-quality camera.** Though a DSLR produces the best quality, a webcam — as long as it can capture HD — works pretty well, as shown in Figure 4-7. Plus, it's simple to use and requires little, if any, setup.

✔ **Use a separate microphone.** It may not always be easy to work with a microphone, but trust us — it's often worth the aggravation. Why have your voice sound tinny and distorted when all it takes is plugging in an external microphone? Even a cheap one will make your voice sound better than the microphone on the webcam or your computer. You can even use a lavalier, as shown in Figure 4-8.

✔ **Be consistent.** If you're looking for an audience, think of yourself as a brand. That means the format and setting should remain consistent with each video. Here's an opportunity to show some originality with props, background, and set.

✔ **Improve the lighting.** If you think the overhead lamp and illumination from your monitor will suffice, think again. We strongly recommend adding some light outside of the video frame. If you don't want to use photo lighting, a plain household lamp (with shade) that's capable of providing bright, soft illumination is your best bet.

Figure 4-7:
Built-in
webcam on
a MacBook
makes
it easy
to shoot
the next
installment
of your vlog.

Figure 4-8:
A lavalier
clipped
to a lapel
can greatly
improve
audio
quality.

✔ **Don't ramble.** The difference between a great blog and a terrible blog
depends on several factors — the host's sense of presence, the subject
matter, and the length, for example — but it's the host not getting to the
point that often acts as the deciding factor for the viewer to move on to
another video. Don't be that person. Instead, plan in advance what you

want to say, and when the time comes to record it, be sure to manage your delivery effectively. Also, be sure to capture several takes so that you end up sounding as fluid as possible.

✔ **Don't count on needing only a single take.** It's not a sport, nor is it something you need to do live, so always take your time and reshoot parts that are not perfect — not just for getting your vocal delivery right, but also to make the video visually more interesting. You can do that by shooting each take from a different angle or by framing your subject a bit differently.

Making an educational video

YouTube has become a great place for people of all ages, education levels, and interests to learn. And why not? It's a central location where viewers can find out about just about any topic; besides, though it's one thing to read about a subject, watching it on video provides a whole new perspective. You'll find history lessons, teaching aids, and coverage of current events all on YouTube.

Here are some tips for producing an educational video:

✔ **Know your audience.** Before Goldilocks tells you that one video was too hard to understand and that another had information she already knew, it's up to you to make it just right. That starts with knowing your audience — knowing what they're capable of and also knowing what your audience most needs to know.

✔ **Keep it simple.** There's no reason to show or tell any more information than necessary. In other words, stay on topic. Have a singular focus and be sure to use lots of strong visuals.

✔ **Be concise in your introduction.** Potential viewers must have some idea of what they can learn. That's why it's important to have a clear description of the video. If you can't explain it in two lines, you should consider reworking your idea.

✔ **Write a good script.** At its core, the educational video is still a movie. And like a great movie, its success begins with having a good script that both entertains and gets to the point. Make sure to write the narration as succinctly as possible and make the visuals consistent with your time constraints and budget.

Making tutorial and how-to videos

Search on YouTube and you'll find endless videos that explain how to do everything from kissing a girl after the prom and drawing a freehand circle to replacing an iPhone screen and making an epic movie trailer. YouTube even has videos on how to make a how-to video. Some of these how-to videos provide lessons that are quite informative; some are also quite entertaining, whereas others simply serve as examples of how not to make one.

If your goal is to make a good vide rather than the typical not-so-good one that's too often found on YouTube, you'll need to heed the following advice:

- ✔ **Know the subject.** It sounds obvious, but some of those less effective how-to videos suffer from a lack of understanding of the topic from the production side. Stick to what you know best and take it from there.

- ✔ **Prepare a script.** A good script acts like a roadmap for making the movie, no matter what the subject matter. So, tutorials are no exception. Though everyone has their own method of tackling a topic, one idea is to create a skeleton of the entire process by writing down every step. After that, you can rewrite it as a script, taking into account video content and (of course) witty puns.

- ✔ **Use title cards.** Title cards are not only cool in an "old school" kind of way, they can also help viewers understand the topic. Using words in your video helps the lesson sink in. You can use title cards to introduce each step, and to provide a summary.

- ✔ **Shoot cutaways.** A *cutaway* is one of the most effective components in a movie. It's basically a break in the current video by the insertion of another shot, one that's often related to the action at hand. Close-up and detail shots provide a clearer picture (pun intended) of the use of cutaways, but don't do them while shooting the actual video lesson. Instead, shoot them afterward, or before if that's the way you roll. Why? So that you have clean shots to edit later. It's often jarring for the camera to zoom in during the lesson.

- ✔ **Shoot multiple takes.** Editing is your friend, so shoot several versions of the same scene to try out different approaches or simply to get it just right. These alternative shots give you enough content to work with while editing.

- ✔ **Make sure the narration is clean.** *Clean* means clear and concise speaking, simple phrases, and no jargon. And one more thing: Read the text many times to get as comfortable with it as possible.

Let's play (and make) gaming videos

Whether you're explaining how to find a settlement on Durotar in *World of Warcraft*, battling the Archadian Empire in *Final Fantasy*, or simply providing some tips in *Clash of Clans*, chances are good that lots of people are looking for these kinds of tips and more on YouTube. So if video games are your thing, and you want to share your exploits and advice with others or perhaps teach them something, why not make your own gaming video?

What's a gaming video without a real example from the game? Boring. So you want to be able to capture the action using a screen capture program. The simplest way is to have your game loaded on a computer rather than on a gaming system.

Here are a few choices that are inexpensive and work pretty well:

- ✔ **Snapz Pro X:** Allows you to capture still images, audio, and video using a few keystrokes on your Macintosh computer. You can download it at `www.ambrosiasw.com/utilities/snapzprox`.

- ✔ **Debut Video Capture:** Works on both Mac and Windows computers and lets you record video (including streaming video) on your computer screen, as shown in Figure 4-9. You can download it at `www.nchsoftware.com/capture`.

Figure 4-9:
Debut Video
Capture.

Making animal videos

Take an informal survey and you'll discover an insatiable fondness for videos that feature animals. People love to watch them over and over as well as share and share. That probably explains why the most viral content is content that features our four-legged friends. The recent Mutant Giant Spider Dog video has already attracted more than 125 million views. And spider dog is not alone. Numerous videos are dedicated to the feline accomplishments, too, like cats answering with meows, fraternizing with dogs, or just being cute.

But the animal video is not dominated entirely by dogs and cats. In fact, you'll encounter every animal imaginable on YouTube. Horses, cows, monkeys, and even lions and tigers and bears are represented on YouTube.

So if you think your pet has what it takes to be a YouTube sensation, it's time to break out the ol' camcorder and make Fido a star.

Follow these tips for making animal videos on YouTube:

- ✔ **Keep it short.** Many of the most-watched videos on YouTube are often less than a minute long. That, apparently, is all it takes for a major dose of cute. And shorter videos attract more clicks.

- ✔ **Find a willing participant.** Some dogs — and other animals, for that matter — are more inclined than others to ham it up for the camera, as shown in Figure 4-10. If you have one with the acting bug, consider taking out your camera because — who knows? You may have a potential star on your hands.

- ✔ **Nail down the right location.** That's what they say it *all* comes down to — why else would they repeat it three times? We're not sure whether that makes the saying triple-ly true, but it does add value to the video when you find the right place. If it's a house pet, that can mean a tidy space in a part of your place that has sufficient lighting and is free of clutter. For outdoor situations, choose an area free of clutter, and make sure the sun is at your back.

- ✔ **Reward the participants.** Dogs and cats work for treats, so when they do a good job, it's important to compensate them.

Capturing sporting events

With the exception of professional sports leagues with a YouTube channel or a news organization granted rebroadcast consent by a professional league, most sports videos found on YouTube consist of extreme events and amateur sports. Because the latter often borders on boring for all but those connected to it (family members, participants, sadists), the former provides the best opportunity for the ambitious videographer.

These days, capturing extreme sporting events and activities has gotten easier, thanks to the GoPro. This durable little camera helps provide a fresh perspective by putting the viewer directly in the middle of the action, making

Figure 4-10: Windee the Airedale gets ready to shoot a scene.

GoPro videos some of the most compelling videos on YouTube. Besides, the GoPro is waterproof, captures amazing quality, and can mount to just about anything. (For a deeper dive into GoPro cameras, be sure to check out *GoPro Cameras For Dummies,* written by John Carucci and published by John Wiley & Sons, Inc.)

Here are some (extreme) ideas:

- **Skateboarding:** Since it's a popular sport among young people, chances are good that there's a good audience for your skateboarding video, as long as it's compelling to watch. You can shoot with anything from a dedicated camcorder to your iPhone, or mount a GoPro to the board itself, as shown in Figure 4-11.

- **Skydiving:** Here's another situation that was changed by the GoPro camera. Just mount the camera to your helmet and capture a perspective that has rarely been seen until now.

- **Skiing:** Wow, it seems like a lot of extreme sports begin with the letters *sk,* and although skiing is more common, it can be every bit as extreme, especially when a parachute's involved and you're skiing off a cliff. You can provide your audience with the skier's perspective by mounting your GoPro in a variety of places, including your helmet, on a chest harness, or directly on your ski pole.

- **Water sports:** Attaching a waterproof video camera to your surfboard or raft or on your person while waterskiing can result in some compelling video content of places that a camera dared to tread — assuming, of course, that you don't wipe out after the first three seconds.

Figure 4-11: You can easily attach a GoPro to a skateboard to get a board's-eye view of the scene.

✔ **BMX:** The possibilities are endless because you can mount cameras anywhere from the bike itself to your helmet to strategically placing cameras on the course and from the crowd.

Film and animation

YouTube has liberated the stage or, more appropriately, the screen for film-makers of all levels by allowing them to reach a global audience. Not that long ago, you would make a short film and then physically show it to your friends and colleagues in a dank screening room, a classroom, or (more than likely) your own basement.

On a good day, the screening may have seen scores of people. That would mean you would need dozens of showings, if not hundreds, to duplicate the reach of your YouTube channel moments after you upload a movie. Besides exposure to a large audience, you can also enter your film in various online film competitions.

Here are a few types of movies you can find on YouTube:

✔ **Film shorts:** One traditional gateway to directing a feature film comes from making a film short. But how a person actually ended up seeing one of these films remained one of the great mysteries in filmmaking. We all hear whenever they're nominated for an Oscar, but never knew where you could see one. Nowadays you can view short films of all genres on YouTube, and maybe even see a future Oscar nominee.

- ✓ **Web series:** These (mostly) scripted series are the YouTube version of a television show. And just like their broadcast cousins, they cover a wide range of topics, situations, and subject matter. Instead of the standard 30- or 60-minute episode blocks, however, the web series is broken down into installments that range from five to ten minutes each. Popular web series include *Between Two Ferns* with Zack Galifianakis, the hipster comedy adventure, *High Maintenance*, and the award-winning series *The Guild*.

- ✓ **Animated movies:** If you're a fan of animé or you want a place to show it off, YouTube can help you reach your audience. Whether you're going old school with cell animation, doing stop-motion with objects, or venturing into computer-generated imagery, YouTube provides a great place to share your work with the world. You can even create an animated web series.

Entertainment

Most videos should entertain the viewer in some way, and that includes the ones that are about entertainment. Content that covers celebrities, movies, music, theater, and television should entertain the viewer beyond its subject matter. So although all video should be entertaining, videos on areas associated with the entertainment industry should be doubly entertaining.

Though entertainment covers a wide ranges of topics, here are some of the areas you're likely to see:

- ✓ **Celebrity interviews:** These can cover a wide range of subjects, including comments on specific projects, opinions on current events, and humor interest.

- ✓ **Red carpet coverage:** Stars attending their movie premieres, arriving at award ceremonies, or supporting their favorite charities are popular subject matter, as shown in Figure 4-12. Many make comments to the press, and some show off their fashion sense.

- ✓ **Entertainment news:** This one covers the news side of the industry, with coverage of areas like obituaries, divorces, babies, and impaired driving arrests.

News and information

YouTube offers far more content for viewers than perusing the latest music videos, marveling at people doing truly weird stuff, or looking at dogs dressed in costumes. Though these provide a pleasant escape, you can also use YouTube to stay informed when it comes to news and current events. It's not live news, but that doesn't really take the news out of it. Instead, it consists of replays of newscasts, editorials on every imaginable topic, and news segments and packages that cover anything from business and national news to entertainment and health issues. That's why almost every major news outlet has a YouTube channel where you can look at clips and watch video segments.

Figure 4-12:
Red carpet action, captured at the Toronto International Film Festival.

Here's a brief list of news organizations represented on YouTube:

- ✔ Associated Press Television
- ✔ ABC News
- ✔ NBC News
- ✔ BBC News

Viral Videos versus Evergreen Content

One phenomenon created by the Internet is the spread of viral video. Just like a virus (except that it's the good kind that won't make you sick), a viral video spreads rapidly online and can garner a million views in a relatively short time.

On the opposite side of the spectrum lies the *evergreen* video: As its name implies, videos with this distinction usually remain fresh and vibrant for longer periods, providing a timeless quality to the content.

Your channel's objective depends on being able to bring as many viewers as possible to your content. Sometimes that comes from a single, albeit extremely popular video, whereas at other times it's more about having a healthy lineup of relevant content.

Creating a single viral video can bring a great deal of attention to your channel, and those visits can quickly monetize into big bucks, especially with a video that garners a couple of million views. On the other hand, evergreen videos (see below) lend themselves to less dynamic, though more steady buildup through a variety of content that keeps people coming back.

Don't bet your YouTube strategy trying to create a viral video. When it comes to viral videos, there's a random element to their success that cannot always be duplicated the next time around. Nevertheless, you can do some things to make success just a tad less random — we tell you more on that topic in the nearby sidebar "What makes a video go viral?"

Viral content

Viral videos usually consist of some trendy or contemporary aspect that allows it to build a huge audience quite quickly. For example, a new dance craze or music video sometimes makes for the most watched video, but it can also consist of a dramatic news event or wild stunt that people can't stop talking about. Sometimes it fades away as quickly as it started, whereas at other times it sticks around.

Evergreen content

Like a tree of shrubbery that never turns brown, the evergreen video remains popular with its niche audience for a long time. That's because it consists of content that people are going to search for often and over an extended period. If YouTube were a refrigerator, comparing the two, a viral video would have a shorter expiration date to more evergreen content. Though there's less pressure to creating a successful evergreen video, it still requires a lot of work to gain a following. You have to let people know that it's out there while keeping it relevant for them to venture out and find you.

The types of content that may have (potential) evergreen value include

- Instructional videos
- Educational videos
- Travel videos
- Overviews of holiday traditions
- Biographies of famous people

Most evergreen content — instructional videos or content associated with a historical event, for example — doesn't usually go viral but can enjoy a longer run of popularity because the content will continue to attract a steady stream of viewers.

What makes a video go viral?

Viral videos usually have a humorous or quirky feel to them, and though most of the time they unintentionally gather a mass following, some corporations have managed to produce successful viral videos quite intentionally. But there's no guarantee that your video will find success, even if it's a promotional video with big money behind it.

Like the countless grains of sand, millions of videos are uploaded to YouTube — but only a few become viral sensations. As with winning the lottery, the success of a viral video is more "hoped for" than "planned for." Still, you can improve your chances by considering some attributes that other viral videos have displayed.

Consider these suggestions:

- **Engage the viewer.** You have to grab their attention before they know what hit them.

- **Be relevant.** Trends and pop culture references have a wide appeal to audiences, so why not integrate them into your video?

- **Add humor.** Make 'em laugh and they'll keep coming.

- **Be brief.** After grabbing viewers' attention and holding their interest, don't take a chance on losing by going on too long or having a lull in the action.

- **Use popular subjects.** The biggest YouTube video of 2014 showed a dog dressed as a giant spider. So consider animals as one popular subject.

After completing and uploading your video, here are some aspects that will help it along its viral path:

- **Spread the news over social media.** Tweet out your video link, post it on Facebook, and ask friends to share it.

- **Send out emails.** Send out an email blast with the YouTube link.

- **Blog about it.** If you have a blog, then blog about your video. Also reach out to other bloggers and ask them to do the same.

- **Listen to feedback.** It's no secret that comments found on YouTube can be hurtful, but some are actually helpful. Try to sift through them to find what people like about your video.

Chapter 5

Making Plans Both Large and Small

In This Chapter

▶ Mapping out your viewers' experience with your YouTube channel

▶ Determining what content will best engage your audience

▶ Understanding how and why scheduling is critical to channel success

YouTube is a truly massive online community with over 6 million hours of video watched each month, where millions of new subscribers are added each day, and where a significant proportion of subscribers (both new and old) not only engage with YouTube creators but also frequently take some sort of action while on YouTube, such as buying a product. With so much content to choose from, you need to be authentic, well organized, and consistently active for your channel to attract a growing fan base. Effective planning and a continual review against your goals is critical to success on YouTube. Fortunately, getting your plan together is straightforward, but your goals need to be measured and adjusted on an ongoing basis.

Proper planning is about looking at the big picture first and then working your way through the details in a methodical way. YouTube audiences know the difference between great channels and mediocre ones because the best ones are always well planned. Planning makes all your other YouTube and marketing activities more efficient. You may feel the need to rush out and produce some videos, but you'll be better served — and get better results — if you step back and think about how audiences, channels, and content all come together. This chapter is about planning your YouTube strategy.

Go back to the basics if your existing channel isn't attracting or engaging viewers. Effective planning isn't only about creating new YouTube channels and uploading more videos — it's also about laying the groundwork for some cool marketing strategies. Fortunately, planning ahead goes a long way toward getting your present channel moving and your audience excited about your work. Don't be surprised if some of your viewers want to collaborate and offer to help you out.

Establishing Your Channel's Mission

Your YouTube channel is a great way for you to present yourself and your brand to an audience (that's potentially massive). You may balk at considering yourself a "brand," but we're here to tell you that it doesn't matter whether you're an independent creator, a Fortune 500 company, a cutting-edge digital agency, or a local business — every organization and YouTube creator has its own brand, whether they know it or not. Your brand value is tied to its uniqueness and how it appeals to your viewers. That's why YouTube is so important and effective for showing what you or your company represent, far better than words can ever do.

Successful YouTube strategies incorporate a channel presence well beyond simply uploading your videos for free. Your channel is a place where viewers should come regularly to discover and consume content. This is an opportunity to grow, engage, and inspire communities of passion.

Upon arriving on your YouTube channel, viewers should quickly understand what you and your channel are all about. The success of your channel is tied to making your brand and channel mission resonate loud and clear. Khan Academy, shown in Figure 5-1, is an excellent example of YouTube integration with its brand. Visit the channel at www.youtube.com/khanacademy to see a live example of a YouTube channel with a clear mission.

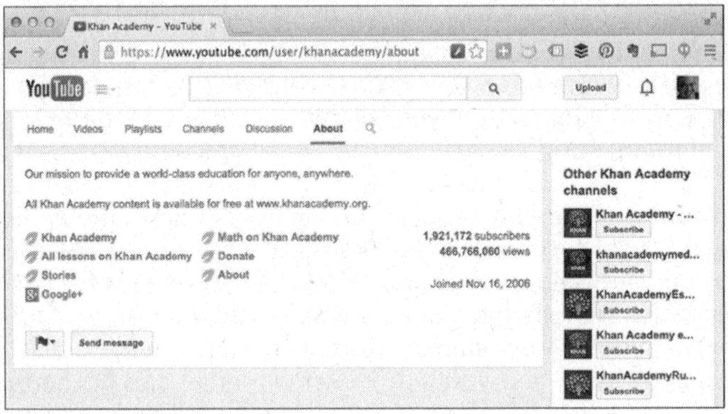

Figure 5-1:
Khan Academy's mission aligns with its YouTube content.

If you have other online properties, such as a website, Facebook page, or Twitter account, make sure your YouTube channel has consistent branding and messaging that aligns with all your social networks and websites. Viewers commonly move across these properties as they engage with you, so your mission must be unified and clear.

Determining your goals

Your YouTube channel showcases something you're passionate about. What drives you to create a YouTube channel and content isn't so different from what motivates you to do other things in life, such as

- ✔ Host a fundraiser
- ✔ Write a blog
- ✔ Support a cause
- ✔ Give something back to society
- ✔ Earn some income
- ✔ Learn a new hobby

The reason that YouTube is such a great place for you to share your passion is because video is a supremely effective medium for getting your audience to engage with you. Learn to put that medium to use for you.

Though building your channel is one major goal, you'll likely have additional goals. Here are some other reasons for creating your YouTube channel and the content it contains:

- ✔ **Build a brand.** There's no better way to show who you are, either as an independent creator or as an organization, than by way of a video or series of videos on your channel. The content might include different types of videos — something you've created, straight news, information about you, or a combination. Your motivation for brand building could be to obtain a new job, attract attention from industry luminaries, or make people feel good about your products.

- ✔ **Educate your target audience.** Most people love to learn, and much of the successful content on YouTube revolves around education and tutorials. Educational content includes home repair, product configuration, justification for social causes, and many more topics. Educational content also helps drive brand awareness.

- ✔ **Entertain the crowd.** People love to laugh, enjoy music, and get engrossed in a good story. These genres are all forms of entertainment, and all work especially well on YouTube.

    Many forms of entertainment are highly subjective, so be sure to tailor your content so that it connects with the specific audience you're trying to reach.

- ✔ **Sell something.** It doesn't matter whether you have a product to sell, a subscription to offer, or a candidate to elect, your YouTube channel is a great way to demonstrate to your audience that they want what you're offering. People are turning to YouTube to make buying decisions about future purchases. Make sure you understand that YouTube is now a primary source of information used to influence a sale. In the past seven years, YouTube searches for video reviews have more than doubled.

✔ **Earn a living.** We've explained that your videos can make money by driving and influencing sales. You can also earn a living from people watching your YouTube videos by monetizing your channel (as explained in Chapter 14).

Don't quit your day job — at least not yet. Making money from YouTube takes time, creativity, and persistence. Even the best-laid plans can't guarantee results if you don't (or your content doesn't) resonate with your target audience. Don't fret: Your YouTube channel may be a nice source of supplemental income, eventually.

Don't feel that you have to keep your goals separate. Michael Stevens' popular Vsauce channel (www.youtube.com/Vsauce) does a great job of combining educational goals with entertainment to keep his audience (almost 8 million subscribers) coming back for more.

Embrace discoverability

At the end of the day, YouTube is about one thing: getting people to watch your content. Simple, right? In theory, yes, but your challenge is to help viewers find your channel and your content. That's what discoverability is all about: placing your content in front of the right viewers so that they can watch. Unfortunately, YouTube doesn't share the secret sauce for getting found, but you can help improve the odds of your videos showing up in YouTube and Google Search as well as in Suggested Videos on the Watch page. What can you do in the planning phase for aiding discoverability? Make watch time an important goal.

Watch time is one of the most important factors that trigger YouTube to put your content in front of viewers. In 2012, YouTube made watch time more important to discoverability than the number of views the video received. So what exactly *is* watch time? In its simplest form, *watch time* is the total amount of time viewers spend watching your videos. People who watch your content are telling YouTube, "Hey, this is important stuff; make sure similar viewers know."

Watch time doesn't indicate whether your viewers watch the *entire* video (although that's a good thing, too) — it indicates that a relatively high percentage of the video is being viewed. How much? Again, YouTube isn't specific. Note that it doesn't matter whether your videos are short or long; what's important is that viewers are engaged. The secret is to make legitimately good content. Good content increases watch time, which increases discoverability.

Creating viral videos shouldn't be your goal. Betting your YouTube strategy on producing viral videos is like betting your entire retirement savings on winning the lottery. Attain your goals through proper planning and execution, not through chance.

Being different, being valuable, being authentic

YouTube has over 1 billion unique visitors every month, and this number continues to grow. Now, that might sound intimidating, as in "How can I get anyone to notice *me?*" but our advice to you is to jump right in. The trick is that, you simply have to be different enough and interesting enough for people to care. Your content (or the content of those videos you choose to curate) must connect with your audience while tying into your brand. In an increasingly congested space, you need to be authentic to establish credibility and aid discoverability.

Yes, it's possible to make a little money in the YouTube world by hiring yourself out as a spokesperson for a third party, but being a paid spokesperson is a risky strategy. You'll find that your YouTube audience is rather astute and will quickly weed out channels that lack authenticity from their subscriptions and playlists. If you get paid to include product placements in your videos, be sure to notify YouTube when updating your monetization settings. You *must* follow all of YouTube's ad policies if you're paid to include product placement in your editorial content. For more on monetization settings, see Chapter 14.

Surveying the YouTube landscape

Your channel-planning blueprint must include a clear understanding of the community you're aiming to reach. Ask yourself these questions:

- ✔ **Who are the influencers and thought leaders?** Discover spokespeople who share your passion to determine their tone, style, and content approach. Determine how they engage with their fan base and with whom they collaborate.

- ✔ **What channels are popular?** Use YouTube Search to determine which channels are the most popular with the subject matter planned for your own channel. Enter keywords into the search bar to discover popular channels and videos. Look at the number of subscribers, views, likes, and comments. Find out why these channels resonate by looking at style, branding, publishing, scheduling, collaboration level, and personality. See how the channels organize videos and playlists, repurpose content, and promote new videos.

✓ **How engaged is the community?** You need to gauge how viewers are reacting to the content they watch. Determine what normal levels of likes/dislikes and comments are for your target audience. Identify the vocal members of the community and capture their constructive criticism and content recommendations. Comments are a great source for telegraphing audience needs.

✓ **Is my idea different enough?** Figure out whether there are gaps in the content being produced. Assess whether your approach covers some of the fan base content recommendations now unfulfilled by existing channels.

The YouTube community is quite collaborative, especially among better channels and viewers. If you're in a competitive market, your audience will provide a competitive advantage by promoting your channel and making content recommendations. If you have a product or service, don't be surprised if your audience gives you feedback on that as well.

With more than 100 hours of video now being uploaded to YouTube every minute, you'll realize that you'll have to search through, watch, and analyze a good deal of content so that you can determine whether your YouTube strategy is sound. YouTube is the second-largest search engine in the world, so take a reasoned and disciplined approach to determine where you fit — or where your organization fits.

We recommend visiting comparable channels, watching their videos, and then exploring the video recommendations to determine whether your channel will be unique enough to build a following. You can use YouTube Search to track down the competition, or you can try one of the specialized tools recently made available, such as Pixability's Video Marketing Software (www.pixability.com).

YouTube provides some valuable options to discover content that is important to your target audience or relevant to your discovery. Working directly from the YouTube search bar can be helpful; anytime you begin typing a search query into YouTube, you see a list of possible search results displayed; these are the high-volume searches that YouTube feels may be relevant to your current query.

YouTube's basic search feature is a good tool to use if you want to gauge whether you're creating content that is in high demand. Using the advanced search filters, however, is much more efficient if what you want to do is find specific channels and videos. Figure 5-2 shows an Advanced Search Filter query for the term *monster trucks*. (Note that it has nearly 1.2 million relevant videos — who knew?)

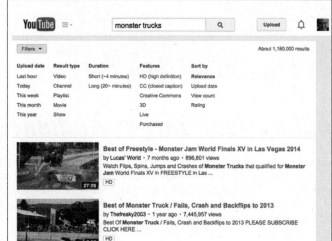

Figure 5-2: Using YouTube advanced search filters.

Mobile YouTube viewing and mobile search must be significant parts of your channel strategy. Understand that not all mobile apps have complete functionality, including the advanced search filters referenced.

Be sure to look at recommended videos under the What to Watch section of the guide we describe in Chapter 2. Your previous viewing and search patterns influence what shows up under your recommendations, so you may see a blend of content from different searches, both professional and personal.

Just as independent software tools, such as Adobe Creative Suite and Apple Final Cut, are important to the video production process, new independent tools, including Pixability (www.pixability.com) and Tubular Labs (www.tubularlabs.com), are quite valuable to the channel discovery process on YouTube. These third-party products often combine YouTube data with information from social media sources, to offer a more granular analysis of important channels, demographic information about your targeted fan base, and a detailed look at what your audience watches and shares. Figure 5-3 shows the critical channels around a specific topic base.

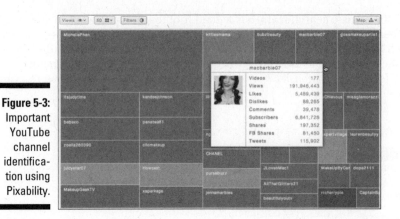

Figure 5-3: Important YouTube channel identification using Pixability.

Understanding Your Target Audience

Your channel's success is linked to how well you know your audience. In Part III of this book, you can find out all about building your audience and determining whether they're finding and hanging out on your channel. Your core audience on YouTube is a community of passionate individuals who collectively care deeply about a specific subject.

To be truly effective on YouTube and get your audience to engage, you need to share their passion and be creative enough with your content, channel, and social interaction that your commitment comes through loud and clear to them. Your goals are to be either part of the community proper or an expert who provides value to the community.

Going narrow versus going broad

Sharing your passions most effectively often means focusing on your niche. Many aspiring YouTubers feel that going after the largest audience possible to start with is the clearest path to success. Not necessarily. In fact, we want you to consider a few factors that may make you reconsider your plans to try for the broadest audience possible:

✔ **Getting found:** It takes time for your channel and content to infiltrate a popular subject area. You're likely competing with millions of videos, some of which have proven immensely successful and will dominate search results for some time.

✔ **Producing unique content:** With so many videos in a popular category, you'll definitely have challenges standing out — at least initially. Channels that have been covering your topic space have also had time to refine their brands, another factor that makes their content stand out.

✔ **Reaching influencers:** Popular and important industry spokespeople and personalities are constantly being bombarded by creators and viewers. You'll have a tough time attracting their attention at the beginning, no matter how insightful your vision or how creative your content.

✔ **Having help:** The channels at the top have lots of promotional help from subscribers or other advocates in social media. That didn't happen overnight. Invest time in developing relationships and proving that you bring value to the table.

Start off being the big fish in the small pond, and choose a specific topic space carefully. Your channel and your content will be more discoverable and increase the likelihood of connecting with both key influencers and the fan base.

Knowing why your audience matters

Treat your audience as an adjunct to your marketing department, public relations firm, sales organization, and design group.

The right audience will

✔ **Spend time on your channel.** The length of time that your audience spends viewing your content is important. Videos that receive more watch time are more likely to appear in YouTube search and watch recommendations.

✔ **Share your YouTube content with peers.** Everyone dreams of having a popular video with millions of views. A video becomes successful when it's unique and compelling enough with the target audience that one viewer eagerly shares it with peers, who then just as eagerly share it with other peers, and so forth.

✔ **Subscribe to your YouTube channel.** Subscribers watch twice as much of your content as nonsubscribers. They also receive updates about your channel activity (new videos, comments) in their subscription feeds, keeping them informed about all the exciting stuff on your channel. Ask your viewers to subscribe in the video, and include annotations where appropriate to subscribe to your channel.

✔ **Engage with your channel.** Likes (or dislikes) and comments comprise the avenue for building a community around your channel. Motivated audience members may also include your content on their own channels or websites, expanding your reach and your opportunity to build your audience even further.

✔ **Be your creative advocates.** A great audience truly cares about the channels they subscribe to and can be an important source of great ideas and content. Encourage your viewers to use the Comments section below the video to submit ideas; this strategy gives you more content ideas and helps engage viewer interest for the current video.

Defining your target audience as precisely as possible is an important component of channel success. A target audience of "15- to 55-year-old men" is far too broad. Add a layer of detail to define a more targeted audience — for example "people who like cooking" is a much more defined audience.

Finding out the nitty-gritty about your audience

If you haven't yet thought about your online audience, we recommend *Video Marketing For Dummies*, by Kevin Daum, Bettina Hein, Matt Scott, and Andreas Goeldi (John Wiley & Sons, Inc.). It provides a more in-depth look at audience needs and identification than we can offer here, but we do want to offer some food for thought. When planning your YouTube channel, have an image of your targeted fan base in mind at all times. Ask yourself these questions:

✔ **Who are they?** Marketing people like to use the term *demographics* to describe some of the characteristics of their target audience. Think about your audience and attributes such as age, gender, and interest. If you're selling baby products, for example, your audience may be new mothers between 24 and 36 years old. Be specific.

YouTube now attracts more 18- to 49-year-olds than most cable networks. However, if you're going after seniors, it may be a bit more difficult than if you were targeting a slightly younger audience. Fortunately, even some of our older friends are discovering YouTube as well!

✔ **Where are they?** YouTube works as well for small local business as it does for the big, international companies. Your social media efforts around your YouTube channel should involve influences in the geographic location you serve.

✔ **How do they get their information?** Make an effort to understand what your audience reads, where they go on the web for information, and what events they attend. This will influence the direction of your channel and its contents.

> ✔ **Who influences them?** What bloggers or YouTubers do your targeted viewers connect with? Pay attention to the style of how these web celebrities communicate.
>
> Be authentic. Don't feel that you need to mimic an influencer, because your audience will see right through it.

If you have other properties, such as a website, Facebook page, or Twitter account, you likely have much of the audience information you need for your YouTube planning process. As your channel grows in popularity, don't be surprised if your audience changes as well.

Defining Desired Actions

Your channel-planning blueprint must spell out the type of action you want your audience to take. That's *activation.* You need clarity around the type of action you want because it influences the type of content you create and the steps you want your audience to take. We cover both of these topics in detail later, in Chapter 10, but you should identify these actions during the planning phase.

No matter how intelligent and independent your fan base, you need to guide them through the experience with your channel and its contents. Believe it or not, your viewers want you to tell them what to do. Some of that supervision may be as explicit as a Subscribe button, or more implicit with the automated viewing of a playlist.

This is an area where many people and organizations struggle. Define what you want the viewer to do and determine how you'll help them do it. If your audience is aligned with your mission, they'll entrust you to guide them through your channel and give them a call to action (CTA, for short). Look at the following CTA options and determine which one sums up what you want your viewers to do:

> ✔ **Subscribe to your channel.** Subscribers are much more valuable viewers because they statistically consume more content and engage more on YouTube and social media.
>
> Don't be shy! Make sure to ask viewers to subscribe.
>
> ✔ **Watch more of your videos.** Content is often related. If a viewer has just watched a video of yours on house painting, chances are good that they'll watch a video on paint options or brush selection *if you ask them to.* In Chapter 10, we show you that playlists and annotations can help you guide viewers to watch more.

✔ **Do something**. What do you want your viewers to do? Vote? Volunteer? Run marathons? Cook Thai food from your recipes? Video is a strong motivator, so use that factor to drive your viewers to take action.

✔ **Make a purchase.** YouTube is now one of the places that people go to make buying decisions. If you're selling something, ask them to buy what you're selling, and be sure to let them know where they can close the sale — whether it's a physical location or a "virtual" store on the web.

✔ **Share their experience**. If a viewer enjoyed your channel or content, help them tell others about it. It's another helpful way to attract subscribers and views.

Planning an Outstanding YouTube Channel

YouTube rewards you with higher search rankings and supplementary video recommendations based first and foremost on your channel and individual video watch times. In addition, YouTube looks at factors such as viewer engagement and video sharing rates. Your job in the planning process is to identify and coordinate each component so that you're in a position to keep your channel active.

Having a spokesperson

Okay, you've analyzed your target fan base and figured out what motivates them on YouTube. Now you need to determine whether a specific channel spokesperson would be the right fit for your target fan base. This is a critical decision for both independent creators and organizations.

Typically, an audience gravitates toward either a personality or content, but not toward any old personality or content. Whatever you choose to prioritize, it has to have a high level of authenticity. If the viewers in your topic area engage more with personality, for example, be sure to choose a spokesperson with credibility and appeal.

Aim for the same voice across your content because it will provide the consistency that your audience needs across different types of video.

A good example of a brand with a consistent voice is the personal care company e.l.f. Cosmetics (www.youtube.com/eyeslipsfacedotcom), which consistently uses Achelle Dunaway as the voice of its videos. Achelle isn't terribly famous, but the fans of e.l.f. have come to know her and expect to see or hear her in every video the channel produces. They trust her and associate her with the e.l.f. brand. Often, they give her both feedback and praise in the individual video comments.

Branding

Branding can be a large and complex topic, but we're going to keep it simple: Branding is about naming and design that is unique to you. Need an example? Think about Apple. You see consistency in all its products, naming conventions, website, and packaging. Over time, that branding symbolism — the look and feel — becomes synonymous with who you are. Want to learn more? Check out *Branding For Dummies*, by Bill Chiaravalle and Barbara Findlay Schenck (John Wiley & Sons, Inc.).

Your YouTube channel and videos are powerful extensions of your brand. If you have an existing website, logo, or color pattern, bring it over to your YouTube channel and use it for the branded elements of your videos as well. If you give your viewers a great experience on YouTube, chances are that they'll end up on your website, too. Keep the branding consistent. Your viewers will appreciate it.

Planning the channel layout

Your channel must be visually representative of the video content you create. When a viewer first visits your channel, it's important that they understand what kind of videos your produce or curate. You also want viewers to be in a position to quickly find out when new content is expected from your channel. A great design layout makes these tasks a lot easier.

When coming up with a design layout, keep these elements in mind:

- **Channel art:** The banner you see across the top of your YouTube channel's home page is the welcome mat for your viewer, so make it as appealing as possible. A good channel art design is *device agnostic* — it looks good on mobile devices, desktops, smart TVs, or what-have-you. To help you make the creation of your channel art easier, you can download a customized graphical template for your YouTube channel at `https://support.google.com/youtube`.

- **Channel trailer:** The channel trailer is the first video that visitors see when viewing your channel. This is where you need to captivate your new viewers and get them to subscribe to your channel. You can customize the channel trailer for subscribers or nonsubscribers.

✔ **Channel icon:** This icon indicates who you are when you post a comment, release a new video, or show up in search results and many more locations across YouTube and Google+.

The channel icon can be changed only from the Google+ account associated with your YouTube channel.

✔ **Channel links:** The small icons that live in the lower-right corner of your channel art direct viewers to your other digital properties, such as Facebook, Twitter, or Pinterest. The complete list of digital properties is under the About section of your YouTube channel, and you can choose whether to display icons for some or all of your properties.

✔ **Custom sections:** Visually dividing your channel page into sections is a great way to help your viewers find the most relevant content on your channel. One way to customize your sections is to create unique playlists or groupings of videos per section.

✔ **Custom thumbnails:** Thumbnails are visual snapshots of your video, similar to a poster for a movie. They are chosen by default by YouTube — three optional frames from the beginning, middle, and end of your video are provided for every video asset that's uploaded. You can, however, create a custom thumbnail for each video. If you do so, choose a thumbnail that is illustrative of the content in the video.

Thumbnails have a tremendous impact on a video's view rate. With that fact in mind, always choose or create a good thumbnail, especially for videos shown in sections.

✔ **Featured channels:** Channels that you own or like or that are simply relevant for your audience are best included in the Featured Channels section on the right side of your channel page.

Under Featured Channels, you control the additional section **Related Channels**, which YouTube populates with channels that it considers to be like yours. Though YouTube doesn't disclose the exact criteria, it's likely based on content type and what viewers search for. You can turn off this feature, but by doing so, YouTube won't put your channel on the Related Channel feeds of other users. You benefit only by keeping it on.

✔ **Verified name**: A verification badge, identified by a gray check mark, signals viewers that a channel associated with a celebrity or brand is legitimate. You need a Google+ account with the name authorized to receive a verified name for your channel.

With so many channels on YouTube, viewers may think they're viewing the appropriate channel for an organization or famous personality. The verification badge shows up to the right of the channel name and helps alleviate any viewer concerns about the legitimacy of the channel.

Crafting a Content Strategy

Coming up with a mission for your channel is important, as is defining your audience and planning how your channel could best serve your target audience's needs, but at some point you have to define the content that brings it all together. Well, there's no time like the present, so get ready to tackle that task.

Recognizing that content includes video and more

When establishing a content plan, consider these factors that influence how your audience discovers your content and what action viewers take as a result of watching:

- **Video:** The *channel trailer* is the first video visitors see when viewing your channel. This is where you need to captivate your new viewers and get them to subscribe to your channel. You can customize which channel trailer is shown for subscribers or nonsubscribers.

- **Intro and outros:** Create consistent intro and outro styles for your videos. Think of intros and outros as what you see at the beginning and end of your favorite television show. In the first five seconds, a viewer should know that this is one of your videos; this consistency can be something as simple as the way you say hello and greet your viewers or as complex as an animated logo. Outros should be similar across your channel as well — a goodbye ritual or animated end cards, for example.

- **Metadata:** Metadata, or the words you use to describe your video, include the video title, keyword tags, and video description. In Chapter 9, you can see how to add and modify your metadata content.

  Though the term *metadata* sounds like something out of a *Star Trek* episode, it's important for discovery and YouTube Search. Viewers can also find more information about the video or links back to your website if they want more information.

- **Thumbnails:** Thumbnails need to be descriptive of the content that a viewer could find in your video. Make custom thumbnails to help viewers discover your content above the rest.

- **Annotations:** Annotations are overlay elements that you can add to your existing videos. They allow viewers to do something when they click on the annotation, such as subscribe or get more information about you or view more content.

Don't worry about the nuances of making your videos interactive with annotations. You can see how easy this task is and understand the art and science of annotations in Chapter 10.

✔ **End cards:** An end card is a collection of one or more annotations at the end of a video that drives viewers to do what you want them to do when the video is completed. As part of your branding, you want your end cards to be consistent in both their layout and CTAs.

✔ **Links:** Use clickable links in your video description to drive viewers to a specific location on the web or somewhere within YouTube.

Your planning process should consider the viewer who wants more information from a specific video. Providing links in the video description or annotations is a great way to give the audience more information when they want it.

✔ **Web assets:** Where you send your viewers after they click on a video description or annotation is important for both your viewers' experience and for your channel goals. Your planning must take into account where you send your viewers and what you expect them to do when they arrive at your chosen destination. Be creative! Your target might be a Facebook contest, a Twitter page, a scientific journal, or anything else you can link to that is relevant for your viewers.

Looking at content formats

If you've been mulling over jumping into the YouTube world for a while, we're pretty sure that you've spent a lot of time wrestling with how to produce all that content to keep your channel fresh and active. With YouTube, you have several options for your content strategy:

✔ **Creation:** Regularly produce your own content. You can certainly build a channel without a stitch of your own content, but if you're going to stand out, your viewers need to see your genuine stuff.

✔ **Curation:** Mine the YouTube universe for content that complements your channel, and organize it in a logical way using sections and playlists for the viewer.

Think of curation in terms of what a museum does: Collect all this great art *(content)*, and then pull it together into a themed exhibit. The YouTube playlist is the museum's exhibit. That's why museums put French Impressionist paintings together: because it's all about the viewer/visitor experience. Would you want to see an impressionist painting together with contemporary pottery? Probably not.

Channel owners generally love it when their videos are included in playlists, because it helps promote their channels and gets viewers watching their content. Done right, your curation favor will be returned many times over.

✓ **Collaboration:** You don't have to do everything yourself! Team up with other channel owners and create joint content. It's a popular and effective way to grow an audience and gain subscribers. Since a YouTube video can be associated with only one channel, your collaboration planning should take into account content that you'll own (create) and content that you'll help share (collaborate).

Here are some examples of different types of content you can utilize for your channel:

✓ **Episodic content:** The idea here is to have reoccurring content that creates a series or a body of work on a specific topic. This is great content to produce for your channel because it's highly attractive to channel subscribers. Subscribers can be notified every time you release a video.

✓ **Short- and long-form content:** Creating a mixture of short- and long-form content can help you understand the sweet spot for your viewers. YouTube Analytics (described in Chapter 11) helps you plan better by identifying the optimal total run time for your videos. If you're creating ten-minute videos with short watch times, consider adding in annotations to lead viewers to a different video on a similar topic where you start to see the watch times decline.

✓ **Create new edits, recycle footage**: Don't be afraid to think outside the box when it comes to content creation. Reuse video outtakes, behind-the-scenes, and additional footage (called *B-roll*) to make new edits. Recycle your content when it makes sense for your viewers.

✓ **Playlists**: Reengage viewers with old videos in new playlists. Highlight videos that are still relevant on your channel page and in new playlists. You can choose to include your playlist updates in your channel feed to update your fans.

✓ **Plan for Mobile**: Mobile viewership accounts for 40 percent of global YouTube video consumption. Make your content easy to consume on mobile devices. Easy-to-see thumbnails and text onscreen are important for your mobile audience. Shorter titles are easier to read and understand on mobile as well. In Chapter 11, you can see how to use YouTube Analytics to check your channel traffic sources and understand what percentage of views are from mobile.

Above the beauty crowd

We conducted a major research study of the Beauty category on YouTube, analyzing 168 companies and their YouTube channels, 45,000 independent creators and their channels, and more than 800,000 total videos. We found that even in this very crowded part of YouTube, channels with a clear but authentic and differentiated mission had far superior channel performance. They had more views, subscribers, and engagement than many much larger beauty brands. The more savvy beauty brands, though, were quick to understand this new dynamic and then began including content from independent creators.

For example, Bobbi Brown, the beauty brand, put together an additional YouTube channel dedicated to beauty vloggers looking to create inspiring looks for their viewers. Check it out at www.youtube.com/ilovemakeupOFFICIAL. The brand provides products and inspiration to the vloggers, and the vloggers then go on to create videos for the I Love Makeup channel. This may sound convoluted, but it works well because each of the vloggers already has a dedicated audience following their content, each one is a trusted advisor to their audience on all things beauty, and now their fans watch them create content for one of their favorite cosmetic brands. It's a win for both vloggers and the brand.

Curation recycling

Multi-channel networks aggregate many similarly themed YouTube channels and personalities. Frequently, they help promote their managed channels' content on a single primary channel. To see what we mean, check out Tastemade (www.youtube.com/tastemade), which is a great example of an MCN *curating* its channels' content — they group videos from different channels into a unified theme and make it much easier for viewers to watch them. You don't have to own or be affiliated with a YouTube video to include it in your own channel playlist lineup. You can simply enjoy recipes and collect and curate them from your audience. There are no limits to what you can curate, although some content will resonate better with your audience.

 Create sections and playlists on your channel that include videos from other creators. As long as it makes sense for your channel to include outside content, curating content is a great way to expand your channel's appeal and keep it active even if you aren't creating unique content.

Adidas, for example, has a ton of channels; it made a conscious decision to link many of its subchannels to sections and playlists on its primary channel, at www.youtube.com/user/adidas. Doing so encourages cross promotion of its other assets and channels.

Programming for Success

Suppose that you create a good channel and produce ten excellent videos that your audience would likely watch, share, like, and comment on. Uploading those ten videos all at one time translates into only one measly real event for your audience, meaning that you've left nine marketing opportunities unexploited.

The moral of the story? Don't rush to upload all your content to YouTube at one time. You'll get better audience engagement if you space out your uploads, in essence delivering your content on a regular basis. Programming dictates how best to deliver your content to your fan base.

Keeping your subscriber feeds active is an important part of programming strategy, but it doesn't need to be video based. Your other channel activity (such as playlist modification) and engagement (which includes likes and sharing) also keeps your subscriber feed flowing.

Delivering content consistently

A famous philosopher once spoke rather disparagingly about foolish consistencies and the danger of conformity. That may be a good philosophy for your branding and content, but not for your YouTube channel programming. Though YouTube differs significantly from broadcast television and cable networks, your viewers will want consistency and predictability of content scheduling.

The better YouTube creators put up content on their channels regularly. That's what a publishing schedule is: your upload plan. Check out the grid shown in Figure 5-4 — it shows the publishing schedule for Dulce Candy (www.youtube.com/DulceCandy87), a beauty-and-style personality with a popular channel. From the pattern, you see a continual stream of content being added. Her average is every 3.1 days between uploads.

Figure 5-4:
The Dulce
Candy
publishing
schedule.

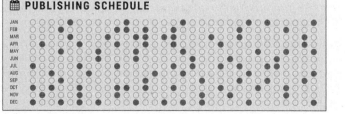

Upload regular content weekly. Don't hide it. Let the audience know your publishing schedule on YouTube, and use social media to alert them when your content is live.

In addition to your social media outreach, remember that your channel feed will alert your subscribers whenever you upload new content.

Being flexible and reactive

Just because you're producing regular, addictive, episodic content that amasses both subscribers and views doesn't mean that you can't generate some additional excitement around your channel. You may want to consider certain triggers:

- ✔ **Tentpole events:** Significant cultural or industry events may play well into your channel and content strategy. If you sell zombie paraphernalia, Halloween is a perfect tentpole event for you. Identify regular events or happenings in your topic area. If your channel covers auto racing, consider certain events such as the Daytona 500 and Le Mans as tentpole events. Industry events may be a great way to capture footage with industry leaders and personality.

  Make sure you have important YouTube apps installed on your mobile devices, especially at tentpole events. There are several apps available on both Android and IOS that allow you to work on the fly. Use the Capture app to record, edit, and upload video on the fly. Manage your channel with the Studio app. Just want to watch some YouTube videos? The YouTube app is great for that.

- ✔ **Reactive:** You should be prepared to leverage nonplanned events for your channel, which should drive additional traffic and viewership. Nonplanned events are about news, but only if it's relevant to your channel. Marques Brownlee (www.youtube.com/marquesbrowlee) is a major video reviewer who covers the consumer electronics business. If someone announces a new smartphone, you can be sure that Marques will have something on YouTube relatively fast.

  Time-sensitive content may help you in search and recommended videos because YouTube likes to put trending content recommendations in front of relevant viewers.

- ✔ **Momentum:** You can repackage your content into video trailers to help drive channel promotion. Just did a YouTube live event? Put together a highlight reel to keep your channel active and your subscribers' channel feeds flowing. Don't be afraid to craft outtake videos, behind-the-scenes content, and more personal pieces to let your audience know that you're excited for this new content. This will help personalize and enhance the authenticity of your channel.

Going live for more engagement

You can deliver a much more interactive experience with your most passionate viewers by taking advantage of YouTube live events. You can live-stream any number of events, but remember that they should align with your channel's mission.

There are channel restrictions and some technical requirements for live streaming. Ensure that your account is in good standing with no strikes and that you meet the technical requirements. Don't forget to test sufficiently before using this service.

Consider the following statements before adding live streaming to your YouTube programming mix:

- ✔ **Promotion is important:** YouTube live streaming is clearly different from regular YouTube video — your viewers must show up for the live event to experience it as it happens. If they don't know about it, they won't show up, and all your prep work may be for naught. Be sure to get the word out, and don't be shy about asking your YouTube subscribers to help.

- ✔ **Adjust in-flight:** Your audience will provide feedback on the fly as your event occurs, so be sure to watch the comments and respond accordingly.

- ✔ **Repurpose event content:** A livestreamed event is a great way to capture rich and engaging content for use on your channel. Figure out how it fits into your channel after the event is over.

Reuse your livestreamed content and divide it into multiple videos if it makes sense. If you're going to include the event on your channel, don't feel the need to save the event as one video.

Before you use content derived from a live event on your channel, you will in some circumstances need the legal right to use the content. Don't worry: You won't need to hire a lawyer, because you can read all about it in Chapter 16 when you'll learn all about copyright.

Planning Doesn't End

Your channel is live. You created great content. You have views. Your audience is engaged. It's all smooth sailing, right? Hopefully, yes, but as the saying goes, "You have to inspect what you expect." Look to see whether your audience

✔ Watches your videos all the way to the end

✔ Stays on your channel and views more content

✔ Comments and provides creative suggestions

✔ Shares your work on social media

✔ Includes your videos in their playlists

"Well, how do I all that?" you may ask. Fear not: You'll find the answers to all these questions (and to a few others as well) when we help you explore YouTube Analytics in Chapter 11.

The YouTube world constantly changes with new channels, new contents, new personalities, and new trends. Your channel makes you part of this world, and you're responsible for adapting to changes in order to stay relevant. Pay attention to what the viewers are telling you, and feed it into your ongoing planning process.

Chapter 6

Acquiring the Tools of the Trade

· ·

· ·

*L*et's face it: Making video is easier now than it has ever been, and that trend is growing. Cameras, editing software, and computers that can edit video are now relatively cheap and available, which means that, following a few best practices, almost anyone can make a decent YouTube video with equipment they may already own. This chapter looks at a few of those best practices and helps you make a decision about price versus quality by examining the advantages of new camera and recording formats. To close out the chapter, we also take a look at the production tools you'll need in order to produce great video for YouTube.

Checking Out Your Camera Options

Let's get the good news out of the way right off the bat: There's a good chance that you already own a High Definition (or HD) camera. Video cameras are everywhere. According to the Pew Research Internet Project, as of January 2014, 58 percent of American adults own smartphones. Pretty much any modern smartphone has an HD camera, as do most modern laptops and all-in-one desktop computers. But just because access to cameras is easy doesn't mean that choosing the right camera is simple. Quality varies widely, and there are some tools and techniques that can help even a basic camera shoot good video. We talk about several types of cameras specifically, but you have to take a few (mostly universal features) into account when shopping for cameras. For the most part, we talk about these three types of cameras:

- ✔ **Camera phone:** We use the term *camera phone* as a catchall term for a camera built into a mobile device. (So don't write in to tell us that your tablet or music player isn't a phone; we are well aware of that fact.) When we say *camera phone,* you should see in your mind "a camera that is built into your iPhone or Android or Kindle Fire or whatever." A camera phone may not produce the absolute best images out there, but when the moment comes to capture the footage of one of your dogs sitting on your other dog and howling the tune to "Total Eclipse of the Heart," the best camera is the one in your pocket that you can start shooting with immediately.

- ✔ **Camcorder:** The venerable standalone camcorder was for many years the average person's entry point to the home video market. In recent years, camcorders have been pressured from both sides because camera phones are generally good enough these days to satisfy the needs of the casual video shooter, and the very high quality (and dropping price) of digital single-lens reflex (DSLR) cameras has captured the interest of shooters who are interested in higher video quality and feature control. Camcorders can be quite convenient, though, and the best of them offer a happy medium between features and ease of use. Camcorders also range widely, from the most basic entry-level devices to full-blown professional machines that cost tens of thousands of dollars.

- ✔ **DSLR:** DSLRs have exploded in popularity in recent years. DSLRs have traditionally been used for still photography, but now all DSLRs include an array of video features and settings. You can capture great-quality video and easily stay under a $1,000 budget for your camera gear.

Working through the (camera) basics

Before getting into a detailed discussion of the pros and cons of the different camera types out there, we want to talk a bit about a few features and elements that *all* cameras share. That way, we can get some terminology out of the way that may prove helpful when you're comparing cameras:

- ✔ **The sensor:** The heart of any digital video camera is its sensor. The larger the sensor, the better the image quality. That's because a larger sensor has larger pixels, which capture more light, resulting in higher image quality. Currently, a "big" sensor is a full frame sensor measuring in at 36x24mm, the same size as a 35mm film negative.

When people talk about megapixels, that's something of a red herring. A 10 megapixel camera with a larger sensor can likely capture better-looking video than a 12 megapixel camera with a smaller sensor. Though this description can be confusing and technical, the important thing to note is that a larger sensor is generally better.

✔ **The lens:** The pros will tell you, it's all about the glass. The lens in a camera is a huge factor in image quality, and it's a factor that can be difficult to understand. The most important feature of any lens is its *aperture* capability. The aperture of a lens controls how much light enters the camera body and hits the sensor. Basically, along with shutter speed and ISO, this is the control that makes the picture brighter or darker.

The aperture is also called the *f-stop* (or *t-stop* on cinema lenses), and aperture ranges are denoted as f2–f24 or similar language.

The most popular look on YouTube currently is an f-stop of 5.6; this draws the viewers' attention to the foreground, keeping it in sharp focus, while leaving the background soft.

Try to use lenses that have a fixed f-stop, not a variable f-stop. Such lenses often are a much higher quality — with a price tag that reflects that fact. A Canon 50mm 1.8 is a great starting lens and usually will cost you around $100.

✔ **Resolution and format:** The YouTube player supports High Definition (HD) video and you really should have an HD camera to take advantage of that support. Most modern video cameras are capable of shooting full 1080p HD (1920x1080 resolution), and that is what you should look for. Some cameras have variable frame rates, but as long as they can shoot the standard rates, such as 24p, 30p, and 60i, you should be able to find something you like. Look for all these numbers in the specs when shopping for cameras.

The numbers before the letters indicate how many fields per second are shown. As for the P, it stands for *progressive,* where the video image is drawn progressively line after line. In 30p, to take one example, one whole frame is typically shown every 1/30 of a second. The I stands for *interlaced,* meaning the odd or even rows in the picture show every 1/60 of a second. 60i is typically used for sports or fast paced videos, because it results in less of a flicker feel. 30p is often perceived as higher quality for less action-based footage because its resolution brings with a clearer image. 24p is the frame rate of film — but getting that "film look" also depends on lighting and composition.

The latest and greatest DSLRs can shoot in the format *4k* (4k is short for 4,000 pixel resolution), which is a much higher resolution than 1080p HD. Though footage shot in 4k is beautiful, the cameras that shoot 4K tend to be expensive. The reality of shooting video for YouTube is that 4K resolution is, for the moment, overkill. The site can display 4k, but the vast majority of views are on computer screens or mobile devices incapable of displaying 4k or 8k content.

✔ **Codecs:** Most cameras compress the captured video to save space on whatever recording media you're using. The compression software that the camera uses is a *codec.* In the past, different codecs could result in wildly variable performance when the time came to edit. Often, footage would need to be transcoded to a different format in order for the editing suite to understand it. Thanks to improvements in editing software and hardware, transcoding is largely a thing of the past. All the major editing packages these days can handle just about any codec you care to throw at them. Just be sure to record in the highest quality codec for your device — which generally means the least compressed video.

✔ **Monitoring:** You need to be able to see your video as you shoot it. Most modern video cameras have an LCD screen for monitoring video. Usually, manufacturers talk about these screens in terms of pixels. When choosing a camera, make sure you can tell if the image is in focus from the view on the LCD. Built-in focus assist options will also help when using a smaller LCD. If you cannot tell if your image is in focus, you may need an external HD monitor or you may want add an EVF (electronic viewfinder) from a third party for monitoring.

✔ **Zoom:** Zoom involves changing the focal length of the lens to make it seem as though the camera is closer to its subject. Though it's a somewhat familiar concept, one important thing to remember about zoom is the difference between optical and digital zoom:

- *Optical zoom* is the actual telephoto effect produced by the physical change in the focal length of the lens, and it is the only zoom you would ever want to use. It allows you to zoom in on the subject with no significant degradation of picture quality.

- *Digital zoom* is usually a very high, seemingly impressive number, but it is a feature to avoid. Digital zoom doesn't actually change the optics of the camera; it simply scales the image up, which produces a lot of noise and artifacts in the picture. Stated simply, it won't do anything but make your footage look bad.

✔ **Memory, tape, and hard drives:** Pay attention to how your camera is storing the footage you're shooting. Each of the following formats has upsides, and downsides.

- *Tape:* Cameras that record on tape are less common these days, but there are still a few out there, and many used ones are available. Tape has a few upsides, in that it is durable, but its downsides are many. Generally, tapes are expensive because it's really not a good idea to reuse them. After you use them once, the quality degrades significantly upon a second use. Tape also degrades over time, so it turns out not to be a great place to store your footage. Tape can also be difficult to deal with. Generally, taped footage has to be captured to your editing computer in real time, which is quite time consuming when compared to tapeless workflows.

- *Flash memory formats:* The video industry is rapidly moving toward the use of the standardized flash memory cards for all kinds of cameras. These cards are inexpensive, almost infinitely reusable, and easy to use for both capturing and transferring footage.

There are still a few competing standards when it comes to memory cards, so make sure you purchase the right card for your camera. The two most popular memory card types are Secure Digital High Capacity (SDHC or SD, the more common title) and Compact Flash (CF). Both are excellent. They're relatively cheap, reliable, and ubiquitous. You can buy them just about everywhere.

Our recommendation when it comes to memory is to choose your camera first — that will often determine what kind of memory card you need to purchase. When purchasing your memory card, either SD or CF, choose a card that can read and write data as quickly as your camera. An example of a write speed is 1000x; this means the card reads and writes at approximately 150MB/s.

- *Proprietary digital memory card:* Many high-end professional camcorders use proprietary memory cards. For example, Panasonic's pricey pro camcorders use either the P2 or Sony's SxS-1 format. Though these cards perform well, they work with only *their* cameras, and they're extremely expensive. These formats tend to be used on cameras that are also quite expensive, so it may not be a problem encountered by the YouTube beginner. But as your skills progress, you may want to upgrade your camera, so keep this information in mind.

✔ **Image stabilization:** Higher-quality cameras often offer image stabilization, a feature that does just what it says — it stabilizes images. One hallmark of footage from people who are new to videography is shaky footage. Image stabilization can help with this problem, and it comes in a couple of different flavors:

- *Optical image stabilization:* This type of correction features gyroscopes and moving elements inside the lens itself. When the camera shakes, the lens detects the movement, and the lens elements roll with the punches, so to speak. The lens parts move to correct for the motion, and the sensor captures a stable image.

Internal gyroscopes can be noisy, so be sure to use an off-camera recording device when using optical image stabilization. (An internal camera mic is sure to pick up the noisy gyroscope sounds.)

- *Digital image stabilization:* This correction uses various software algorithms to reduce the impact of shaky hands on your video. Unfortunately, some to the tricks it comes up with aren't that aesthetically pleasing. For example, the most common way digital image stabilization corrects an issue is by removing the edges of the frame. More often than not, you end up with a degraded image that's just not worth keeping. Yes, you may be able to correct in post-production, but your best bet is to collect the highest quality image while recording in the field.

✔ **Manual controls:** An important feature to look for in a camera is easily accessible manual controls. Though at first you'll probably want the camera to manage most aspects of image capture for you, as your skills as a videographer develop, you'll inevitably want to take control of the camera's controls. The manual controls have to be easily accessible — ideally assignable to physical buttons on the outside of the camera. These physical buttons allow you to change settings quickly, which can be important when you're trying to capture a moment. Controls that are buried deep in the camera's settings menus aren't truly useful.

Looking at DSLRs

DSLR stands for *d*igital *s*ingle-*l*ens *r*eflex, but its initials are not the key concept to understand here. The big reason that DSLRs are massively popular these days is that they can produce great image quality for a relatively low price; the many happy DSLR owners out there probably don't know — and don't care — what the initials stand for.

As with any camera, the DSLR has both upsides and downsides. The upsides are clear:

✔ **The big picture:** By a large margin, the most important advantage that the DSLR affords a filmmaker is the large sensor. Some DSLRs even have a sensor that is roughly the same area as a traditional frame of 35mm film — these are *full-frame* sensors. Without getting too technical, the larger the sensor, the better the image quality. Also, the large sensor, when combined with the right lens settings, produces a shallow depth of field, which is desirable if you want your video to have that sheen of professionalism. This depth of field effect is, put simply, the phenomenon in which the subject of the video is in focus but the background is out of focus, which makes the subject feel separate from the background. This out-of-focus background — called *bokeh* by all the arty film school types — is an important trick to have in your repertoire.

✔ **The lenses:** Another great feature of the DSLR is its interchangeable lenses. A DSLR allows the operator to choose the type of lens that is required for the shot. Some lenses are better for action shots, and some lenses are great in low light; macro lenses shoot subjects in extreme close-up, and zoom lenses allow you to capture distant subjects. This sort of flexibility, which is crucial in higher-end filmmaking, can really improve the visual quality of your videos. A nice bonus is that each manufacturer has a standard lens mount that most of its cameras use. For example, if you start with an entry-level Canon camera and obtain several lenses for it, those lenses also fit the fancier Canon camera if and when you decide to upgrade.

✔ **Manual settings:** Most serious videographers will tell you that capturing the best image requires understanding and using the camera's manual settings, and setting characteristics such as ISO, aperture, and shutter speed. We don't get into explaining all the details of how to use a camera in this chapter. The important point here is that even entry-level DSLRs have robust manual controls that are usually easy to use and under- stand. Advanced videographers want to make changes to these settings quickly and easily, and most DSLRs have dedicated buttons on the camera body to change each of these settings quickly.

As proof that not everything is hunky-dory in DSLR-ville, check out these things that folks love to hate about DSLRs:

✔ **The sound:** Though this situation is slowly changing, DSLRs have tra- ditionally been reviled for their inability to capture sound well. Audio is extremely important to making a watchable video, so this is kind of a big deal. We will say up front that no DSLR on the market today has an acceptable built-in microphone. We believe that you should not use the built-in mic on the camera when you can avoid it — we recommend you buy more stuff to accompany your camera. There are a couple of ways around this problem.

• *An external microphone:* This is the simplest solution to the DSLR audio problem. Most DSLRs have a connection that allows the user to plug in a separate microphone. Because this audio problem is widespread in the DSLR market, quite a few options are available that are designed to work specifically with DSLRs. There are many choices in this space, but we find one solution to be the Rode Video Mic Pro; it has an excellent cost-to-value ratio.

• *An external audio recorder:* Even with an external microphone, many DSLRs still don't have a great way to monitor the audio you're recording. This is a very big deal. If you don't know what the audio sounds like as you're recording the footage, you can quickly ruin the shoot and waste a lot of time and resources. A number of digital recorders on the market are designed for this very purpose. These recorders come in a wide variety of price points, but they do confer a lot of advantages. Going down the list, they offer bal- anced inputs (eliminating hiss and hum noises), phantom power for professional mics (recommended is the mkh416), more control of audio levels, and compressors and limiters for keeping levels from clipping.

Recording the audio externally does mean that you have to synchronize the footage and the audio recording in editing, which introduces more work and an opportunity for problems to arise. Just because you're using on off camera recording device doesn't mean you should turn off the in camera audio recording. You'll want audio from both devices captured for reference when syncing in post production.

✔ **Manual settings:** Extensive manual controls can be both a blessing and a curse. The best part about shooting manually is the amount of control you have over the quality of light in every shot. You can choose how bright you want the shot to feel based on the emotion of the scene, whereas if you use an automatic setting you may lose some of the mood you could have created with your lighting setup. The sheer number of settings and the fine gradations of adjustment can be overwhelming to an inexperienced user. Though DSLRs generally have a full automatic mode that will allow you to point and shoot quickly, we recommend working in the manual controls and maintaining control over the quality of each shot, even if it takes more time.

✔ **Record time limitations:** One long-standing complaint about DSLRs is that all of them have some kind of record-time limitation. Admittedly, popular cameras like the GH4 or a7s do not have duration limits, but in some cases, a camera can shoot only 29 minutes of continuous video.

Before planning a long video, be sure to check the upload limits for your particular YouTube channel. To do so, point your browser to `https://youtube.com/my_videos_upload` to check your limits or extend your limits.

✔ **No autofocus:** Not all DSLRs can autofocus while shooting video. This can be inconvenient, especially when you're shooting a moving subject with a shallow depth of field. The fact is, it doesn't take much for your subject to move in and out of focus; it doesn't have to move far at all. This is most problematic when shooting scenes with lots of action and movement at low aperture settings.

✔ **Manual zoom only:** The only way to zoom with most DSLRs is to manually adjust the zoom ring on the lens barrel. This can cause a number of problems while shooting video. Touching the lens more than likely is going to produce a shaky image; it takes a steady hand to make a smooth manual zoom. If you're planning to do lots of zoom shots, a DSLR may not be for you.

✔ **The expensive aftermarket:** A lot of the issues we've described with DSLRs *do* have solutions, but you're going to have to pay a pretty penny for them, or try to build them yourself.

For most YouTube video creators just starting out, a DSLR may be just the ticket for you. If you have no experience with video production or photography, be patient, the DSLR will have a learning curve. The inexperienced creator often can use a simple webcam to get started. If you do have experience creating video, and you're making content that requires the best image quality for your buck, a DSLR is the way to go.

Several manufacturers are in the DSLR market, including Canon, Sony, Nikon, and Panasonic. Though all these companies make good DSLRs for still images, we generally recommend the Canon DSLRs for shooting video. In our estimation, they offer good features for the price. Start by looking at some entries in the Canon line:

- ✔ **Canon EOS 5D Mark III:** Though this option is a bit pricey, running around $3,000 for the camera without a lens, this is a truly excellent camera choice for shooting video. The 5D Mark III has made huge improvements to its video capture capabilities, and its full 35mm sensor gives you the ability to capture beautiful video. As with any DSLR, you need to have at least an external microphone, and maybe even an external audio recorder; but as far as image quality goes, the 5D is hard to beat. The latest Canon DSLR cameras have done a lot to improve the on-board audio capture quality.

- ✔ **Canon EOS Rebel t5i:** The Rebel series is Canon's more affordable DSLR line, and the t5i is certainly cheaper than the 5D. The t5i is widely available for under $600, and it delivers excellent image quality. It features a somewhat smaller sensor than the 5D, but the sensor is considerably larger than can be found on any camcorder.

- ✔ **Panasonic GH4:** Currently the only DSLM (digital camera without a mirror) that shoots 4k video. This camera is known for reduced noise and great color reproduction. This is a great camera for both novices and professionals at around $1,500.

- ✔ **Sony a7s:** Sony's very popular a7s, coming in under $3,000, is currently the world's smallest full-frame camera with interchangeable lens capabilities. Since lenses are truly the part of the camera that you can continue to invest in, it's best to stick with one camera manufacturer. Most DSLR lenses can be used on many different models within the same manufactures products. Double-check your manufacturer of choice before making large investments in lenses.

Checking out camcorders

A *camcorder* is an all-in-one camera that is dedicated solely to shooting video. For the vast majority of users, a camcorder is what comes to mind when they think about video cameras. Camcorders have traditionally recorded to videotape cassettes, but pretty much any camcorder you can buy these days uses some sort of file-based system utilizing digital media.

There are generally two types of camcorders that are at all relevant to YouTube creators. The *consumer* camcorder is the type of camera available at big box electronic retailers. *Prosumer* is the term for cameras that add many of the features of professional cameras while retaining at least some semblance of affordability.

The professional range of video cameras tend to be the cameras that are designed for news gathering for television stations; those cameras can run into the tens of thousands of dollars, and they aren't really cost effective for creating YouTube videos. For the purposes of this book, we focus on consumer and prosumer camcorders.

The consumer camcorder

First off, let us point out that consumer camcorders have come a long way in the past ten years. The video cameras that you can buy in an electronics store these days affordably deliver a lot of great features. They have some downsides, but if you're just starting out shooting videos, excellent consumer camcorder choices are out there. As usual, these cameras have positives and negatives.

First, the positives:

- ✔ **Low cost of entry:** The greatest appeal of the consumer camcorders is by far the price. The market for these types of cameras is competitive, which means that manufacturers have really packed a lot of features into these cameras for very little money. A basic camera is less than $200, and the best of the best consumer cameras generally cost less than $1,000.

- ✔ **Ease of use:** Consumer camcorders are designed to be easy to use. They are intended for consumers who may not know a lot about shooting video, and, as a result, they do a lot of work to make up for that. These cameras generally have effective automatic settings that do a good job of capturing usable video in a wide variety of situations. Both the video and the audio recorded by these cameras tend to be pretty decent. It won't win any cinematography awards, but it can get the job done, depending on the job. Especially for vlog-style videos, these consumer camcorders may be all you need.

Now for the bad news:

- ✔ **Picture quality:** If you already have experience in shooting video, and you like to control the image, you'll find a consumer camcorder annoying. These cameras generally have unremarkable lenses, and very, very small sensors. This means that anything you shoot on these cameras will likely look like a home video. That works for some formats, but if you're making short art films, this may not be the camera for you.

✔ **Lack of manual control:** Part of the consumer camcorders ease of use, which is generally a positive, can be a negative for someone who wants to manually control settings. For the most part, manual controls are non-existent, and if a consumer camcorder does have manual controls, they can be very hard to use. They are often buried in onscreen menus and are difficult to operate. Users who want to fine-tune their footage won't find much to love here.

✔ **Feature bloat:** One of the most annoying aspects of the consumer camcorder market is the feature arms race that goes on between the various manufacturers who operate in this market. Rather than improve lenses or sensors on their models year over year, they focus on silly features like built-in projectors, Wi-Fi connections, digital zoom, and near field communication. All this stuff is useless when it comes to improving your footage.

The prosumer camcorder

Prosumer camcorders aim to be a true all-in-one solution for capturing video, and most of them are flexible enough to address a wide variety of shooting scenarios with aplomb. We tend to think of prosumer camcorders as the happy medium of video cameras. They combine a lot of the ease of use of a camcorder and can produce a picture quality that can rival some DSLRs. They have weaknesses and trade-offs, of course, as does any camera.

Here's why prosumer camcorders have a dedicated fan base:

✔ **Picture quality:** In almost all cases, a prosumer camcorder will produce a better image than a consumer version does, primarily because of the larger sensors and the better lenses that these models tend to have. Any decent prosumer camcorder will capture a sharper image than its consumer counterpart.

✔ **Ease of use *and* manual control:** The best of the prosumer camcorders are straightforward to use and have a lot of useful automatic settings. Videographers are able to capture images on the fly without a lot of fuss. However, they also have extensive manual controls. On the good ones, those controls are operated with buttons on the camera body.

✔ **Robust audio capture:** Most prosumer camcorders do a good job of capturing digital audio, and they often have a robust set of inputs for getting your audio into the camera. In most situations, you'll use an external microphone, and a prosumer camcorder should have plenty of connections for those mics. As a bonus, the external mic audio is often recorded on a separate track from the internal camera microphone — both in the same video file. That means you don't have to sync the audio and video later.

- ✔ **Long record times:** Unlike the DSLRs with their recording time limitations, most prosumer camcorders can record as much footage as your memory cards can hold. This makes them suitable for shooting longer events and in other situations calling for longer recording times.

- ✔ **Excellent monitoring:** The prosumer camcorder niche seems to be crowded with cameras that have bright, clear, articulate displays that swing out from the body of the camera. This makes monitoring what you're shooting a breeze, with no need for an external monitor.

Here's why prosumer camcorders have generated some critics:

- ✔ **Image quality:** The relatively small sensors found in prosumer camcorders is the most common complaint. Though they do have larger sensors than consumer camcorders, their sensors are dwarfed by the DSLR sensors. Although this is not always the case anymore, it is important to point out that Canon c-series cameras have super 35mm sensors, as do the Sony NEX cameras and all in the prosumer camera range.

- ✔ **Being stuck with one lens:** The vast majority of prosumer camcorders do not allow for interchangeable lenses. This rule has a few exceptions, but generally the only cameras that have this feature are expensive. (Many videographers will use adapters to add on a better lens on those less expensive models.)

- ✔ **Non-modular:** In camcorders, it's all or nothing. None of the parts are usually interchangeable, which means that after part of your camera is obsolete, the whole thing is obsolete. With a DSLR, at least the lenses can transition to your new camera when you upgrade (as long as you stick with the same camera manufacturer).

The mighty, miniature GoPro

Many specialty cameras are available in addition to the types we discuss in this chapter. One that is hugely popular for making YouTube videos is the GoPro. The GoPro is often used in extreme sports videos. It is extremely small, durable, affordable, and it comes with a waterproof case. It also happens to deliver excellent HD video, considering its miniature size and miniature price. The GoPro isn't only for sports, though. It can be useful for capturing risky shots for which you may not be willing to use your fancy DSLR or camcorder. This can provide you with some freedom to try interesting cinematographic techniques. (Check out the features of the GoPro at http://gopro.com/cameras.)

Settling for smart phones

We won't argue that the camera on your phone should be your primary camera. Smartphones aren't the best video cameras, they can be difficult to stabilize, and the footage files they produce can often be difficult to work with. Still, sometimes in the heat of an amazing moment unfolding in front of you, the best camera is the one in your pocket. It may not have much in the way of manual control, and it may not produce the most beautiful image, but in a lot of cases, being quick on the draw is more important.

The specs for smartphone cameras are a moving target. Smartphone manufacturers are constantly trying to outdo each other by packing more powerful cameras into phones. We won't make a specific recommendation, but we know pretty much any high-end or flagship smartphone has a camera that can shoot passable HD video.

In many ways, choosing the camera that works for you is a matter of personal taste. If you're just getting into videography, you should watch a lot of videos. Find the stuff you like on YouTube, and find out how those videos were made. The beauty of YouTube and social media is that the barrier is much lower for reaching out to creators. Find creators that make stuff you think looks good, and then ask them nicely how they shot it. Though you may not get a response from a creator with millions of subscribers, smaller creators are often happy to help out. Give it a try.

Stabilizing the Shot

One of the most important things you can do to give your video an air of professionalism is to stabilize your shot. Nothing says amateur video like extremely shaky handheld video. We've all watched home videos that induce motion sickness as the camera whips around. Many tools can help you lock down your shot:

- ✔ **Tripod:** The most useful stabilizing tool is the simple tripod. It has three legs; you attach your camera to the top, and your shot is as stable as stable can be. Tripods are readily available online, at camera stores, and at electronics stores, and they have a wide variety of price points. We recommend investing at least $50 here. It can be helpful to get one that has a built-in level to keep your shots from being crooked.

When you're shopping for a tripod, make sure you choose a model that has a fluid panning head. At some point, you'll want to add a few camera moves to your repertoire, and you'll need that fluid head when that time comes. A basic still photography tripod may be cheaper, but you're going to regret it when you need to move the camera during a shot. Tripods with nonfluid heads cannot replicate the smooth motion that a fluid head can provide.

✔ **Dolly:** A dolly is simply a set of wheels for the camera. The simplest dollies attach to the bottom of the tripod, and — voila! — your camera is now on the move, allowing you to create interesting motion and following shots.

✔ **Steadicam:** A number of handheld Steadicam rigs are available these days, but they can be a little expensive. They also require a great deal of skill to use effectively. That means practice. If you want to get good handheld shots using a Steadicam rig, you have to practice, practice, practice to get the hang of using the thing. If you do put in the time and get good at it, you can create some pretty cool shots with these devices.

✔ **Sliders/cranes/jibs:** A wide variety of devices are also on the market to create moving shots. Sliders allow the camera to move on rails, providing a sense of smooth motion in the shot. Cranes/jibs allow the camera to move from side to side *and* up and down in space, creating a smooth sensation of flight. Many of these are available as add-ons to tripods. Though they aren't absolutely necessary, a few nice moving shots do provide a feeling of high production value to almost any project. Sliders start at around $200; if you are ready to build something in order to save money, search YouTube for some DIY glider videos.

Seeing Your Way with Light

Another super-important aspect of creating a video with some level of professionalism is lighting. You don't need to win any lighting awards, but decent lighting goes a long way toward making a watchable video. There are a couple of ways to approach lighting: You can buy specialized lights, which will probably produce the best results, or you can work with the lights you already have. Just using lamps from around the house isn't ideal, but it can get you started, and there are ways to improve your video's look just by putting some thought into light placement.

Setting up 3-point lighting

The simplest and generally most useful lighting setup for shooting a person inside is *3-point lighting*. As its name implies, this lighting setup involves three lights, and it illuminates a subject in what is considered a traditionally pleasing way.

We describe the three lights that are involved (see Figure 6-1) in the following listing:

- ✔ **Key light:** The key light is the main (and brightest) light in a 3-point lighting setup. It is usually placed to the right or left of the camera, and it points directly at the subject from a 30- to 60-degree angle. The height of the light should ideally be set so that it points slightly down on the subject's face, but not so high that it creates shadows on the face. It should point down from slightly above the subject's eye level.

- ✔ **Fill light:** The fill light is a generally a softer light that should be pointed at the subject from the opposite side of the camera. The fill light shouldn't be as bright as the key light. It is there mainly to create a more even light on the subject. Using only a key light would usually result in creating dramatic shadows on the subject's face, and unless you're shooting a horror movie or a serious drama, you probably should want to stick with somewhat even lighting.

- ✔ **Back light:** The back light (sometimes called a *hair light*) shines from behind the subject and casts a thin outline of light around the subject's head, almost like a halo. This isn't intended to give the subject an angelic look — it's intended to create depth and separate the subject from the background. The back light can be directly behind the subject, but it can also be placed at an angle to the subject. Be sure not to get the light in the shot if you're going to place it directly behind the person.

- ✔ **Background light:** We know, it's confusing to add a fourth light into a section about 3-point lighting, but the reality is that most 3-point lighting setups also use a background light. This light does what its name implies — it lights the background. This is sometimes used to call attention to the background, but it is most often used to light the background separately from the subject. This can help create a sense of distance between the subject and the background, and can help enhance the separation between the two.

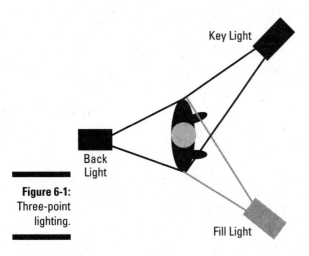

Figure 6-1:
Three-point
lighting.

Key Light

Back
Light

Fill Light

Working with the lights you have

Your video will look best if you have actual video lights. The problem with this strategy is that video lights are expensive. So why can't you just use the lights you have in your home? The good news: You can. You can create a simple 3-point lighting system using lamps from around your house. If you use them, though, you should follow a few guidelines:

✔ **Move the lamps.** Using home lights is the easy way out, but it's usually not quite as easy as just turning on the lights and rolling the camera. You need to move the lights around into something resembling the 3-point setup. You also might have to move some lamps from other rooms because house lamps don't have the same brightness as video lights.

✔ **Standardize.** When possible, try to use the same type of bulb in all the lamps you're using to light the scene. LED lights are very popular with a color temperature you can manually change. Mixing fluorescent and incandescent lights can cause weird-looking results in your picture, so you should choose one or the other and make sure your bulbs are all the same color temperature (color of the light is measured in temperature). Each different type of light bulb emits a different temperature; mixing bulbs can make skin tones look very unnatural for example.

✔ **Lose the shades.** Lampshades can cause uneven lighting, so you should take those things off while you're using your lamps as video lights. This will also help with maximizing the limited power of household lighting.

Setting up high-key lighting

Another viable, if less popular, lighting scheme is *high key lighting*. This involves using multiple high-powered key lights and turning them all on very brightly. This setup basically floods the subject with light. Though this setup lacks subtlety, we recommend it because it is simple. It also allows for quick production, as pretty much all shots require the same lighting setup. No one will comment on your beautiful lighting if you use this setup, but it does make things easy.

Capturing Sound

A crucial factor in creating an air of professionalism in a video is the sound. In this sense, audio is truly king. Capturing good audio to accompany your video is essential. Good sound is, in most cases, transparent. If you're able to record your talent's voice clearly and cleanly, the audience won't notice, which is exactly the reaction you're looking for here. If you record echo-laden bad audio, the audience will notice, and not in a good way.

Looking at microphones

The single biggest thing you can do to improve the audio in your videos is to obtain a decent external microphone. Though some camcorders do have a decent built-in microphone, you'll almost always obtain better results by using an external microphone. You can use a few different types of microphones:

✔ **Lavalier:** The lavalier mic — or *lav mic,* for short — is also known as a *lapel mic.* A lav mic's primary advantage is that it is small. The microphone can be attached to the speaker's clothing, and it's small enough to be unobtrusive. Most viewers are accustomed to seeing newscasters and other video subjects with visible microphones, so it isn't generally off-putting for the audience. Lav mics are usually omnidirectional, which means that they pick up sound from every direction: You cannot only hear your subject, but you'll also hear every sound in your recording environment.

Lavs work best in quiet environments or controlled studios. The nice thing about the lav mic is that it is, for the most part, a set-it-and-forget-it solution. After the lav mic is attached correctly to the talent and the levels are set, you only need to check periodically to ensure the levels are maintained.

✔ **Shotgun mic:** A shotgun microphone (or *boom mic*) is a highly directional mic that is often used to record voices in videos. The shotgun mic is designed to record audio from a single direction, and it's less sensitive to sound coming from behind the mic, to the sides, or elsewhere around the subject. This type of mic is especially useful for isolating sources in noisy situations, where background noise can overwhelm the subject's voice. Shotgun mics, which are a lot larger than lav mics, need to be pointed at the talent from just off camera, no more than a foot from the speaker's mouth. This is usually accomplished by a boom operator, who is a human who holds the shotgun mic attached to the end of a pole and points it at the talent, or a c-stand with a clamp.

✔ **Handheld:** You often see onscreen talent using a handheld microphone. A handheld mic can be a practical solution for capturing audio, but it is clear that the talent is using a microphone. This is completely acceptable in newsgathering situations, and it can be a great solution for videos of that type.

Wired or wireless?

Most microphones for video can be purchased in either a wired or wireless version. The wired version is connected directly to the camera with a microphone cable, and the wireless version uses some kind of radio signal to send audio to the camera or audio recording device without wires. The wireless option can be very useful, and it certainly feels futuristic, though it can be impractical. As with any device that relies on radio transmission, interference can be a problem, especially in crowded urban areas. Wireless devices also use batteries, and dead batteries can be just one more thing to go wrong. Wireless mics are necessary for applications where the subject moves around a lot, or is far from the camera, but in other situations, it may be wise to consider wired mics. They may not have the same level of tech appeal, but they can remove a couple of layers of complexity from your shoot.

Capturing good audio

Capturing good audio is important, so it's worthwhile to look at a few factors that go into capturing it. You may already know that you need a decent mic, but a couple of other factors go into it:

- ✔ **The recording environment:** Modern audio-editing software allows you to make quite a few changes and fixes to your audio after the fact, but the best way to end up with good audio is to *capture* good audio. A huge part of capturing good audio is controlling the environment in which you shoot. If you shoot your video in a busy coffee shop, it's difficult to keep the sounds of the coffee shop out of your video. Make sure you've chosen a quiet place for your video recording, away from traffic, refrigerators, air conditioners, pets, crying children, televisions, and so on.

- ✔ **Monitoring your audio:** Another key aspect to capturing good audio is to listen to what you're recording while you're recording it. Though a good camera will have an onscreen monitor visually representing the audio you're capturing, it is essential to listen to the audio in headphones as you're recording. Ensuring that everything sounds good, and retaking shots with audio glitches and noises, is much more time-effective than trying to fix all that stuff in post-production.

Chapter 7

Putting It All Together to Capture Some Video

*T*he big day has arrived and it's time to shoot some video! You're ready to stride onto the set as the big-shot director or producer and yell "Action!" It's all a breeze from this point, right?

Not quite. A video shoot can be an incredibly high-pressure environment, with too much to do and too little time to get it done. You must perform an amazing juggling act that keeps the cast, crew, camera, script, set, props, costumes, and all those inevitable but unplanned events all moving forward to get your video "in the can" by the deadline.

The good news is that a video shoot can also be one of the most creative and rewarding experiences you'll ever have. When all the elements click and you see that outstanding performance or fantastic camera angle, you'll feel a sense of deep personal satisfaction and pride that you nailed it. When the shoot is going well, the payoff far outweighs the pain.

This chapter explains how to prepare for the shoot — from developing a checklist the night before to setting up on the big day. We lay out the steps involved in every good camera take, and we list the little details that every first-class director must keep an eye on in order to capture the outstanding footage you need.

Setting Up for a Shoot

Directing or producing a video is similar to running a marathon — you must be rested and ready before you can go the distance. The night before you run 26.2 miles, for example, you don't want to begin wondering whether you should have bought new running shoes. Similarly, the night before the big shoot, you want to be as prepared as possible. The more you prep, the smoother your shoot — and the better you sleep the night before.

Getting organized

Buy a production notebook to make your film or video production extremely well organized. We recommend a good old-fashioned, three-ring binder, the type often carried by schoolchildren. It's the perfect one-stop spot to store all your shoot-related information, and it will soon become your new best friend.

Stock your production notebook with these items:

- **Dividers:** Add instant organization, and make the items you need during the shoot easy to find.

- **Pens and pencils:** Pens are the first thing you lose, so be sure to have more than one.

- **Blank paper:** You may need scratch paper or sheets of paper to illustrate shots.

- **An envelope:** Store the receipts from your expenditures.

Completing your checklists and "shoot sack"

After you have the basic items for your production notebook (as described in the preceding section), expand its contents by storing these items in it as well:

- **Script:** Your copy of the dialogue to be used in the shoot should always stay with you so that you can make notes, change the dialogue, or stay abreast of scenes that have been shot.

- **Call sheet:** This is a list of your cast and crew's arrival times on set. If you expect them to arrive at different times, keep track of their schedules.

✔ **Cast and crew contact sheet:** This list of contact information (such as email addresses and phone numbers) is the easiest way to ensure that participants can contact each other.

✔ **Schedule:** A schedule is useful when a number of cast or crew members are arriving on the same day and you want to better schedule the shoot, by determining which scenes to shoot and when, and when to let everyone take a break.

✔ **Storyboard:** This series of panels shows the individual shots within a scene. Keep the storyboard handy to show your crew the shots you want.

✔ **Prop and costume list:** Double-check this list after the shooting day ends to ensure that all items are returned to the appropriate person or place.

✔ **Script breakdown:** List cast members, props, costumes, and types of shots for every individual scene, and specify whether the scene is an interior or exterior.

✔ **Cast breakdown:** This reverse version of the script breakdown lists actors and the scenes in which they appear. Creating this list helps you schedule the shooting order of scenes.

Though the script breakdown and cast breakdown may be unnecessary for a simple shoot, if you have multiple scenes and actors, consider the breakdowns as insurance against losing important elements of the shoot. (We've seen actors released from a shoot for the day only to find that they were still needed for another scene later the same day.)

The night before your shoot, complete these tasks:

✔ **Charge all batteries.** Charge up all related devices, such as your camera, lights, laptop, and cellphone.

✔ **Clear out any reusable media.** If your camera records video to SD or CF cards, format them (otherwise known as erasing them) and clear some space.

✔ **Double-check your equipment.** Quickly test your camera, lights, and audio equipment. Ensure that every item works and that you know the exact location of all your equipment and accessories.

✔ **Pack props and costumes.** Don't wait until the morning of the shoot to pack everything!

✔ **Make copies of the script.** While you're at it, take the extra step of labeling every copy individually for your cast and crew.

✔ **Stock up on petty cash.** Withdraw cash from a nearby ATM so that you can purchase food, water, extra batteries, last-minute cab rides, coffee, and any other necessities you may need for the shoot. This is where the receipt envelope comes in handy.

✔ **Confirm call times.** Call, text, or email all participants to ensure that they know when and where to show up.

✔ **Check the weather forecast.** Make sure that the atmospheric conditions will not affect you adversely. Pay attention to rain forecasts, storm warnings, and make sure you're prepared for all conditions.

While you're charging batteries and anxiously awaiting the last of the cast to confirm their call times, turn your attention to another vital element of the shoot: the *shoot sack*. Simply fill a gym bag, large backpack, or (our favorite) rolling suitcase with the following essential items, and then you can take this film-production survival kit with you anywhere:

✔ **Batteries and chargers:** Store any batteries that aren't already installed in your equipment, and add any extra AA or AAA batteries you may need.

✔ **Extension cords:** Bring along at least two heavy-duty cords.

✔ **Power strips:** Bring two of these also.

✔ **Gaffer tape:** This heavy-duty tape has a million uses.

✔ **Lights and mic:** As long as these items fit into your shoot sack, add them.

✔ **Screwdriver and knife:** You never know when you'll need to tighten the tripod plate or cut some rope on set.

✔ **Gloves:** The lights may get too hot to touch after being on for a while.

✔ **Tripod and monopod:** Even if these items don't fit in the bag, pack them as part of your preparation ritual. (A monopod is a one legged tripod, typically used for shots requiring a more dynamic feel, or a quick paced live event or production.)

✔ **Laptop (and optional external hard drive):** These devices are likely to have separate cases, but you should make them part of your preparation ritual, too. You may need them for transferring footage among cards on the set.

Take a moment to look over everything you've packed. You've created a production notebook, double-checked equipment, charged batteries, confirmed schedules and locations with your cast and crew, and made for yourself the world's best shoot sack. You're ready to go, so take a deep breath, and get a good night's sleep.

Arriving on set

Whatever call time you've given your cast, plan for your crew to be on-site at least one hour earlier. Even if the hour is more time than you need to set up, having enough time to get ready without feeling pressured starts the shooting day on the right note. Besides, you'll quickly fill that hour.

Every shoot requires these three distinct spaces:

✔ **Shooting area:** This area should be ready for use when you arrive on the set so that you can begin setting up camera angles and lighting. Be polite but firm about claiming your space, and remove any items that don't belong in the scene.

✔ **Equipment area:** Designate a quiet corner in which to store equipment, props, and costumes and to serve as a charging station for batteries.

✔ **Green room:** Give your cast and crew (and perhaps certain equipment) a place to relax — and stay out of the way — between takes. In an office space, for example, a conference room is the perfect spot, but you may have to take whatever you can get. The green room is also a good spot for setting up an alcove to serve coffee and water to your cast and crew.

After you determine the boundaries of your space, you can set up the following equipment in it:

✔ **Charging station:** Plug in a power strip, and set up your camera's battery charger (and the chargers for light batteries, if you're using them).

✔ **Data station:** Plug in your laptop and external hard drive so that you can periodically "dump" footage.

✔ **Camera, tripod, lights:** After you unpack these items, you can start setting up the first shot. Check the natural ambient light in the room by looking at the camera's viewfinder to see what adjustments you need to make. Experiment to find the camera angles that work best.

Planning a realistic shooting schedule

When you watch a short scene in a video, you may believe that creating the scene was a simple task. And if the video is no good, it probably was a simple task. Virtually anyone can flip a switch on a camera and ask an actor to speak. Finding a unique and memorable way to shoot a scene takes time to prepare and pull off — even for simple scenes — and this amount of time has to be figured into your shooting schedule.

Two forces are at work in every film and video shoot: the creative need to make the production special, and the technical need to complete the production as quickly and inexpensively as possible and still look good. These needs are equally important. If you can't complete the shoot on schedule, you'll have nothing to show, but if you rush to complete the video with no regard for creativity, what's the point in even making it?

We would love to boil down the standard schedule to the simple mathematical formula "*x* number of shots divided by *y* setup time equals *z*," but scheduling simply doesn't work that way. (Besides, math is not our forté.) To come up with a realistic estimate of the time you need, consider these factors:

- ✔ The number of shots your production needs
- ✔ The length of each shot
- ✔ The amount of time you need to realistically set up, shoot several takes, and break down the set

Shooting usually takes longer (often, *much* longer) than most people anticipate. The technical setup can be complex, and actors may need a few takes to nail their performances. If you're working with non-actors, you may want to add an extra 30 to 60 minutes to their scenes, just in case it takes longer to get the performance you need.

These guidelines can help streamline the shoot:

- ✔ **Spend no more than 5 minutes setting up a shot.** A 5-minute limit keeps the setup process lean and mean. You should have enough time to adjust the lights and position the camera. Obviously, some shots require more time than others, but when you're working on a deadline, time magically passes faster than normal.

- ✔ **Shoot scenes out of order.** Few film productions shoot scenes in the exact order they'll appear in the finished product. Usually, the shooting schedule is created by determining which resources (such as locations, actors, props, or lighting) can be reused in other scenes. Those scenes are then filmed consecutively.

  By shooting out of order, you can schedule certain actors' scenes one after the other and then release the actors when they finish, leaving fewer people to manage as the day progresses.

- ✔ **Shoot "big" scenes first.** If you're shooting a crowd scene or another type of complicated shot, get it out of the way early in the day. Your cast and crew will be more energized, and you'll have that worry out of the way as the day wears on and pressure grows to wrap up the shoot.

- ✔ **Experiment.** Once, anyway. If you want (or a cast member wants) to try a radical idea, just to see whether it works, do it. But shoot the scene as specified in the script, too. Don't get *too* creative at the expense of the clock.

- ✔ **Cut freely.** If you find that your schedule is overstuffed, pull out the script and storyboard and cut some shots. Not scenes, mind you, just shots. We generally encourage you to shoot scenes with multiple shots (called *coverage,* which we address later in this chapter, in the section "Determining the best shot"). If time is running out, be prepared to change the shot list.

✔ **The fewer people who are on the set, the faster you can shoot.** The more people who watch a scene, the more your shoot can turn into a party rather than a production. When something strange or funny happens on the set (and suddenly everyone is laughing or chatting and no longer working), you have to play the role of benign dictator. Firmly, but with a friendly smile, ask all bystanders to clear out — pronto. When you have a camera, you wield power!

Practicing good habits before a shot

Your camera is set up, your actors are in place, and all eyes are on you. You're ready for the first take of the day. What do you say and when do you say it? You can actually set up a smooth, productive workflow by using a series of commands to move through each shot within a scene.

Draw from this handy list of words and phrases to communicate with your cast and crew — and to help them to communicate with you:

✔ **"Quiet on the set."** When you let everyone know that you're about to "roll camera," the only audible sound should come from whatever is happening in front of the camera. Side conversations, coughing, and mobile phones can all spoil a take, and you should have zero tolerance for them.

✔ **"Roll camera."** When your actors and crew are set, cue the camera person to start shooting.

✔ **"Camera rolling."** The camera person should reply to "Roll camera" with this phrase after shooting begins. If you're doing the shooting, just say "Camera rolling."

✔ **"Sound rolling."** Someone who is listening to sound separately on headphones says this phrase to indicate that the audio sounds good.

✔ **"Action."** Finally! This famous cue tells actors to start the scene and lets everyone else know to remain quiet. Wait a few seconds after the camera and sound are rolling to say it.

✔ **"Hold."** If a sudden event (such as a passing police siren) interrupts a shot, call "Hold" to let everyone know to stop what they're doing until the interruption ends. Then call "Action" again.

✔ **"Cut."** After a scene ends, wait a few seconds to say this famous cue so that the crew continues shooting video and recording sound until the moment you say it.

After a few tries, your cast and crew will have the order and rhythm of these cues down pat, and your set will quickly sound professional (as long as an actor doesn't announce, "I'll be in my trailer").

Every take of a shot should have *handles* on it — a waiting period of a few seconds before you say "Action" and after you say "Cut." This way, an editor (who may be you) who works on the scene in postproduction has a clearly defined segment of video to work with. "Action" and "Cut" are also cues for them.

Don't wait to press the Record button immediately after calling "Action" or "Cut" (a mistake typically made by novice filmmakers). This bad habit leaves the editor with a scene that is potentially missing its first and last seconds — a huge amount of editing time. (Applying a cool transition effect, such as a dissolve or a fade-in, during the editing process is then impossible.) Also, actors shouldn't break character until you say "Cut." As they finish their lines, they should remain in place until you stop shooting.

Maintaining continuity

Continuity is the purely technical requirement of maintaining a consistent look and action in every shot, including the background and lighting of the set and the actors' costumes, hair, and (most frequently) movement. A mobile phone that's held in a character's right hand in one shot and shifts to the left hand in the next shot jars the audience out of the moment.

If continuity mistakes happen to you, you're in good company. Many successful Hollywood movies are full of continuity mistakes. Throughout *The Wizard of Oz,* for example, the length of Judy Garland's hair and dress changes several times. If that type of huge production can slip up, your video can, too.

A simple way to keep an eye on actors' positions between shots is to call "Hold!" (refer to the list in the earlier section "Practicing good habits before a shot") and quickly set up for the next shot. You can also show actors an earlier take so that they can position themselves to match their own movements. If your characters are drinking from a glass, for example, make the liquid level consistent from shot to shot (to prevent the audience from wondering how the glass was seemingly refilled). If you're shooting over several days, take a photo of your actors in full costume so that they can match their looks for the next day.

Continuity has an additional meaning for actors. It refers to their characters' mental and emotional states from scene to scene. When you're shooting scenes out of order, matching these states from the previous scene can be challenging. As a director, it's your job to keep actors on track from scene to scene by reminding them of their previous circumstances, such as where they're coming from, what has just taken place, and where they're headed. You can even draw a timeline for reference. Actors should see the big-picture view of their entire performances *and* their scene-to-scene progress.

Shooting a Great-Looking Video

To say that camerawork is a technical process, and not a creative one, is a mistake. Film and video are visual media, and the camera resembles a paintbrush. A huge dose of creativity determines where to place the camera. If you look at the camerawork in the films of Alfred Hitchcock, Steven Spielberg, or Peter Jackson, for example, you see one stunning memorable image after another. This section tells you how to use your camera effectively, from choosing angles and specifying movement to framing scenes and capturing extraordinary imagery.

To illustrate the techniques we describe in this section, we use the following familiar scenario to show how to use the camera and the *frame* (the rectangular image you see on a movie, TV, or computer screen) to better tell a story: When a young child plays ball in the house and his mother warns him to move outside, he ignores her request and instead breaks an expensive vase. Oops! The child's unhappy mother confronts him.

Composing and dividing the screen

Composition is the process of creating a picture that helps to effectively tell a story within the camera frame for each shot. Just as a photo needs composition to possess more visual power, a moving picture needs composition to help tell the story more powerfully.

The *rule of thirds* (a visual arts composition guideline) divides a rectangular picture, such as a camera frame, into nine smaller rectangles of equal size — three across and three down. Though this concept originated in photography and painting, it has its place in film and video production.

Using the rule of thirds to position the subject one-third of the way from the edge of the frame (rather than in the center of the frame) makes the picture stronger and more interesting visually.

Because the rule of thirds also applies to framing the background of an image, you can create beautiful, symmetrical images in outdoor shoots by positioning the ground across the lower third of the frame and positioning buildings and trees and the sky in the upper two-thirds of the frame.

The rule of thirds is an artistic concept related to the way the human brain interprets imagery. It simply makes images "look better."

In the example, you can create tension in the shot (again, because of the way the brain processes images) by moving the camera so that the child is one-third of the way from the edge of the frame. When the child tosses the ball, you see the nearby empty living room, full of breakable objects, and you start to anticipate the ball flying from his hands and into Aunt Bertha's expensive Ming vase.

If you have a photo camera, try this experiment for capturing a better, stronger image. Frame the subject in the center of the shot, and take a picture. Then move the camera to frame the subject approximately one-third of the way from the edge of the shot, and compare the photos.

Determining the best shot

Your selection of camera angles, or *shots,* is limited, technically, only by your imagination, though you should master the basic principles before trying any fancy tricks. This section explains the building-block shots you see in most film and TV productions, and most scenes are built using a combination of these shots. In Hollywood, *coverage* is the practice of shooting a scene from various angles.

When you start shooting video, take these types of shots first:

- **Master:** The master shot is the foundation of your coverage. It shows everything — every important element of your scene. Place the camera far enough away to capture all the action, and shoot the entire scene from beginning to end. You can always cut back to the master shot to remind the audience where the characters are located in relation to each other.

- **Medium:** The medium shot moves in to show characters (or a single character) in an area from roughly just above their waists to a little over their heads. The medium shot is commonly used because it shows facial detail but still conveys a sense of the bigger picture.

- **Close-up:** In the close-up shot, the camera moves in tightly on a subject's face or on an object, such as the bouncing ball in this section's running example. The close-up is a powerful tool to show lots of facial detail and to build tension and emotion in a scene.

- **Extreme close-up:** In this type of shot, the camera (obviously) moves in even more tightly on a subject to show lots of detail. A shot of a character's eyes or of fingers drumming on a table or of a doorknob turning slowly shows an intimate level of detail to drive home a particular moment. Though an extreme close-up is rarely followed by a master shot (it's too much of a leap for viewers to make from small to large), you can follow it with a close-up or a medium shot.

These steps show one way to break down the scene in the bouncing-ball example:

1. The master shot shows a child tossing a ball in the living room. The shot is framed to show the child positioned one-third of the way from the edge of the frame. You can hear his mother say, "Don't play ball in the house!"

2. Cut to a medium shot of the child watching the ball move up and down. He smirks and says "No problem, Mom."

3. In the master shot, the child throws the ball high into the air. Uh-oh.

4. A close-up shot of the child shows him watching the ball begin to descend.

5. Cut to a close-up of the child's hand reaching for the ball — and missing it.

6. An extreme close-up shot shows his eyes widening as you hear a vase shatter.

7. Cut back to a medium shot of the child looking at the floor, horrified.

8. A close-up shot of the broken vase shows the ball lying in the middle of the glass shards.

9. Cut to a close-up of the child as he gulps and his mother scolds him.

10. Return to the master shot, as the child turns to face his mother and blurts, "It wasn't my fault!" while she crosses her arms angrily.

These steps break down a scene, moment by moment, into shots that underscore the emotion of every beat of the scene. We won't win an award for this scene, but we can probably make an audience feel tension (and make them laugh at the child's excuse). That's how you "paint" a scene with your camera and the camera frame.

In any scene you shoot, keep your shots smooth and steady. In the age of point-and-shoot video cameras, people have a tendency to start the camera rolling and then point it at various characters in a scene, in one long take. They often attempt this all-over-the-map approach with a shaky hand so that the scene ends up looking like an earthquake just occurred. Unless you're shooting *The Great Quake of the 21st Century,* we recommend that you simply place the camera on a tripod. If your scene involves a lot of camera movement, shoot it with a smooth, steady hand.

Moving and grooving the camera

Anyone can put a camera on a tripod, turn it on, and shoot the scene before them in a single shot. But this style amounts to simply recording a scene, which is boring, rather than true directing, which uses the different shot choices that are available to tell a story, controls what an audience is seeing from moment to moment, and moves the camera to achieve great-looking images.

You can choose from a few basic camera moves:

- **Pan:** Simply move the camera from side to side, along the horizon. If the child in the bouncing-ball example enters a room, spots the ball on a table, and walks to it, you can follow his movement by panning from the doorway to the table.

- **Tilt:** Move the camera laterally, along a vertical plane. In the example, you would tilt the camera from the child's hand grabbing the ball and then lifting it to his chest as he looks at it mischievously.

- **Track:** In this tricky-but-fun shot, you simply follow the subject throughout the scene. You can track the child from an outdoor starting point, keep him at a distance, and then follow him right up to the ball. The tracking shot, which is used in lots of Hollywood films, can be an effective way to show off. (A famous 3-minute tracking shot from Martin Scorsese's *Goodfellas* follows Ray Liotta's character through the hallways and kitchen of a nightclub.)

You can pan and tilt by either using a handheld camera or placing it on a tripod or monopod. Tracking shots are typically accomplished with the use of a steadicam or dolly. To add a slick touch to your video, work out a brief tracking shot of one character.

Matching your eyelines

An *eyeline* is the invisible line leading from the eyes of a character on camera to a person or an object that the character is looking at off camera. The cut that you make to the next shot showing the off-camera person or object must be placed within the shot where the brain would expect it to be. If a character is looking upward, for example, you should then cut to the object that the viewer sees, placed above the camera. If the character's eyeline and the object's position don't match (if they look down at an object that you then see hanging over their heads, for example), the audience becomes disoriented and disconnects from the scene. The eyeline makes a subtle but crucial difference when cutting between two people who are speaking to each other within a scene.

In this section, we explain how to add two medium shots to the bouncing-ball example. One shows the mother furrowing her brow at her child, and the other shows the child lowering his head after being scolded. For these two shots, you can shoot the actors in this scene separately or even on different days because they don't appear in the frame together in this particular moment. Above all else, you have to match the eyelines of the mother and her child.

Suppose that the child looks up at his mother towering over him and then you cut to a shot of her face. Rather than look downward at him, as your brain expects, she instead looks directly across the shot at an object at the height of her eyes. Your brain would automatically connect the two shots to make you wonder what she's looking at (another person in the room, for example). Because she's the taller of the two, her eyes should aim downward at him, at a spot that's as close to the same spot in the frame where his eyes were looking up in the previous shot.

A character who looks off-screen at another character should be looking at the spot where the other character would stand. If you *reverse* the shot (to show the other character), the second character's eyes should be focused on the spot where the first character is positioned. Any well-made TV show or film has examples of shooting proper eyelines. In one with incorrect eyelines, you cannot determine where characters are oriented in a scene.

To ensure matching eyelines, position an off-screen actor behind the camera so that the on-screen actor can look at that person and deliver her lines. Encourage actors to stand immediately off-camera, even when they aren't part of a shot, to help make eyelines match. It also helps a cast member with her performance to speak directly to her scene partner, even if the partner is standing off camera.

Following the 180-degree rule

The 180-degree rule is a critical guideline in how scenes are shot in a film or video. When you watch a movie in which two characters are speaking and the cut moves from one to the other, you're likely seeing the *180-degree rule* in action: It establishes the spatial relationship between characters or objects within a scene, specifically when the scene cuts between shots of them. Most viewers aren't aware of the 180-degree rule when it's followed; but when it isn't, viewers can become disoriented or confused about where characters are standing or sitting in relation to each other.

To use the 180-degree rule to construct a scene, imagine a straight line running down the middle of the characters, as shown in Figure 7-1. To avoid disorienting the audience, choose *one side* of the 180-degree line on which to shoot all your shots, and don't cross the line. Understanding this concept can be confusing, so we will walk you through an example.

Rather than show each actor individually, such as in the bouncing-ball example, you can use the popular Hollywood technique known as the *over-the shoulder* shot. For a shot of the child in the example looking up at his mother, you place the camera over her left shoulder and aim it at the child so that part of her left shoulder and hair frame the shot of his face.

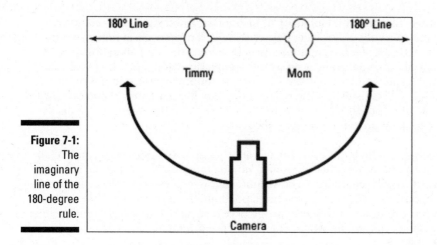

Figure 7-1:
The imaginary line of the 180-degree rule.

Cut back to the mother looking crossly at her child. If you place the camera over his *right* shoulder, pointing up at the mother, who is towering over him, his right shoulder and hair frame the shot of his mother looking cross. Then you cut back to the first shot over her *left* shoulder, of the child looking remorseful.

In the example, we stay on one side of the line, over the mother's left shoulder and over the child's right shoulder. If we had moved from her left to his left, we would have crossed the line and confused the audience, because they wouldn't know where the characters were standing in relation to each other.

In another example, you see a shot of a train flying down the tracks, moving from right to left in the frame. Cut to a person waiting for the train, and then cut back to the same train, except that now you've crossed the tracks and you're shooting from an angle on the other side. The train is now moving from left to right! Your brain believes that it's another train, heading directly for the first train, and suddenly you've made a disaster film!

The 180-degree rule has one exception: If the camera is moving, you're allowed to cross the imaginary line if the shot itself moves across it. Then the audience will understand why you switch sides in the next shot.

Shooting an interview

Shooting an interview is a fairly easy task. In the world of marketing videos, you'll likely shoot a lot of sit-down interviews.

Follow these steps to shoot a simple but professional-looking interview:

1. **Set up two chairs.** One is for the subject, and one is for the interviewer (who may be you). The subject should be seated.

2. **Set up your camera on a tripod.** Place the tripod to the side of your chair, facing your subject.

3. **Frame the subject.** Use a medium shot, moving upward from mid-torso or slightly closer.

4. **Light and mic your subject.** This topic is covered in Chapter 6.

5. **Have your subject look at you, not at the camera.** Looking into a camera lens tends to make a person self-conscious. You can conduct an excellent interview that has a conversational flow by having the subject speak to you. The camera serves to record the conversation you're having. (The most common camera style on YouTube is to have the subject speak directly into the camera; we recommend this style only if the subject can appear natural.)

A person who is verbose the first time he answers an interview question may want to answer a question a second time, after having the opportunity to find the best wording for his answer. To avoid being heard asking the interview questions, you can edit yourself out, by having the subject rephrase your question within the answer, as in this example:

You: "How long have you been the president of Smith Industries?"

The subject: "I have been president of Smith Industries for 40 years."

Encourage your subject to answer as simply as possible, always including the crux of the question within the answer, and you'll have a professional-looking, easy-to-edit interview that you can replicate with different subjects.

Shooting extra footage and B-roll

Watch any political thriller (especially one with Harrison Ford or Morgan Freeman as the commander in chief) and you're bound to see an impressive shot of the White House while ominous music plays in the background. Did you know that the shot wasn't filmed by the movie's director? It may not have even been filmed by anyone working on the movie. That shot of the White House is a classic example of an *establishing* shot (that shows you where you are) and is a member of the family of B-roll footage.

B-roll footage is supplementary, traditionally used to accompany a documentary or TV news story. For example, in an interview with the president of

Smith Industries, during an especially dry segment, you can *cut away* to show the Smith Industries factory floor or show workers picketing the president's office.

You can shoot and use B-roll to support the main storyline in your video. Film anything related to your business, or to the storyline of your video, and *intercut* it (cut back and forth) with your main (or *A*) storyline.

B-roll can be shot quickly, using your camera's internal mic. Shoot lots of footage until you find shots that blend well with the main part of your video. You can also shoot establishing shots of various buildings or areas where your scenes take place.

Capturing the perfect take — several times

Whether you're shooting a scripted scene or an interview, you probably won't get the perfect take the first time every time. Someone may flub a line or slam a door off-screen, a dog may begin barking, or a sudden rainstorm may interrupt a romantic picnic scene. Or, the "magic" just isn't happening right away and your actors need a few takes to warm up and discover the best way to play the scene. In any case, if you have to do it again, shrug your shoulders, yell "Cut," and prepare everyone for another take.

Shooting multiple takes can be demanding because actors have to repeatedly speak the same lines and hit the same marks. However many takes you shoot of a scene, the acting always has to seem fresh. One way to achieve this goal is to let the actors vary their line readings slightly on every take. You can always revert to an earlier take if you don't like the revised version.

After you capture an excellent take, shoot a *safety* take immediately afterward. This extra version ensures that your editor has two good takes to work with, just in case something goes wrong with the footage during the postproduction process.

Working with Voice

When you shoot video, it's easy to get caught up in the visual aspect of each shot. However, you must also keep audio quality in mind at all times. See Chapter 6 for details about audio, but aside from mics and audio capturing devices, you have another tool in your audio arsenal that is provided for free by your actors: their voices. Whether you're dealing with seasoned or first-time actors, you can get the most from the mouths of your talent in a few ways, as described in the following sections.

Practicing diction and dialects

William Shakespeare, no slouch himself in producing one or two quality scripts, had some good advice 500 years ago for video actors: to speak their lines "trippingly on the tongue." In other words, he suggested good *diction,* or the proper enunciation of the words in a script. Your actors need to practice diction in order to get your message across. Even unscripted interviewees can stand to use good diction.

Diction is all about several distinct vocal areas:

- ✔ **Volume:** Actors should speak loudly enough for the mic while still sounding believable. (Our experience tells us that nearly every actor can stand to be a bit louder.)

- ✔ **Clarity:** Determine whether actors are speaking unclearly, such as pronouncing words incorrectly or dropping sounds off the ends of their words. Most of us do this when we're speaking casually. Make sure that actors practice pronouncing the trickier words in your script. No one should sound like Mary Poppins, but every word should be clearly understood.

- ✔ **Pace:** Make sure that your actors aren't speaking too quickly or too slowly. Many people tend to rush through sentences when they're excited or stressed — which is exactly how actors will feel with the camera on them. Take time to rehearse the scene, and find an appropriate speaking pace.

- ✔ **Vocal energy:** Not to be confused with volume, *vocal energy* refers to the quality of an actor's voice, such as whether he's speaking with passion and animation or in a tired monotone. Because the camera is fairly close, actors don't have to speak the way they would to a crowded auditorium, though their voices should possess energy and make the dialogue sound authentic and believable.

Everyone speaks in a *dialect,* or regional accent. There's no universal, unaccented way to speak. A dialect can add huge amounts of believability and variety to a performance and truly drive home the content of your video. A dialect that's too strong, however, especially if an actor seems to be struggling with the lines in a script, can also detract the audience from engaging in your video. The key is to ensure that the words in your script are striking the audience as clearly and effectively as you need.

The power of the pause

People who speak to large groups or, worse, in front of a camera tend to barrel through their lines in an effort to reach the end of the script as soon as possible and stop speaking. Because they simply forget to *pause,* they're missing out on the most powerful audio tool available.

A well-placed pause carries a lot of weight. For a brief moment, suspense hangs in the air. The words you've just heard settle for a second, and then you hear more. A pause used by actors can add drama, dimension, and structure to the words they're saying.

Work with actors to find two or three spots to pause the dialogue. Don't overdo it, and don't make a pause last forever. Make sure that it's real, however, where the speaker can take a breath and feel in control of her words, not the other way around.

Managing crowd audio

Keep this Hollywood secret between you and us (and everyone else reading this book). Watch a crowd scene in a movie or TV show — a restaurant or bar scene is perfect. Notice how you hear the main characters speaking clearly while the crowd around them is quiet. How do the creators *do* that? Yes, mics are being used, but the bigger trick is that the *crowd is completely silent during filming.* All their talking is pantomimed, and the sounds are later added by editing.

Hollywood uses stock crowd sounds, which is why (if you're paying attention to these sort of things) you sometimes hear the same voices on different TV shows. When you're shooting a crowd scene, stock crowd sounds are available for different group sizes, and you can find the one that best suits your scene.

You can also direct the crowd to simply speak more quietly than normal. Depending on how many people you're working with, this suggestion can be an easy solution or a tough one to manage. The key is to get a great sound level from your main actors while retaining a believable amount of background noise. Remind crowd members that they're adding to the authenticity of a scene and offer to throw a party after the shoot is complete.

Chapter 8

Fixing It in Post: The Edit

. . . .

. . . .

*E*ven the simplest modern editing tools are powerful applications. If you want to edit your own videos, expect to spend some time learning how to use your tool of choice. If you've ever worked with Word or PowerPoint, for example (from the Microsoft Office suite), you may recall that you spent some time learning how to use that program. Let's be honest: Most people discover new features and new ways of doing things in these programs all the time.

To edit a video, you need to get familiar with the software and some foundational editing techniques. In this chapter, we describe both of these and how to turn your footage into a polished video.

Choosing Editing Software

Editing programs are sophisticated tools for content creation with a lot of powerful features. The best way to approach them is to first read about the basics, or you may take a class to get started. Then just dive in and complete a project. Most people become comfortable using their chosen editing tool during the first few days.

The first item to consider when choosing editing software is your existing operating system on your computer. In other words, if you use Windows, you need editing software for Windows; if you use a Mac, you need editing software for the Mac.

Mac tools

The selection of editing tools on the Mac is somewhat smaller than on the PC, but that isn't necessarily bad news, because of the high quality of Mac-based programs:

- ✔ **Apple** itself provides two industry-leading editing applications:
  - *iMovie:* Entry level
  - *Final Cut Pro:* Professional level
- ✔ **Adobe,** the market leader in creative software, offers a full line of tools for the Mac.

iMovie

If you have a Mac, you already have iMovie. This powerful little editing application comes preinstalled on every new Mac. We highly recommend this for your YouTube video editing because it is very easy to use.

Upgrade to the latest version of iMovie, if you can. If your version is older, you can buy the current edition online at the Apple App Store. It's more than worth the price.

iMovie covers virtually everything you need for normal video editing, and it comes supplied with helpful templates for impressive titles and neat visual effects.

The main drawback of iMovie compared to professional-grade applications is that it can deal with only a single video track and a single track of background sound. You can use background music and a voice-over narration track at the same time, but using more elements isn't possible. This restriction isn't a big deal for most videos, though it can be limiting on ambitious productions.

A good companion product for iMovie is Garage Band, which comes preinstalled on Macs as well. You can finish up your visual edits in iMovie and export right into Garage Band. It lets you put together soundtracks for your videos and provides some useful background music tracks that you can use immediately. Be sure to check on the copyright for any existing or canned background music tracks you pull from Garage band. Your video monetization may be affected when using tracks with existing copyrights.

Final Cut Pro

Final Cut Pro is the professional-grade editing application from Apple that covers most capabilities that an editor needs. It's used by many professionals, including such legendary editors as Walter Murch (*The Godfather, Apocalypse Now*).

Final Cut Pro is a major upgrade from iMovie. Its user interface is quite similar to iMovie, and old iMovie projects can be imported directly. It offers much more flexibility, such as unlimited video and audio tracks, many more visual effects, a feature-rich footage management system, and sophisticated audio editing.

If you're going with Apple editing programs, start with iMovie and then upgrade to Final Cut Pro X when you run into limitations.

Adobe Premiere

Apple's primary competitor on the Mac platform is Adobe and its Premiere editing programs — note the plural form here. You have a choice between two Premiere products:

- **Premiere Elements:** The entry-level Adobe editing program, Premiere Elements, an application designed for consumers and business users.

  The advantages of using Premiere Elements over the free Apple iMovie program are that it:

  - Supports multiple video and audio tracks
  - The additional power is useful if you edit more complex projects, such as footage shot with multiple cameras simultaneously
  - Offers a more sophisticated way to organize large collections of raw footage
  - Provides more flexibility in dealing with photos and other images

- **Premiere Pro:** The Adobe program for professional video editors, Premiere Pro offers all the same professional features of Final Cut Pro. Some editors like it better because:

  - Its user interface is optimized for a professional editor's typical workflow.
  - It has broader support for the file formats that professional and consumer-level cameras produce. It allows you to work with files natively — no transcoding needed.
  - It integrates the workflow as a one-stop — you can take a project entirely through the Adobe Creative Suite, including color correction, motion graphics, and audio finishing.

Windows tools

Dozens of editing programs of all sophistication levels are available on the Windows PC platform. The following five sections describe a few of the most popular.

Windows Movie Maker

Much like iMovie on the Mac, the free editing tool Windows Movie Maker covers basic video editing needs. It lets you quickly import footage and pictures, arrange and trim clips, add music, and apply basic visual effects and titles. If your Windows PC doesn't have Movie Maker installed, you can download Movie Maker for free at this Microsoft website: `http://windows.microsoft.com`.

Movie Maker is a helpful way to get your feet wet with video editing. Most people working on advanced video projects quickly run into its limitations, such as having only one background audio track, one video track, and limited visual effects. Furthermore, its particular way of handling the start and stop points of clips isn't ideal for precision editing.

Adobe Premiere

The people behind Photoshop also provide their video editing program, Premiere, for Windows PCs. The Premiere version you need depends on your goals.

Premiere can work with multiple video and audio tracks, which allows for the easy arrangement of footage and complex narrative structures. That's an important advantage over the free Windows Movie Maker.

Here are your Premiere choices:

- **Premiere Elements:** A strong editing application for consumers and business users, Premiere Elements improves upon Windows Movie Maker by packing in a ton of features that let you edit your videos in a much more sophisticated way. It organizes footage more intelligently, it can stabilize shaky footage, and it comes supplied with a huge selection of transitions and visual effects. It can even handle green-screen effects and animated graphics.

- **Premiere Pro:** We discuss Premiere Pro, Premiere Element's larger sibling, in the earlier Mac section "Premiere Pro." The Windows version is largely identical, and it's a highly respected tool for professionals.

Sony Vegas Movie Studio

Sony's aggressively priced Vegas Movie Studio editing software is an interesting alternative to Adobe products, positioned between Premiere Elements and Premiere Pro. It offers features that are comparable to some of the best editing software on the market. If you're looking for the most bang for your buck, Vegas is worth a serious look.

Pinnacle Studio

This product is significantly more sophisticated than Premiere Elements. It boasts unlimited video and audio tracks, animated titles, broad format support, sophisticated audio editing, and a ton of professional-level special effects.

The price is reasonable, and the product even comes with a green-screen backdrop and software for Blue-ray disc authoring. Pinnacle Studio is a good choice for people who want to do frequent, sophisticated editing and are willing to endure a bit of a learning curve.

CyberLink PowerDirector

Another tool competing with Premiere Elements is CyberLink PowerDirector, priced similarly to Premiere Elements. The PowerDirector feature set is comparable to other products in this market segment, but its performance tends to be somewhat faster, and its user interface is nice and clean.

The drawback to using PowerDirector is its somewhat weaker media organization functionality, which can be a problem for people with a lot of footage. But thanks to its speed, it's one of the best programs on the market.

Where to Get Started with Editing

At first, the task of editing video may seem confusing and somewhat scary. The process has many technical expressions to understand, many software features to use, and many concepts to grasp. The best way to deal with this complexity is to simply dive in.

Attempting a test project

After some preparation, there's no better way to get up to speed in video editing than to simply try it. Select a topic for a test project, and try to put together a simple video about it. This gives you firsthand experience with the editing software before you try to create your first real video.

Reading books and watching videos

As a starting point for editing video, you may want to read a book about your editing software of choice. A book can help you understand the basic concepts that your editing application is built on, and it can provide a quick overview of all its features. In addition, good books have step-by-step guides for more advanced features.

Several books in the *For Dummies* series explain how to use some of the most popular editing programs, and we highly recommend them.

Apple and Adobe products generally have the biggest selection of good instructional books available, though some of the less popular editing applications aren't covered as thoroughly. Before you decide on a particular editing program, look at what kind of information and support are available for it. Don't forget to check out YouTube for editing tutorials, there are many channels dedicated to this topic.

If you have some video footage from your last vacation or family event, that's a good place to start, because your family can then enjoy a watchable, well-edited video. Or if you want to dive right into marketing-oriented videos, shoot some quick footage about your business and use existing pictures.

Avoid overthinking your first project. Your goal isn't to produce a master-work of cinematic storytelling — it's to explore the features of your editing tool and experience the basic process of editing.

Your first project should follow these guidelines because you find these elements in most serious video projects:

- ✔ Import, view, and organize multiple clips of raw video footage.
- ✔ Use pictures and graphical elements, such as a logo, in your video.
- ✔ Experiment with different title styles.
- ✔ Try variations of background music to see how music can influence the mood of a video.
- ✔ Explore basic visual effects, such as transitions between scenes.
- ✔ Record a voice-over narration track.

Make a short video first, maybe a couple of minutes long. Don't forget to share the video with a friend for feedback; you'll be surprised at what you notice when you're sharing a project.

Handling file formats, resolution, and conversion

Video used to be supplied on magnetic tape. Though it was available in several formats, such as VHS and Betacam, figuring out what you had was fairly simple. The digital world has brought about a dramatic cost reduction (video professionals no longer have to own a VCR for every cassette format), but it also brought about more complexity. Dozens of different digital video file formats are now used in the industry.

Fortunately, modern editing programs handle much of this mess for you. Almost all editing tools handle the most common dozen or so formats. But if you work with video footage shot by someone else, you still may occasionally encounter an exotic format. That's why you should understand the basic principles of using video file formats.

Sorting out the file formats

Digital video produces extremely large files. These files would be even larger if not for the heavy compression that's applied to the original video signal. Video compression uses some fancy calculations to squeeze high-quality moving pictures and sound into files that are as small as possible. To give you an idea, your video files would be between 5 and 50 times larger without compression.

The compression process is managed by a coder/decoder, or *codec*. This piece of software squeezes the video into a smaller digital format when it's recorded and decompresses it again when it's being watched. Because a codec typically isn't compatible with other codecs, you can't watch a video recorded via codec A on a device that supports only codec B.

Some of the most popular video codecs are

- ✔ Apple ProRes
- ✔ Digital Video (DV)
- ✔ H.264 (a more modern version of MPEG-4)
- ✔ MPEG-4
- ✔ Windows Media (WMV)

The data generated by these codecs is stored in a file that contains additional information, such as the title and description of the video, synchronization markers that sync audio and video, subtitles, and more.

You see these file formats, or *container* formats, on your PC or Mac. These container formats and their file endings are the most popular:

- Flash Video (`.flv`)
- MP4 (`.mp4`)
- MPEG (`.mpg`)
- QuickTime (`.mov`)
- Windows Media (`.avi`)

Don't let yourself become confused: Container files can contain several different codecs. For example, a QuickTime file can contain a video in Apple ProRes, DV, or H.264 format. Each format can be matched with a number of audio codec formats, such as AAC, AIFF, or MP3.

In other words, if someone asks you for the format of your video files and you respond "AVI" or "MOV," the person doesn't know much more about the format than before he asked. Any container file type can contain any of dozens of different codecs.

The only way to determine what you have is to open the video file in a player application, such as QuickTime Player or Windows Media Player. Then use the menu command that shows you details about the file. In QuickTime, it's Window⇨Show Movie Inspector. In Windows Media Player, it's File⇨Properties.

Converting formats

Modern editing programs can work with most widely used video file formats. However, if you use footage in a more exotic format — material provided by someone else, for example — you may encounter roadblocks. Your editing application may not be able to work with unusual formats directly.

In this case, convert these files to a more standard format by using a video conversion program. Your editing program may even have one already.

You can find many free or inexpensive conversion programs. If you have to deal with an exotic video file format, the time savings are definitely worth the price. On Windows PCs, AVS Video Converter (`www.avsmedia.com/AVS-Video-Converter.aspx`) and Any Video Converter Pro (`www.any-video-converter.com/products/for_video`) are good choices. On the Mac, AVCWare Video Converter (`www.avcware.com/`) and Wondershare Mac Video Converter (`www.wondershare.com/pro/video-converter-pro.html`) are recommended products.

Editing Your Video

Editing is the art of telling a story using video footage, pictures, and sound. Editing is often called *the invisible art* because the best editing isn't noticed by the viewer.

A well-edited video brings the viewer into the story, none of the elements of the actual edit should be seen unless your goal is to show off a digital effect on the footage.

Even when you plan a video shoot meticulously, surprises and changes take place during editing. An idea that seems outstanding at first may not work in the final video. On the other hand, unexpected moments of excellence may show up in your footage to give your video an extra boost.

Editing can make or break your video. This section tells you how to approach this essential process. We use the Apple iMovie editing software in the examples, though other editing programs work similarly.

Recognizing videos that need no editing

Some types of video can stand on their own with no significant amount of editing. You can prepare the following types of videos for publishing with a minimal amount of trimming:

✔ **Talking head:** A talking-head video shows a person simply speaking into the camera to make an announcement or to explain a concept or an issue. This technique isn't terribly interesting visually, but it can be effective if the speaker has interesting material. If your talent can complete the statement in one take, you typically don't even need to edit.

✔ **Speech and presentation:** Sometimes, you can tape a representative of your company or an outside expert presenting a relevant topic at an event. You can typically use this footage without editing if the presentation is brief. But remember that presentations on video tend to be less interesting than the ones you see in person.

✔ **Simple product demonstrations:** A salesperson, or even a CEO, may be able to give a killer product demonstration in only one take. Sometimes, a charismatic salesperson can be more convincing than a slickly produced product video. A competent camera person can show details of the product by zooming in or moving the camera.

Logging your footage

After you return from a shooting location, follow these general steps to log your footage — the most important step in preparing for the editing process:

1. **Download the footage to your computer.** Using a modern camera, this process can be completed quickly — just copy the digital video files from the camera. Shooting on tape is more time-consuming because you have to let the tape run so that your editing program can capture all footage digitally. Refer to your camera's instruction manual to find out how.

2. **Import the footage into your editing program.** You may already have completed this step if you downloaded the footage using your editing software, but in other cases, you first have to import the footage manually.

3. **Organize your clips.** After you have a bunch of clips that cover different parts of your project, start by organizing them to better see what you have. Group clips that are related to the same scene. Editing programs offer different methods to help, such as folders or "bins" in which you can store clips, labels and tags that you can assign to clips, or "events" that group related clips.

4. **Watch your footage.** Review all your clips to determine what you have. If you have a lot of footage, there's no way to avoid this time-consuming step.

5. **Remove unwanted material.** If you have clips that are clearly unusable, remove them immediately. Don't delete them — just store them in a folder labeled Unusable in your editing program or in your computer's file system. Sometimes a clip that looks unusable now can come in handy later.

6. **Take notes.** The best way to find your footage quickly during editing is to take the time to take notes about every clip. Add a few simple words about the content of the clip and its level of quality. Notes can be taken in the editing software directly in line with the clip you are referencing in most programs.

7. **Mark the best clips.** If you have multiple takes of a scene, mark the one you think is best. Many editing programs let you use a special Favorites functionality, or you can simply make a mark in your notes. Also mark B-roll footage that you think looks good, and make notes of the best sound bites in interview clips.

Logging your footage may seem like a tedious and time-consuming process, but investing time in it pays off later. During editing, you can waste a lot of time hunting for a particular clip that you somehow recall but didn't mark properly.

Trimming video clips

Clips often tend to be too long. If you want to use a one-take video, you can simply trim off unwanted pieces at the beginning and the end. Fortunately, trimming a clip on your computer is fairly easy. The best tool depends on the platform you use:

✔ **On the Mac:** Mac users already have QuickTime, a preinstalled media player that has basic editing features.

If you want to trim a clip, open the video file in QuickTime, and then choose the Edit ➪ Trim command. A timeline showing the entire clip appears. Drag the yellow handles to mark the start and end of the clip, and then click the Trim button. The resulting clip can be saved or exported for use on YouTube or on your website. Figure 8-1 shows how to use the trim function in QuickTime.

✔ **On the PC:** PC users can select from a variety of video processing tools that provide the trimming function.

An easy way is to use Windows Movie Maker (described earlier in this chapter). This simple editing application is free, and it works well if you want to trim only a few clips.

In some editing programs you will need to save the trimmed video as a new clip, or else you lose the rest of your footage.

Some simple video programs even let you assemble multiple clips into a longer clip. For example, QuickTime lets you add a clip to the end of the current clip by choosing the Edit ➪ Add Clip to End command. On a PC, use Windows Movie Maker and simply drag and drop the clips to the storyboard. This method works for assembling two or three clips, but don't expect it to replace an editing program. As soon as you want to move beyond the simplest trimming level (and save time in the end), invest in quality editing software.

Figure 8-1: The trim function in QuickTime Player.

Making a rough cut

The first step in determining what your video will look like is to make a *rough cut,* in which you line up all the good footage to figure out what works. A rough cut is typically much longer than the final product, and it lacks many of the elements from the final video, such as titles and visual effects.

To make a rough cut, first log your footage, as explained earlier in this chapter, in the section "Logging your footage." Then follow these steps:

1. **Review your storyline in sequence.**

   Tackle every scene separately.

2. **For every scene, find the best takes that you marked during logging.**

3. **Mark in and out points for every clip to trim it to the part you want in the video.**

   In and *out points* are indicators you set on the individual clips that make up the scene. An in point is the frame in the clip where you would like to begin viewing, an out point is the frame you would like to end the clip with.

   Don't worry much about the exact timing. It comes later. In and out points can easily be changed once your clip is in your timeline.

4. **Insert the clip in your editing program's timeline, in any order you want.**

   Figure 8-2 shows what a rough cut looks like in an editing program. It's just a sequence of clips with no further treatment.

5. **Repeat this process for all scenes to assemble a sequence of clips that tells your intended story.**

When you watch your rough cut for the first time, it probably looks bumpy, overly long, and <ahem> rough. Your goal is simply to figure out how well your material works when it's assembled.

Figure 8-2:
A timeline with a rough cut in an editing program.

If it's possible in your editing program, make a safety copy of your first rough cut, of either the timeline or the whole project. This copy may come in handy later in the editing process, when you don't see the forest for all the trees and you need a fresh perspective. Making a copy can also be a helpful way to find raw clips quickly if you have a lot of footage.

Switching it around

The great thing about modern editing software is that you can experiment by moving clips and entire sequences to find the best combination of clips and scenes. Be careful: You can easily get lost in the experimentation process. First consider why you would want to change something, and if you have a truly good reason, do it.

Try some of these suggestions:

- ✔ **Use different versions of the same take.** Sometimes, a take that you think is best when you watch it in isolation no longer works well with the rest of the material. If you're unhappy with a take, try using a different take of the same shot to see whether it improves the entire scene.

- ✔ **Drop clips or entire scenes.** Shorter is typically better in editing. If you feel that a particular clip or an entire scene doesn't add much value to the video, drop the clip entirely and watch the video without it. If you don't miss it much, your audience will likely never miss it.

- ✔ **Change the order of scenes.** Particularly in documentary-style and educational videos, scenes don't necessarily have a natural fixed order. You can also change the sequence completely for dramatic effect. For example, if you sell lawnmowers and you want to show how your latest model performs, you can grab your viewers' attention if you first show the pristine lawn that results from using your product and then demonstrate how your product was responsible.

Editing is storytelling, but stories don't always have to flow linearly. Early in your video, specify to your audience that you have something interesting to say. Learn from the pros: James Bond movies, for example, don't start with a boring explanation of the villain's latest evil plot, but rather with a high-octane action scene that grabs the audience's attention immediately.

Creating cuts

A rough cut is all about finding the right way to tell a story with your video. In a written document, the rough cut would be the equivalent of the outline and first draft. But there's more to editing: Just as you would refine a written text for style and powerful language, refine your video edit with better timing, transitions, additional material, and refined cuts.

Working on these elements is the style aspect of video editing, and it makes all the difference between a video that's barely watchable and one that excites viewers.

A *cut* in film editing connects two shots. One shot ends and the next one begins, and between them is a cut. The word *cut* comes from the act of physically cutting celluloid film in traditional movie editing. Today, in the age of digital editing, no cutting is taking place, though the name stuck.

Different types of cuts serve different purposes. Depending on the effect you want to achieve, use one of these cut types:

- ✔ **Hard:** This is the most basic (and by far the most frequently used) type of cut. One shot ends, and the next shot starts immediately. Both the picture track and the sound track are cut at the same time.

- ✔ **Transition:** One shot flows into the next with some kind of visual effect. The simplest form of transition is the *fade,* which softly transitions one picture to the next. You can use many different types of other transitions, some of which can look quite elaborate; use such transitions with caution, since the editing should be felt not seen. You don't want to take away from the viewing experience with star burst transitions every minute.

  Use transitions to suggest a special relationship between two shots, such as a scene transition.

- ✔ **Cross fade:** This cut type can be used between shots as a softer replacement for hard cuts. If you want to edit to slow music and achieve a flowing pace, the fade is a useful technique.

  Figure 8-3 shows what a cross fade between two shots looks like in the context of a video. On the left, you can see the timeline with the vertical bar that shows which part of the video is playing. On the right, the preview pane shows the two shots that the cross fade combines.

- ✔ **Jump:** Cut from one view of a person or an object to another one that's only slightly different. You should generally avoid using the jump cut, but it can be used occasionally for dramatic effect. It's also used in interviews or talking-head videos to shorten a statement or to add visual variety. For example, the person who's speaking can be shown in a medium shot while you cut to a slightly tighter shot for the next sentence.

Your rough cut probably uses plain hard cuts exclusively, but as you start refining your video, you may want to consider using these other types of cuts to help advance the story and make the viewing experience more sophisticated.

Figure 8-3:
A cross fade transition.

Many beginners in video editing overuse fancy transitions. Modern editing programs are supplied with dozens of different transitions, and spicing up a video with all that eye candy is tempting. But don't forget that most viewers are more impressed by good storytelling than by overused special effects. A good rule of thumb is that 95 percent of your cuts should be plain hard cuts. If you use more than a handful of fades in your video, you're probably overdoing it.

Filling the gaps with B-roll

The term *B-roll* describes supplemental footage that can be used to provide additional context for the viewer or to fill gaps in the main storyline. We talk about how to shoot B-roll in Chapter 7. Having plenty of good B-roll is always a good idea because it makes an editor's life easier.

Use B-roll in your video in these common scenarios:

- Illustrate what a speaker or an interviewee is saying by showing the subject of the explanation.

- Add a bit of rhythm and visual polish to an otherwise long and visually boring scene.

- Separate scenes in a scripted video to give the viewer breathing room. Many TV series use a few pieces of B-roll between scenes — for example, in shots of the city where the story is taking place.

- Hide cuts in an interview or another continuous scene. If you have only one perspective of an interviewee, shortening the interview is difficult. Cutting directly looks jumpy and indicates that you've omitted material. If you cut instead to a piece of B-roll while the interviewee is still talking, you can easily mask the cut.

- Disguise small flaws in the footage. Did the camera suddenly shake in the middle of the interview, or did the subject move briefly out of focus? No problem — simply use a bit of B-roll to hide the mistake.

If you use B-roll only to disguise mistakes, your use of it may become too obvious. Use B-roll frequently to make your video more interesting and varied. But also avoid using B-roll that has nothing to do with the subject and doesn't add true value.

Polishing Your Video

After you refine your rough cut into a well-timed, well-trimmed video, it's time to apply the final layer of polish. A bit of further fine-tuning makes the difference between an acceptable video and one that looks truly professional.

Fine-tuning your edit

Videos can benefit from a number of relatively simple steps you can follow to improve certain aspects that viewers may not even consciously recognize:

1. **Tweak your cut timing.** If a cut seems even a little bit off, spend some time fine-tuning it. Even placing a cut a frame or two earlier or later can make a difference.

2. **Add music.** You may have already worked with some temporary music tracks during earlier editing steps, but now is the time to finalize all of your audio and background tracks.

3. **Clean up the audio track.** Most audio tracks can use some additional work. Be sure that the levels are correct and consistent throughout the video. Viewers don't like viewing one scene that's too loud followed immediately by one that's barely audible. Some editing programs have the Normalize Audio function, which optimizes audio levels automatically. Also, hard audio cuts rarely sound good. You can add a dissolve transition to the audio track while still applying a hard cut to the picture track.

4. **Use color correction.** Scenes in general should have a consistent look between shots; different video cameras can pick up different color influences. The color-correction feature in most editing programs will help fix color inconsistencies between shots and scenes. Color-correction also lets you give your video a unique and more interesting feeling. For instance, bluer light or colder light is used in many crime scenes, more yellow or warmer light is typically used in more romantic movies.

Adding bells and whistles

You can add a number of elements, as described in this list, to complete your video and make it look more interesting:

- ✔ **Titles:** A video should have a good title sequence, and editing programs offer a variety of different templates. Try a few different styles to see what works best. A general rule for any text on screen is viewers should be able to read it quickly twice. Be sure your title sequences are not too long, viewers on YouTube typically have less patience than viewers in the movie theater.

- ✔ **Sound effects:** A well-placed sound effect can make certain scenes much more interesting. We aren't talking about explosions, alien ray gun sounds, or Wilhelm Screams, but about basic background tracks or sounds that match the visible content on the screen. Sometimes, your original background sounds for a scene aren't good, and you can use canned sounds to replace them. Some editing programs come with small libraries of sound effects, and you can find more online.

- ✔ **Visual effects:** Most editing programs have effect filters that change the look of your footage completely. Though you should always use these effects sparingly, they may occasionally help make your video look more interesting.

You can experiment with bells and whistles in the earlier stages of the editing process, though you typically should wait until the end of your editing process before trying to use them fully. They're typically time consuming to apply, and if you change your edit afterward, you may have to do unnecessary work.

Adding Music to Your Video

You may wonder why music is even necessary in a video that isn't destined to sell a pop singer's latest album. Music determines a lot about the perception of your message because viewers make split-second, subconscious judgments about the content of your video depending on the type of music you choose.

In contrast to music videos, the music in your marketing video is meant to complement the message you're trying to convey. Music isn't the focus of a video — it's there simply to add color.

You must understand the difference between music you pay royalties to use and royalty-free music. Most of the music that you hear on the radio or buy online is copyrighted and can be used in videos only if you pay royalties to its record label — often an expensive strategy because you must pay for every use of a copyrighted music track. Record labels sometimes even charge more, depending on how many views your video attracts. And, "borrowing" music and hoping that you won't get caught is *not* an option. Videos containing copyrighted music can be banned automatically from sites such as YouTube.

The easiest way to save time and expense is to use only royalty-free music tracks — they're sold specifically for use in YouTube videos or presentations. After you pay a fixed price per song, you can usually use it however you want, as long as you stay within the boundaries specified by the music publisher contract. For example, some royalty-free tracks may be available for use in online videos but not in TV commercials. To choose music for your video, follow these steps:

1. **Determine which emotion you want to convey.** For example, you may want viewers to feel happy, sad, or uplifted — or neutral.

2. **Watch a rough edit of your video several times.** Or, if you're still in the planning stage, simply review the video's storyline in your mind. Do you need fast, aggressive cuts? Are your graphics clean and simple, or more elaborate and flowery? The music you choose must match the video's storyline, aesthetic value, and editing style.

3. **Choose an appropriate genre.** You may want to use a rock-and-roll track or a country track, for example, or perhaps electronic music more closely suits your style.

4. **Set the mood.** The mood of the music you choose has to match the emotion you want to convey. To judge, determine how the music makes *you* feel when you listen to it. If it matches the emotion you chose in Step 1, you're on the right track.

5. **Control the pace of the video by controlling its musical tempo.** A song's *tempo* refers to its speed or pace. The pace of the video also has to fit the emotion you're trying to convey and the overall storyline. For example, should viewers be relaxed or breathless after watching your video? Choose a tempo between these two extremes that creates the impression you want.

6. **Search for a song.** After you choose the genre, mood, and tempo of the music in your video, search for a song. (You'll find out more about music to purchase in the following sections. Or, if you're truly talented, compose one yourself.) You'll likely stick with royalty-free music.

7. **Drop in the music.** After you finish creating the video, you can drop the music into your editing timeline and edit the piece to mirror the pacing of the footage.

Adding built-in music in video editing tools

Most of the video editing software programs we describe in this chapter contain royalty-free song tracks, such as in these two examples:

- ✔ **Apple Final Cut Pro:** Has over 1,000 royalty-free sound effects and music tracks

- ✔ **Sony Vegas Movie Studio:** Contains 400 royalty-free music soundtracks

Some of the songs you can use from video editing software are so popular and overused (because they're free) that you risk triggering unwanted reactions from your audience. For example, a friend once complained to us that his video reminded him of a late-night TV ad containing questionable content. When we watched it, we found that his video editor had used a free, built-in music track that's often chosen by these low-cost advertisers.

Incorporating stock music libraries

If you have only a small budget and you want to sound different from the standard music libraries that come with many editing programs, you can find a good selection of royalty-free stock music to download online. This list describes some options that we recommend:

- ✔ **PremiumBeat (**www.premiumbeat.com**):** Has a great selection of great audio tracks and sound effects. They work closely with composers from around the world. They are very selective so it is easier to search through libraries for what you need.

- ✔ **Audiojungle (**www.audiojungle.com**):** It's less expensive than Shockwave-Sound (www.shockwave-sound.com), the major player in the stock music and sound effects derby, but its selection isn't as large. Songs cost between $10 and $20 apiece.

- ✔ **Footage Firm (**www.footagefirm.com**):** This site sells inexpensive DVD song compilations. A disc usually has only a few good songs, but they're usually worth the price — approximately $10 per disc, including shipping.

If you want to use an iconic song such as Nirvana's "Smells Like Teen Spirit" and you have a limited budget or limited time to secure the rights, you can often find inexpensive but similar-sounding songs on stock music sites.

If you can't find a song that matches the length of your video, don't worry: Viewers don't focus on songs — songs simply enhance the pacing and mood. Therefore, a repetitive song, or looping a song to fit the length of the video, usually works well.

Putting music in your video

After you have selected your music, it's time to insert it in your video.

The mechanical aspect of this task is easy to complete. Follow these steps in your editing software:

1. **Gather into one folder on your computer all the music files you want to use.**

   Using one folder helps you find files easily and helps you back them up after editing. If you store your music on a CD, import the necessary tracks to your computer first by using a program such as iTunes.

2. **Import the music files into your video editing software.**

   Most editing programs can process MP3 files and most other commonly used music file formats.

3. **Add an additional audio track to your editing project.**

   Certain simpler programs, such as iMovie, have predetermined tracks for background music.

4. **Drag and drop your music piece to the new audio track. Then shift its position until it fits the timing you want.**

5. **Watch the part of the video that now has background music in context.** Fine-tune the timing of the music, if necessary.

If you aren't sure which piece of music will work best with your video, simply import into your editing program multiple music tracks that you're considering. Drop one after the other on the audio timeline, watching the video with every piece of music, to quickly find which track you like best.

Adding emotional impact

The main purpose of your music selection is to enhance the emotional impact of your video. Even the specific way in which you use music in your edit affects the video's emotional impact. Try these simple tricks to give your music more emotional impact:

- **Work with the volume level.** Music in a video shouldn't always play at the same volume level. It should be softer and drop into the background whenever it supports dialogue or a voice-over narration, and it should be fairly loud when it stands on its own and drives home an emotional point. Most editing programs let you change the volume of a particular track over time. Dramatically increasing the volume of the music track in a key video scene adds quite a powerful effect — Hollywood movies and TV shows do it all the time.

✔ **Determine the proper timing.** A music track doesn't have to start at its beginning when you insert it in your video. Match the music to the video's visual content. Most musical selections have *hooks* — particularly remarkable and recognizable parts. For example, the hook of Beethoven's Fifth Symphony is the famous "Ta-ta-ta-daaa." Try to match musical hooks with important moments in the video.

Cutting your video to music

When you have a piece of music that matches well the emotional purpose of your video, fine-tune your edit to maximize the effect of the music. For example, you can extend a scene slightly to fit the most dramatic moment with a remarkable hook in the music.

Most editing programs let you lock your music tracks to avoid their being affected by other changes in your video. Follow these steps:

1. **Put your musical piece on its own audio track.**

2. **Time the music so that the music begins exactly where you want.**

3. **Lock the music track.**

   Most editing programs use a tiny padlock icon to indicate locking.

4. **Watch the video and determine how to adapt the timing to best fit the music.**

   For example, shorten or stretch certain shots slightly.

5. **Make your editing changes.**

6. **Unlock the audio track.**

 Precisely matching cuts in a video with beats in the music can create quite a pleasing effect because the picture and music then seem to move in perfect harmony. Avoid overdoing it, though, because an exact match can quickly bore viewers. The best approach is to match a couple of cuts with the music and then purposely skip the next few cuts before matching again. Alternating makes the final product less predictable and maintains viewer interest.

Cutting your music to video

You may not want to alter an edit just to better fit the music. In this case, cut the music to match your video instead.

Another important reason to cut music is to omit parts that may not fit well with the visual side of your video. For example, the piece of music you selected may have a bridge section that has a slightly different mood from the rest of the track, which can be distracting in a video. Eliminate the unwanted section by cutting precisely at the end of the previous part and at the end of the bridge section.

Almost all video editing programs let you cut audio tracks also, which is good enough for completing the basic editing of your music tracks, such as cutting off unwanted intros or endings to the millisecond.

An alternative is to cut your music tracks in advance by using an audio program such as Garage Band or Pro Tools. They let you edit audio precisely, and they provide a wealth of audio effects to help you enhance your music tracks for video use.

Adding Voiceover and Sound Effects

Many videos used for marketing employ *voiceover narration,* using offscreen narrators to tell viewers about the company's products or services. Most video editing programs have a voice-over recording feature, which is useful if you're recording your own voice directly into your computer.

To record your own voiceover, invest in a mid-quality external microphone. You can buy good USB microphones well below $100 — a worthy investment because your voice-over tracks will sound much better.

As with voice-over narration, you can also add sound effects. Most noises you hear in a typical Hollywood movie aren't recorded live on the set, but are added later in the process. Recording sounds on location is tricky and often creates mediocre results.

So, sound effects are most often added during the editing process. This list describes the major kinds of sound effects you can use:

- ✓ **Background or ambient:** Continuous background noises that suggest where the video scene is taking place work well to establish location. For example, a busy city scene needs vehicle noises, lots of footsteps, and the occasional siren. A beach scene needs wind and water sounds. These background sounds are easy to apply.

    If you can, record a few minutes of ambient sound on your video set to capture the audio character of the location.

- ✓ **Hard:** This type of sound effect accompanies visible events onscreen, such as slamming doors or passing vehicles. This type is a little more difficult to apply because they must be synced precisely to the picture, though most editing programs let you do it quite easily.

Most advanced video-editing programs are supplied with a small library of basic sound effects that you can easily use in your edits. Just add an audio track, drag in the sound recording you want, and shift the track around until it fits the scene.

You can find additional sound effects online from stock sound libraries such as Shockwave-Sound.com (`www.shockwave-sound.com`) and Soundsnap (`www.soundsnap.com`). Most of these sounds have specific descriptions, such as "Cars passing by at 25 mph on a somewhat busy street," so you can likely find something suitable.

Exporting the Final Version

When you finally finish editing, you export the video from your editing program so that you can use it later.

Typically, you should export multiple versions of a video because you can use the final product in different ways:

✓ **Export an archive master copy with the highest possible quality that your editing program offers.** You can always decrease, but not increase, quality (and therefore file size). That's why you should store a high-quality copy, in case you want to create other versions later.

✓ **Keep a copy just for YouTube purposes:** YouTube export settings are always changing, so be sure to double check the current best practices for settings directly on your YouTube channel upload page. Typically the settings look like this:

   • *Container:* mp4

   • *Audio Codec:* AAC-LC

   • *Video Codec:* H.264

   • *Acceptable and common frame rates:* 24, 25, 30, 48, 50, 60 frames per second

   • *Aspect Ratio:* YouTube players are all 16:9, a typical resolution is 720p: 1280x720

Most of the editing programs discussed in this book let you directly upload video to your YouTube channel. Uploading this way is convenient, but if you notice a mistake after uploading the video, you'll have to remove it, which can be a hassle. Normally, exporting video to your hard drive first is recommended for backing up and test purposes — watch it one last time, and then upload it manually to gain more control over every step.

Chapter 9

Preparing for Upload Day

It's hard to believe that, not that long ago, the whole concept of video production and distribution was the domain of specialized professionals. In those bad old days, the entire process was not only difficult but often also extremely expensive. Securing broader distribution rights required lawyers, which added another level of complexity and expense, all in the name of keeping great video work out of the domain of creative people and many business.

Fortunately, all that has changed. As computers, cameras, and applications became more powerful — and affordable and a lot less complex — creating a fabulous video could be accomplished relatively easily. So much for the miles of film and expensive production facilities that used to be standard operating procedure — now you could shoot an outstanding video on your mobile phone and then edit it on your laptop in the local coffee shop. The digital video revolution had begun.

Then along came YouTube, and suddenly you could get your video *immediately* distributed to, and in front of, millions of viewers without the aggravation of contracts, lawyers, and distribution partners. Overnight, you could become your own Hollywood studio. YouTube made it powerful and easy by making simplified, video self-publishing a reality. It eliminated nearly all the crazy video file format issues and removed the complicated conversion issues so that you could simply upload a file and people could watch it nearly everywhere without any special software.

Today, video is simpler than ever. But don't be deceived by the simplicity: YouTube gives you powerful tools to do great things with video uploading and distribution. So start off simple and hit the ground running, but be sure to leverage YouTube's additional distribution capabilities as your skills and your channel mature.

Preparing Your Channel for Uploads

Chapters 7 and 8 do a great job of guiding you through the process of capturing and editing great videos for your channel. If you've made your way through those chapters, you may be thinking that you're just a few clicks away from uploading a video, and you'd be absolutely right to think so. That's the great part about YouTube — it makes it easy to get your videos online. However, as Chapter 5 so forcefully puts it, being successful on YouTube requires a bit of planning, so don't rush. The time you invest now getting your channel ready for uploads not only makes your future work easier but also gives your channel much better watch time, subscription growth, and audience engagement.

Checking your YouTube account hygiene

YouTube certainly started a revolution in online video by making it amazingly easy to upload and share content. But there's something more: YouTube is also a community that abides by certain guidelines to maintain order and civility. These rules are divided into two categories:

- **Community guidelines:** YouTube is great place to share your work and do business, but just like your physical community, there are certain rules governing behavior — rules usually having something to do with the type of content you can upload. Just keep in mind that viewers can (and do) use the Watch page to flag what they consider to be community violations. Viewers don't have the last word here — YouTube reviewers will review the flag to make sure that the complaint is legitimate — but violations could lead to warnings, known as a *community guidelines strike*, being issued against your YouTube account.

- **Copyright policies:** Individuals or business are strongly encouraged to upload content that they own or have legal ownership of. This includes both audio and visual content. Uploading content you have no legal ownership of — or content where the legalities of ownership are murky — can be cause for more strikes against your account. Three copyright strikes will result in account termination (Copyright issues can be complicated; for a closer look at YouTube's take on copyright issues, check out www.youtube.com/yt/copyright. For our take on copyright, check out Chapter 16.)

Copyright violations can be flagged one of two ways:

- *Copyright strike:* A *strike* is a legal request by a copyright holder directing YouTube to take down the video and remove it from your channel.

- *Content ID claim:* YouTube will grant some users access to an automated copyright-verification system and database known as Content ID. Claims in Content ID don't result in a strike, because the system gives the copyright owner some control over what to do with violations, such as monetization or blocking.

Simply removing videos with copyright strikes or other violations (if YouTube hasn't done so automatically) doesn't make the strike or claim go away. You can wait for the claim to expire in six months, get the owner to retract the claim, or dispute it with a counter notification. Be diligent in resolving the issue with YouTube or the claimant.

Your success at following these rules defines your account status in YouTube:

- ✔ **Good Standing:** This is where you want to be: no community guidelines strikes; no copyright strikes; and no more than one video blocked by a Content ID copyright claim.

- ✔ **Bad Standing:** If you have violations under community or copyright guidelines, you may be subject to channel customization restrictions as well as upload suspensions and limitations. Monetization and your YouTube Partner Program standing may be at risk, too. Though many issues can be resolved or appealed, continued problems while in bad standing can lead to the removal of your YouTube channel. (For more on monetization issues and the YouTube Partner Program, see Chapter 14.)

- ✔ **Terminated:** In particular circumstances, YouTube will terminate your channel and prevent you from establishing new ones. Repeated breaches of community guidelines or continued copyright infringement will get you booted off YouTube.

Checking your YouTube account status is simple:

1. **In your web browser, go to** www.youtube.com.

2. **Log in to your YouTube account.**

3. **Click the logged-in icon and then choose Creator Studio from the drop-down menu that appears.**

   The Creator Studio main menu should appear on the left side of the browser.

4. Click the Channel section of the Creator Studio menu.

By default, it should go directly to the Status and Features submenu.

You can also bypass these steps by going directly to www.youtube.com/features.

5. Select Status and Features, if it's not already showing.

Doing so loads your account status on the right.

6. Make sure that both the Community Guidelines and Copyright lines show a green status circle and the words *Good Standing*.

The top of Figure 9-1 shows an account in good standing.

If your account is not in good standing, for either community guidelines or copyright violations, you probably received an email explaining why. You can get more detail on the status of your channel when you follow these steps:

1. In your web browser, go to www.youtube.com.

2. Log in to your YouTube account.

3. Click the logged-in icon and then choose Creator Studio from the drop-down menu that appears.

The Creator Studio main menu should appear on the left side of the browser.

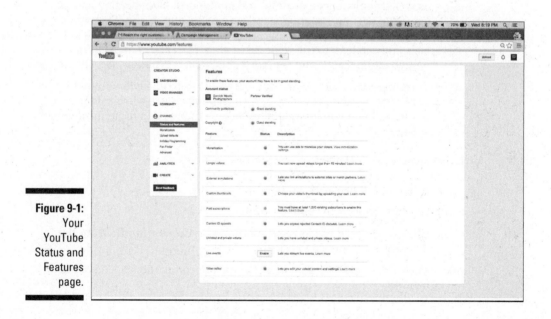

Figure 9-1:
Your
YouTube
Status and
Features
page.

4. **Click the Video Manager section of the Creator Studio menu.**

   If your account is in bad standing, you see selections that aren't normally shown, such as Copyright Notices.

5. **If visible, click the Copyright Notices section of the Video Manager section.**

   You can also bypass these steps by going directly to `www.youtube.com/my_videos_copyright`.

If your account is in good standing but you do have some copyright notices, you'll see those little notices next to your videos in the Videos section as well as in the Copyright Notices section. They are little blue hyperlinks next to the Edit button that generally say Matched Third Party content.

Maximizing the options for accounts in good standing

An account in good standing is much more than a merit badge and a nice pat on the back. It's the gateway to maximizing what you can do on your channel. With a channel in good standing, you're free to

- ✔ Customize your channel.
- ✔ Apply for the YouTube Partner Program. (More about that program in Chapter 2.)
- ✔ Control who can view your uploaded videos.
- ✔ Post videos longer than 15 minutes.
- ✔ Create custom video thumbnails to help get more views to watch.
- ✔ Extend your video licensing rights with Creative Commons. (More on Creative Commons and other copyright issues in Chapter 16.)
- ✔ Stream live events.
- ✔ Provide annotation links to external sites.
- ✔ Monetize your channel.
- ✔ Perform minor video edits on your YouTube channel.
- ✔ Provide a branded introduction to your video or an overlay branding watermark.
- ✔ Appeal Content ID disputes.

You want your YouTube account to be in good standing. Be sure to review the community guidelines and copyright policies every few months.

Enabling channel features

Now that your account is in good standing, be sure to check the rest of the fields on your channel's Status and Features page. Checking which YouTube features are enabled is straightforward:

1. **Log in to your YouTube account.**

2. **Click the logged-in icon and then choose Creator Studio from the pull-down menu that appears.**

   The Creator Studio main menu should appear on the left side of the browser.

3. **Click the Channel section of the Creator Studio menu.**

4. **Select Status and Features.**

   Doing so displays your account status on the right, as spelled out earlier in this section. Now cast your eye a bit below your account statuses and you'll see your YouTube features. More specifically, you'll see three distinct fields for each feature:

   1. *The feature itself:* This lists the name of the YouTube feature — one of the many built-in extensions to YouTube channel functionality that allows for greater channel control, monetization, and enhanced viewing features.

   2. *The feature status:* Your current ability to use these features. Each feature status is binary: Either you've enabled it or you haven't.

   3. *The feature description:* Details on what the feature does.

5. **Click to enable the feature you want to add to your channel.**

   For example, if you want ads on your channel, click the Enable button on the Monetization feature.

Tending to Video SEO Matters

In Chapter 5, we introduce the concept of *discoverability* — helping YouTube get your content in front of the right viewers through recommendations and search so they watch *your* content, rather than somebody else's. Though watch time is a critical part of YouTube's recommendation engine, a video's *metadata* — its title, description, and tags — plays an important role in getting the video found in the first place.

Video search engine optimization (*video SEO,* for short) is all about telling YouTube something about your video. For traditional web SEO, search engines such as Google, Bing, and Yahoo! would analyze the content on your site, figure out what was important, and then offer up your content to the most relevant searchers. Over time, these search engines factored in elements such as links, sharing, and clicks to determine how popular particular content ended up being on the web.

YouTube doesn't work like web SEO because it can't (yet) watch your content to determine what your video is about, so it has to rely on your metadata and how the community reacts by way of watch time, social media shares, and embedded links for the video on external sites.

It's a lot easier to get your video SEO house in order up front, rather than deal with it after you've published all your content.

So what exactly do we mean by *optimization* in *search engine optimization?* Optimization is about intelligently and systematically putting together description words so that

- ✔ YouTube understands what your content is about so it can better offer your video to the most appropriate searchers.

- ✔ Search engines such as Google, Bing, and Yahoo! understand your content and are thus in a position to add your videos to search engine results pages along with web content.

- ✔ Viewers are more likely to click on your content versus other search results offered.

These are the goals you want to achieve. The next few sections spell out how you can achieve them.

A bit later in this chapter, you'll find out where and when to enter information about titles, descriptions, and other important metadata associated with your video. It's important to understand the principles behind all these before you actually upload.

Titles

The video title is the most important piece of metadata that you'll create. As important as the title is to YouTube and the major search engines, you have to also ensure that it works for people. The trouble is that it can't look as though you're trying too hard to grab folks' attention. Fancy click-bait titles, such as "You won't believe what happens to the 12 kittens in this video," may generate more clicks, but the search engines won't bite and they will likely ignore your content. Also avoid breathless wording such as "most epic" or "blow your mind."

You need to strike a balance between attracting humans and attracting search engines when you create and optimize a title for a video.

Your title appears in many places:

- ✔ On the Watch page under the actual video
- ✔ In a YouTube search
- ✔ In Google, Bing, and Yahoo! searches
- ✔ As part of a playlist
- ✔ Under YouTube recommended videos

Selecting a title isn't complicated, but you must be somewhat methodical.

Only 100 characters of your video's title will show up in search results on a desktop computer, while some mobile devices will only show about 40, so you have to make the characters count. Suggested videos show about 75 characters maximum, with mobile being less. You can create a longer title, but it will be visible only on the Watch page. The goal of video SEO is to get viewers to the video in the first place. Being too short with the title is no good either because it may impair search algorithm matching.

Use the following approach to picking a title:

1. **Determine the keywords.**

   These are the important words that people will search for. Make sure they're part of your video content, as well as in the other metadata associated with your video, such as the Tag and Description fields. If you work for Acme Electric and you're marketing the new Z500 convection oven, your keywords would include *Acme Electric, Z500,* and *convection oven.*

2. **Add a descriptive phrase to the title.**

   Your keywords alone may not be enough. Determine why your viewers would be searching for your product or your video. They may want installation instructions or product reviews, for example. Terms such as *how to install* and *product review* will aid you in both search and views.

3. **Move branding keywords to the end of the title.**

   Viewers will search for your brands, but they need to see the descriptive information first.

4. **If your video is part of a series, include an episode number at the end of your title.**

   Even if your videos are part of a playlist, your viewers may end up searching separately, so make it easy and logical for them to find another episode.

Be sure to include your title keywords in the tag and description metadata.

Before you even upload anything to YouTube, it's good practice to rename the video file to a title that accurately represents its content. YouTube will keep the original reference file title on the asset no matter how many times you end up changing the title.

Descriptions

You'll want to make good use of the 5,000-character field that YouTube provides you for describing your video. It's a great place to add details about not only your video but also your channel, along with links for other videos, subscriptions, other channels, and web assets. In other words, it's a goldmine for both metadata and user guidance. (Figure 9-2 demonstrates what we mean.) The viewers who care about your video will read the description, so make it worth their while.

Going long on shortlinks

Chances are, you've seen some rather interesting web names like `bit.ly`, `owl.ly`, `goo.gl`, `pix.tv`, and `is.gd` as you've made your way around the web. Often, these web names are combined with what appears to be a random string of characters to produce something that looks like this: `http://bit.ly/1xUu7KB`. Like any Internet address, this link can be clicked to take you anywhere on the web, including YouTube. You can even click one of these funny-looking strings to get to the Watch page of a specific video.

So what is this funky address? It's called a *shortlink*, and it replaces really long web addresses to preserve valuable space on sites such as Twitter and YouTube. How does this work? A shortlink has an associated target link. For example, in our link example, `http://bit.ly/1xUu7KB`, actually points to `http://www.pixability.com`. When clicking a shortlink, users end up at the associated target. Shortlinks are formally known as shortened Uniform Resource Locators (URLs). *URL* is a fancy way of referring to a web address.

Many free services are available for link shortening. One of the most popular ones is bit.ly, and you can quickly sign up for it at `www.bit.ly`. In seconds, you'll be creating shortlinks to your heart's content.

But there's much more to shortlinks than meets the eye. Services such as bit.ly track clicks so that you can see which shortlinks are the most popular. You can actually have different shortlinks point to the same target address so that you can test which tweets work better or which web pages may be most interesting.

The top YouTube channel managers use link shorteners extensively in YouTube descriptions, channel descriptions, and social media.

Figure 9-2:
A well-constructed description field.

The video description should

- ✔ **Explain** in greater detail what your video and your channel are about.

- ✔ **Extend** the viewer's experience by providing additional detail around what is shown in the video. For example, if you have a video on cooking, the description field would be a great place to include a copy of the recipe.

- ✔ **Trigger** the viewer to do something. That could include watching another video, making a purchase, supporting your cause, and more.

- ✔ **Entice** people to view. The first couple of paragraphs of the description show up in search results, so you have to write compelling — and relevant — content so that the user somehow takes the next step of clicking and viewing. That's also true on the Watch page, where the first couple of sentences appear under the video, compelling the viewer (you hope!) to watch.

- ✔ **Aid** in discovery. A great description can include hundreds of keywords that will help with search. Be sure to use ones that are relevant to the video.

The description field isn't the place for a transcript of your video. YouTube has a special spot for that; we cover that spot a bit later in this chapter.

Include at the beginning of the description a shortlink that leads to a web page that has something to do with the video. Leading viewers to your home page is generally not advised, because they're looking for more detailed information around the video. Follow the shortlink with a clear and concise description, but make it interesting enough that people will feel like watching.

Always consider what information is visible in search results — by being well aware of which devices your audience is using to search. The first paragraph of the description will show up on a desktop search, whereas no description data is currently exposed in a mobile device search.

 Two older terms from marketing and advertising are still quite relevant to today's YouTube description field: *above the fold* and *below the fold.* When people used to receive folded letters or advertisements, they often first looked at the top, which was "above the fold." If the content was compelling, they'd read the rest of it "below the fold." When viewers watch your video, they also see the first part of its description. If the description is compelling, they'll click "Show more" and see what's below the fold. Make what's above the fold in the video description count.

The description field should contain enough shortlinks to answer any questions your viewers might have about your video, your channel, and your business. The About page of your channel should contain links that complement your channel. It's okay to repeat some of these links in the video description as well. The shortlinks in the description field can point to

- ✔ Your channel
- ✔ Other videos
- ✔ Social media sites such as Facebook, Twitter, LinkedIn, Pinterest, or Instagram
- ✔ A website
- ✔ A landing page

Include only one link in the first paragraph if you want viewers to ultimately end up somewhere else. Include all the relevant social links or product page links in the second or lower paragraphs of the description.

 Don't create a custom description field for each video. Put together a consistent framework or template that includes some repeatable information such as subscription information, social media links, programming schedule, and contact information. Customize only the data in your framework that relates to the video itself. Keep everything else consistent. Your audience will appreciate the consistent layout of your field as well.

 Everyone hates email *spam* — unsolicited advertisements filled with overdone and repeated buzzwords. If the description sounds at all "spammy," you'll provoke a negative reaction. Instead, try to be informative by using a lot of descriptive words and appropriate shortlinks.

Tags

Tags are special descriptive keywords or short phrases that indicate what your video is about. They are used by search engines to help potential viewers discover your video. Tags also play an important role in helping YouTube make related video recommendations. (Your description field also has keywords, but tags are used by YouTube to help categorize your video.)

YouTube imposes a limit of 500 characters for the entire Tag field. A tag can contain one or more words, but each individual tag cannot be more than 30 characters long.

Without getting too deep into the math, you may end up with room for 10 to 30 tags. Use as many as you can.

What's the best approach to creating tags?

- ✔ **Be both specific and broad.** Everyone searches differently — some use broad terms like *oven,* whereas others use *Acme Electric Z500 convection oven.* Use both.

- ✔ **Choose synonyms.** Though you may use *oven* only in the description and video, it's okay to use the word *stove* in your tags.

- ✔ **Add an action tag.** Sure, people may be searching for video about the "Acme Electric Z500 convection oven." Think about terms that are relevant, such as *product review, how to install, and how to clean.* Pick one around the video content.

- ✔ **Combine and break up keywords.** Language and people are imprecise, so take that into account and use both keywords, as in *cook top* and *cooktop.*

Tags can be modified. Just be sure that they reflect the essence of the content.

Don't use keywords to mislead or bait viewers. Viewers will realize that they've been misled and stop viewing. YouTube will detect that the watch time is bad and penalize your video and hurt its discoverability.

Thumbnails

Thumbnails are visual snapshots of your video, similar to a poster for a movie. They have a tremendous impact on a video's view rate, so you should choose a good one. Thumbnails by default are chosen by YouTube — three optional frames from the beginning, middle, and end of your video will be provided for every video asset that's uploaded. You can, however, create a custom thumbnail for each video. (See Figure 9-3 for some examples and check out the "Adding Custom Thumbnails" section, later in this chapter, for the specifics on creating custom thumbnails.) If you do decide to create custom thumbnails, it's best to choose a thumbnail that is illustrative of the content in the video. Thumbnails show up in the following areas:

- ✔ Channel page
- ✔ Watch page
- ✔ Playlists
- ✔ Suggested videos
- ✔ Channel guide
- ✔ Subscriber feed
- ✔ YouTube search
- ✔ Web search
- ✔ Mobile display
- ✔ Mobile search

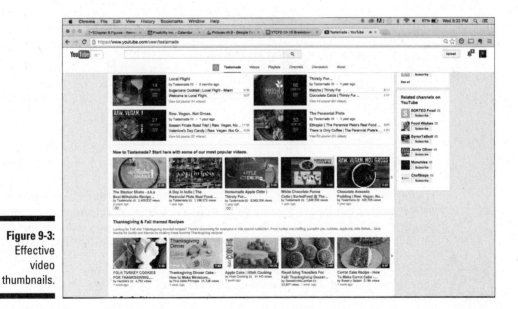

Figure 9-3:
Effective video thumbnails.

Keep the following key considerations in mind when deciding on a custom thumbnail:

- ✔ **Incorporate boldness:** You're competing for viewers, so you need to stand out among the many other thumbnails across YouTube and the web. Color contrast and image quality and visual layout matter.

- ✔ **Add personification:** Show the close-up view of faces, if possible. Viewers will click on faces more than anything else.

- ✔ **Strive for accuracy:** The thumbnail has to relate to the content of the video. Don't use the thumbnail as click bait.

Uploading Your Video

There's always a bit of excitement when you upload one or more videos to YouTube. The feeling is similar to what happens when you see the proverbial light at the end of the tunnel.

Uploading isn't the final step to getting your videos available for viewing by your growing fan base. You still need to *publish* an uploaded video in order to make it live.

Between uploading and publishing, you have several steps to consider. YouTube rewards you with higher search rankings and supplementary video recommendations based first and foremost on your channel and on individual video watch times. In addition, YouTube looks at characteristics like viewer engagement and video sharing rates. Your job in the planning process is to identify and coordinate each component so that you're in a position to keep your channel active.

Picking the source

Before you upload, your videos have to live somewhere. They might be on your desktop computer, laptop, game console, tablet, or smartphone. What's great about having so many choices for uploading is that you can capture and upload content to your channel anytime and anywhere. It's that easy!

Sign in using the same YouTube account from all your different computers, consoles, and mobile devices so that all your videos and channel settings stay synchronized.

The web browser interface to YouTube on your laptop or desktop will have the most complete set of YouTube capabilities for uploading, optimizing, annotating, and publishing. For iOS and Android devices, you can run applications such as YouTube and YouTube Creator Studio to upload videos and manage your channel. iOS even offers an additional application known as YouTube Capture. Though these applications are quite powerful and have most of the features of the computer-based versions, we focus here on the browser-based versions.

Going public about YouTube privacy

New YouTube channel managers and creators often ask, "How do I control who can see my videos?" This is controlled by YouTube's privacy settings, which can be found under Creator Studio's Channel and Video Manager sections. You need to know and understand the three types of privacy settings in YouTube:

- ✔ **Public:** This is the default setting in YouTube — everyone can view your video. Videos set to Public can also show up in all searches.

  After you make a video public, you've officially *published* it. It will show up in your subscribers' feeds. Though you can readily change the privacy settings on your content, be sensitive to how your audience is using and sharing it, because changing settings may suddenly make your content unavailable to them with no warning.

- ✔ **Private:** This setting, the most restrictive one, prevents anyone but you from watching the video without your explicit permission. Private videos cannot be searched and are invisible on your YouTube channel. If your channel is linked to Google+, you can selectively share a private video with specific users on Google+ or within your Google+ circles. If you or your viewers don't have a Google+ account, private video cannot be shared. Video set to Private cannot show up in search results or be viewed by someone even if they have the video URL.

- ✔ **Unlisted:** Unlisted videos will not show up on your channel or YouTube search for viewers. However, anyone with the unlisted video URL can watch the video and share it freely anywhere on the web, including websites and on Facebook, Twitter, and other social sites. Unlisted videos can be included in playlists as well. A viewer does not need to have a Google+ account to view an unlisted video.

  Use unlisted content as a way to share special or exclusive content with select fans or as part of a limited-time promotion or sale.

✔ **Scheduled:** This special setting is reserved for YouTube partners. It automatically sets the video to Private and then changes it to Public on the date and time you specify.

Use scheduled privacy settings for channel programming consistency to ensure that videos are available at a standard date and time, regardless of whether you have access to your YouTube channel.

Your privacy settings also signal to YouTube to begin its magic. When you publish a video, YouTube starts assessing your video by using its algorithms to determine what your video is about, how good it is, and where it should fall in search results. The best practice is to publish a video when your viewers are already on YouTube. Publish the video so that you get immediate views on it; this indicates to YouTube that this video is indeed hot stuff and that it may be a good candidate for YouTube search and recommendations.

Playlists have privacy settings, too. One of your options during the final stages of the upload process is to put your video content into a playlist. Chapter 3 covers playlists and their importance on your channel.

Don't underestimate the power of YouTube playlists, which have become increasingly popular because they not only show up in search results but can also be customized to greatly enhance the viewing experience.

Uploading to YouTube

You should have no problem finding the Upload button on YouTube — it's on every page! You'll find it in the top right corner, to the left of the Sign In button (if you're not logged in to YouTube), or to the left of the bell-shaped notification icon on the top right of the window (if you are logged in). To upload your video content:

1. **Sign in to your YouTube Account.**

2. **Click the Upload button.**

   Doing so brings up the Upload window, shown in Figure 9-4.

3. **Select the video-upload privacy option that you want from the Privacy pull-down menu.**

   The menu is automatically populated with your default privacy setting. If you're happy with the default setting, you don't have to do a thing; just move on to the next step.

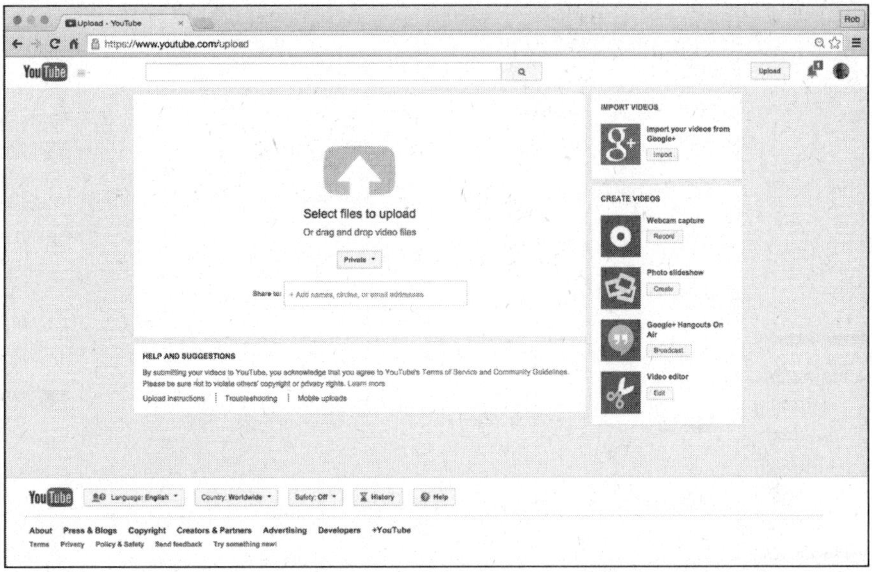

Figure 9-4:
The
YouTube
upload
window.

4. **Still in the Upload window, use one of the following three methods to select the video file you want to use:**

   1. *Select files to upload:* Hover the mouse cursor over the big up-arrow button and click it when it turns red. Then use the Look In dialog box to navigate to — and then select — the file you want to upload.

   2. *Drag and drop video files:* This one's as simple as it sounds: Just drag a video file to the Upload window and drop it when the drag-and-drop video file's overlay turns green.

   3. *Import your videos from Google+:* This option is to the top right of the main Upload window. Start by clicking the Import button there, and then select and upload the video file from your Google+ account.

5. **If your method requires it, click OK to upload.**

   Your files are on their way to YouTube.

6. **Get ready to enter your metadata.**

   In the following section, you'll learn how to add that title, tags, descriptions, and video thumbnails.

With your videos selected and the upload under way, you'll be presented with a new Video Manager editor screen (Figure 9-5) that shows important details about the video. If you're uploading more than one video, YouTube will show you the progress for each upload.

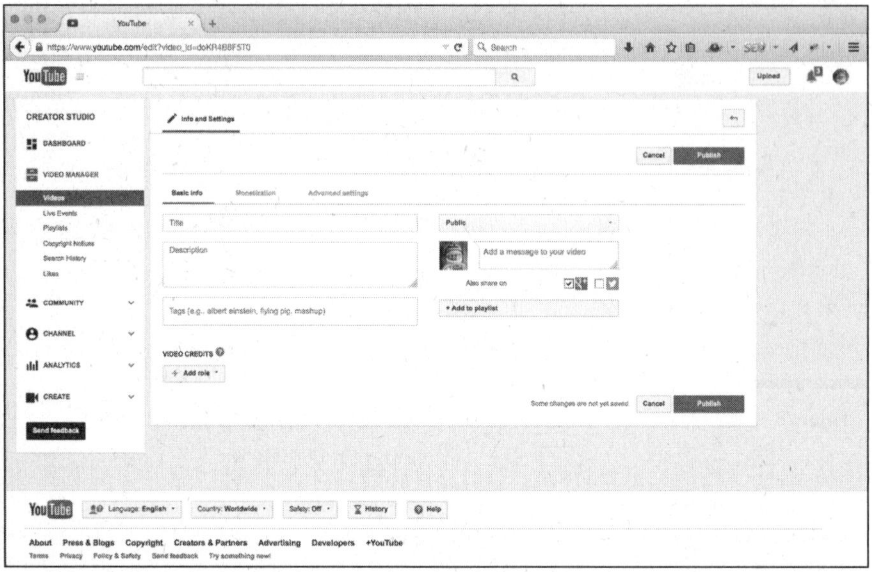

Figure 9-5:
Entering
metadata
through
Video
Manager.

Keeping the upload train moving

Beth Le Manach is the vice president of programming at Kin Community, one of the world's leading online communities for women and lifestyle creators. At Kin, she is responsible for overseeing the original programming strategy for Kin's numerous online properties and the branded content created for its advertising partners.

Kin not only produces its own content for its hub channel (www.youtube.com/kincommunity) but also manages its extremely talented cast of YouTube creators, including baking sensation Rosanna Pansino (www.youtube.com/RosannaPansino).

Along with her full-time job at Kin Community, Beth hosts her own channel, "Entertaining with Beth" (www.youtube.com//EntertainingWithBeth), a channel nominated for three Taste awards; including Best Instructional Web Series. For her channel, Beth creates and shares elegant recipes that are perfect for entertaining guests but simple enough to prepare for a weeknight meal.

Coming from the TV business, Beth knows the importance of streamlining production and shoots several of her weekly episodes during one shoot session. She then edits the content and uploads it to YouTube with the scheduled privacy setting, ensuring that her audience has new content and recipes to try every Saturday. Her upload approach ties in perfectly with her programming strategy. Beth's excellent content is the frosting on the YouTube cake.

The Video Manager editor screen that you see during the upload process is the same one displayed under the Video Manager section of Creator Studio. Having the video manager editor screen here as well allows you to go back later and modify the video settings. This includes such tasks as changing the video description, tags, and shortlinks.

YouTube easily handles most encoding types. If YouTube is having any problems with your file, check out `https://support.google.com/youtube` for more information.

Entering information about your video

It doesn't matter whether your upload is a work in progress or a finished product; you can begin adding the metadata at any time. This process is known as "video optimization." In the YouTube world, optimization involves dealing with three distinct areas:

- ✔ **Basic Info:** This is your most important information because it contains all the important fields for video SEO. This would include title, description, and tags.

- ✔ **Monetization:** Creators who've elected to make money from ads being placed against their video can use this section to specify what types of ad can be shown against the video. Chapter 14 covers this in more detail.

- ✔ **Advanced Settings:** This detailed bucket list contains some esoteric information, such as licensing and syndication, along with some important fields around category classification and distribution.

Edit the basic info first. (Refer to Figure 9-5 to see the layout of the Basic Info section.) Although it isn't rocket science, you'll still want to make sure to cross your *i*'s and dot your *t*'s. Follow these steps to edit your video's basic info:

1. **Make sure the Basic Info section in the Video Manager editor screen is selected.**

   The active section (refer to Figure 9-5) will have a red underline just below the section name. If Basic Info isn't selected, simply click on the name, and the section fields will appear.

2. **Using your newly acquired SEO knowledge, come up with an appropriate title for your video and enter it into the Title field.**

3. **Enter an SEO-friendly description of your video into the Description field.**

4. **Add SEO-appropriate tags in the Tags field.**

YouTube imposes a limit of 500 characters for the entire Tag field. A tag can contain one or more words, but each individual tag cannot be more than 30 characters long. Depending on how you divvy up your 50 characters, you can end up with between 10 and 30 tags.

5. **Add your uploaded video to one or more playlists.**

This step is optional. You can also create a new playlist here. Simply click the + Add To Playlist button and check the playlist you want the video included in. (You can check more than one playlist.)

6. **Add video credits.**

Remember that this step applies only to partner channels. To give credit to your video contributors, click the + Add Role button, choose the title, and then add the person. The person will need a channel user name or URL.

7. **Set the privacy level or schedule your content for publication**.

Click the Privacy button which will show Published, Unlisted, or Private depending your default settings. Make changes, if desired. If you want to schedule a video so that it is made public at a specific time, choose Scheduled after you click the Privacy button and enter the publish date and time.

The best practice is to upload all your videos as Private and then schedule your content. This saves you from the mistake of publishing a video prematurely, often before you've had a chance to set up all the metadata. This has happened to all of us.

If you're part of the YouTube partner program, the Info and Settings page will have a Monetization tab in addition to the standard Basic Info tab, as shown in Figure 9-6. (If you're not bothering with monetization, you can skip this bit and jump right to the Advanced Settings discussion.)

The following steps show you how you can take advantage of monetization opportunities for your uploaded video.

1. **Click to select the Monetization section.**

Doing so displays the fields in the Monetization section.

2. **Click to select the Monetize with Ads check box.**

A menu appears, listing your ad-format options.

3. **Select one or more of the listed ad formats.**

Chapter 14 covers monetization and ad formats in greater detail.

Figure 9-6:
YouTube's
upload
monetization
section.

You've probably figured out by now that YouTube does have a lot of bells and whistles. If you're just starting out, you don't need to mess around with all the settings, because most operations will work fine. As you advance, though, you'll probably want a bit more control. That's what the Advanced Settings page is for (as shown in Figure 9-7).

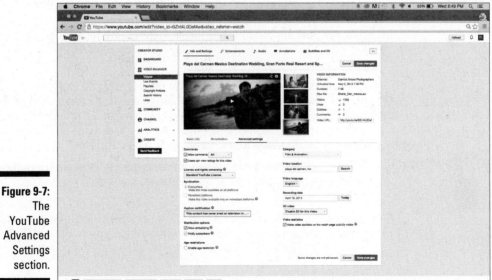

Figure 9-7:
The
YouTube
Advanced
Settings
section.

To manage the advanced settings, do the following:

1. **Click to select the Advanced Settings section.**

   Doing so displays the Advanced Settings section fields.

2. **Modify the settings that are important to your video.**

   Pick and choose from the offerings in this list:

   1. *Comments:* Specify whether you want comments posted automatically or only after approval from the channel owner. Only you can decide what is best for your channel. YouTube viewers generally prefer to see their comments right away and will take note if you require approval.

      You always have the option, as the content owner, of hiding bad comments. Users who posted bad comments can come back to your video and still see their own comments, but no other viewers can see comments you have removed. For more details on comment management, see Chapter 10.

      Keep the Users Can View Ratings for This Video check box selected. That lets users see a video's likes and dislikes — the handy thumbs-up and thumbs-down images.

   2. *License and Rights Ownership:* You have ownership rights for what you create, but you can let other people use your content, even for commercial use. YouTube provides you with some flexibility through the standard YouTube license or Creative Commons. (For more on copyright and your rights options, check out Chapter 16.)

   3. *Syndication:* If you're monetizing your videos, you can control whether your content is shown everywhere or only on platforms that support ads. (Other platforms include mobile applications on iOS and Android, as well as gaming consoles such as PlayStation and Xbox.)

   4. *Captions:* Captions are important to people with disabilities or to others who don't speak the native language of the video. There's no rule that you have to add captions your videos; it depends on whether it's important to use it to connect with your audience. Chapter 10 provides more detail on adding captions.

      If your content has been shown on American television, there may be FCC restrictions around the captions, and you'll need to let YouTube know about it.

   5. *Distribution Options:* Embedding allows people to include your video in their websites. YouTube will provide you with the HTML code for your website. To get the code, click the Share button

under the video on the Watch Page, and then click the Embed tab. Just copy the highlighted HTML and add it to your website. You receive credit for all views, likes, and shares. You can also select the Notify Subscribers option so that subscribers are notified via either their YouTube page or email.

If you're releasing 20 videos in one day and you normally only release 1 video per week, deselect the Notify Subscribers option. Your viewers may see your multiple offerings as spam if they aren't used to this level of activity for your channel.

6. *Age Restrictions:* Certain content isn't appropriate for viewers under 18, and it's up to you as the channel owner to make that call. Selecting this box helps ensure that a video can only be viewed by signed-in viewers who are 18 years of age and older. Understand that this may impact monetization if you're a YouTube partner.

Even if viewing is restricted to audiences 18 and over, community guidelines are still in effect.

7. *Category:* This is the big bucket that you'd put your video into if someone asked you to describe your video in the most general of terms. Think of it as a "super tag," and choose a category that best suits your video. This helps YouTube categorize your video for its search and recommendation algorithms.

8. *Video Location:* Both your users and YouTube may care where you shot your video. Add the location if you think it's important.

9. *Video Language:* Set this to the language spoken in the video.

10. *Recording Date:* Like your location selection, users and YouTube may be interested in when your content was shot.

11. *3D Video:* Some people like 3D content, and YouTube is more than happy to accommodate. Using the options in the Advanced Settings section, you can disable the 3D function for your video, make your video 3D, or upload a 3D video and choose the This Video Is Already 3D option. Viewers can view the video in 3D with HTML5, but they will need to configure the settings.

12. *Video Statistics:* Some channel owners don't mind sharing information about views, time watched, subscriptions driven, and video shares. It's always interesting to see whether views grow slowly over time or have an initial spike and flatten out. It's an indication of whether your content has long-term value to viewers. Uncheck the box if you don't want to share this information. Doing so won't have any negative impact on either your video or your channel.

Setting upload defaults

After you hit your groove and are uploading lots of content, you may tire of having to enter the same information over and over again into your upload screens or through Video Manager. Fortunately, YouTube allows you to set default values on the most common Basic Info, Monetization, and Advanced Settings tabs. Just select the Channel section in the Creator Studio menu on the left side of the screen and choose the Upload Defaults option. Figure 9-8 shows the kinds of things you can set as defaults using this option.

Defaults are simply preconfigured values. You can change values either during the upload process or through Video Manager.

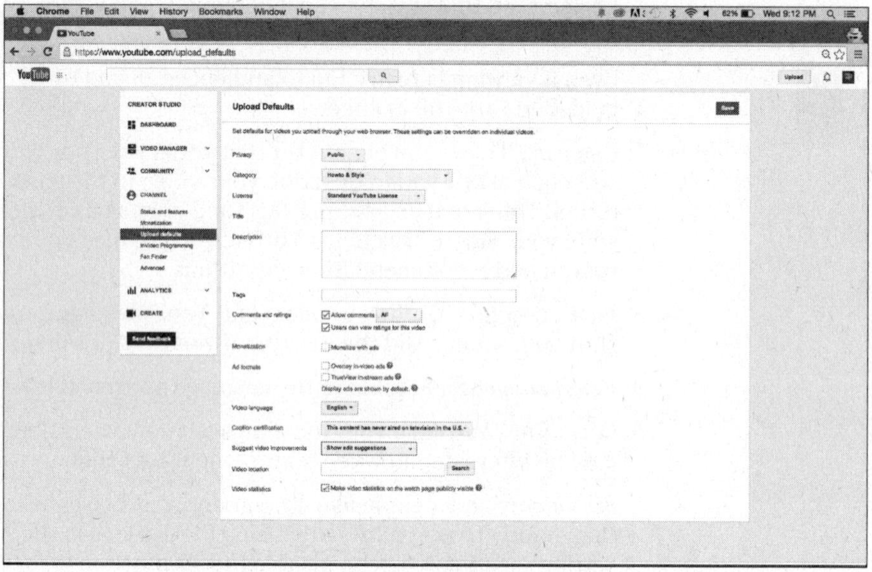

Figure 9-8:
The
YouTube
Upload
Defaults
con-
figuration.

Adding Custom Thumbnails

If your channel is in good standing, you can also provide a custom thumbnail instead of one of the default three images that YouTube recommends for your video. You can only add a custom thumbnail after your video has been uploaded. After the upload is completed, YouTube needs to analyze and process the video before you can add a custom thumbnail.

If you don't pick the thumbnail, YouTube will kindly do it for you. It's always better to pick it yourself or add a custom one.

The thumbnail is your billboard and will have a big influence on whether someone will watch your video.

To add a custom thumbnail to your video:

1. **Log in to your YouTube account.**

2. **On your YouTube page, click your channel icon and then choose Creator Studio from the menu that appears.**

3. **Click the Video Manager section of Creator Studio.**

   By default, it should go directly to the Videos submenu.

   You can also bypass these steps by going to www.youtube.com/ my_videos.

4. **Find the video whose thumbnail you want to customize and click the Edit button next to it.**

   You're presented with page similar to the one shown in Figure 9-9. You'll see much of the information you saw during the upload, but you'll now have more stuff, including detailed video information and a visual representation of the thumbnails.

5. **Click on the Custom Thumbnail button shown under the three default thumbnails chosen by YouTube.**

   Choose the thumbnail from an image file.

6. **Click the Save Changes button.**

   You have a custom thumbnail!

Figure 9-9:
A YouTube video with no custom thumbnail.

Publishing and Unpublishing Videos

As a YouTube channel manager or content creator, your work may well be done when you've uploaded your videos and set the metadata. Publishing is all about configuring the privacy settings that are most appropriate for your users and clicking Save during the upload process or through Video Manager. For most channel managers, that means setting the video to Public at a specified time.

Always set your uploads to Private by default to avoid publishing before you've had the chance to set up metadata, shortlinks, and other parts of the video.

Before you publish, YouTube provides several additional features to help audience engagement, which we cover in greater detail in Chapter 10. You can

- Edit videos without having to upload again
- Add audio tracks
- Add annotations
- Set up captions and transcripts

After you've uploaded a video, you can't simply replace it with another one and use the same video URL. If you need to remove a video from general viewing, you have two choices:

- **Unpublish it.** Set it to Private and remove any Google+ shares.
- **Delete the video.** Remove it from YouTube permanently.

You can only delete videos that you own. To delete a video:

1. **Log in to your YouTube account.**

2. **On your YouTube page, click your channel icon and then choose Creator Studio from the menu that appears.**

3. **Click the Video Manager section of Creator Studio.**

By default, it should go directly to the Videos submenu.

You can also bypass these steps by going to www.youtube.com/my_videos.

4. **To delete one video, click the down arrow of the Edit menu to the right of thumbnail of the video, and select Delete from the submenu that appears.**

   You're presented with a confirmation dialog box.

5. **Select Yes if you want to delete, or Cancel if you've made a mistake or changed your mind.**

6. **To delete multiple videos, select one or more check boxes to the left of the thumbnails of the videos you want to remove, and then click the down arrow on the Actions menu at the top of the Video page and select Delete from the menu that appears.**

   You're presented (again) with a confirmation dialog box.

7. **Select Yes if you want to delete, or Cancel if you've made a mistake or changed your mind.**

   Figure 9-10 shows multiple videos selected for deletion.

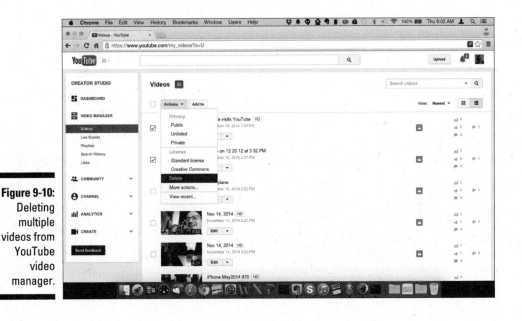

Figure 9-10: Deleting multiple videos from YouTube video manager.

Part III
Growing and Knowing Your Audience

To find out more about how you can grow your audience, check out www.dummies.com/extras/youtubechannels.

In this part . . .

- ✔ Get the word out about your channel.
- ✔ See what it takes to expand your audience.
- ✔ Work with analytics tools to get a better sense of your audience.

Chapter 10

Building Your Audience

*T*here's obviously more to being an excellent channel manager than simply uploading a few videos and arranging a playlist or two. To truly excel as a channel manager, you have to realize that the core of your YouTube channel activities centers on your audience and understanding and responding to their needs. Your audience, whether it consists of one person or ten million people, is coming to your channel and watching your videos for a reason, whether it's education, entertainment, production information, or what-have-you. Building an audience is about catering to the requirements of your viewers.

In the "good old days" of television, content was broadcast to a mass of viewers who were, for the most part, anonymous. It was never truly clear how many people were watching, so companies such as Nielsen provided estimates. The only feedback the audience delivered was either watching or not watching. As important as it was to retain regular viewers, the television networks knew they had to build an audience as well. They did this by putting together good shows and doing lots of advertising. There wasn't much else for the audience to do other than show up and watch shows when the networks decided.

Fast-forward to Generation YouTube, where a completely different set of audience expectations affect not just viewing patterns but also how viewers expect to interact with the stars of the show. In this sense, the YouTube world is a two-way street where the audience expects a back-and-forth exchange with the content providers. Audiences want an experience on their terms.

As a YouTube channel manager, you need to keep that engagement going. If you manage a YouTube celebrity, consider yourself the agent. Got a brand or business channel? You need to put on your Social Media and Press Relations hat. Either way, you need to treat your audience with the same care and attention that you do your own content.

Developing a Community

Your audience consists of the people who watch your videos. As you acquire bigger audiences, YouTube ranks your channel and content higher, greatly aiding *discoverability* — the process whereby potential viewers are led to view your content. It's that simple, and it's why audience development is vital to your channel strategy. You want that newly acquired audience to go to your channel page and experience more of your great content. It's a good pattern to establish.

Deciphering audience evolution

Unless you're already a Hollywood celebrity, you probably won't acquire an audience overnight. That's okay. You need to understand that it may take years to build the right audience. Also remember that your channel may be evolving as well. Where you start on YouTube may not be where you end up. Nonetheless, consider the evolution of your audience and how they engage with your content. That process should (you hope) play out with these characteristics:

- **Interest:** Viewers are interested in something, whether it's Bruno Mars, monster trucks, Indian cooking, radiant floor heating installation, or so much more. They search and come to YouTube to find out more about what they're interested in.

- **Curiosity:** Impressed by watching one of your videos, your viewers then visit your channel to look for more of your stuff. A nicely designed channel and well-organized playlist enhance their experience.

- **Connection:** Liking their experience with you and your channel, they now want to stay current and be informed of updates. They choose to subscribe.

- **Engagement:** Your audience wants even more, so they begin to click that handy Like button on some of your videos and start offering comments. They may engage with each other on the Comments section of your channel.

✔ **Promotion:** They then share your content via Facebook, Twitter, and other social media channels with others who share similar interests and also become part of your audience.

✔ **Collaboration:** In addition to giving you feedback, your most passionate fans may even work with you on content.

Determining what you want your audience to do

Though your final goal may be to become a YouTube celebrity and have your audience request autographed pictures of you, you have some other homework to do before the audience is eating out of your hand. Your audience requirements come down to two simple things you want them to do:

✔ **Watch:** You know the importance of watch time on discoverability. Your audience needs to view your content regularly — and you need to feed them good content regularly.

✔ **Engage:** Having viewers watching content is great, but having them actually do something is the frosting on the cake. Engagement is a broad topic that you can read about at length in this chapter. It includes actions such as liking, commenting, messaging, sharing, and clicking.

Engagement is a two-way street. You need to engage back as well. Holly Casto (www.youtube.com/charmandgumption) is the owner and designer of Charm & Gumption, an online gift shop for bloggers and creative types. Aside from having an interesting YouTube channel that support her business, she does a fine job of communicating with her fans, as shown in Figure 10-1.

As you get more viewers, your watch time and engagement level increase. That's why building an audience for your channel can't be left to chance.

Appreciating the importance of community

Communities have developed around common interests for thousands of years. From medieval guilds to book groups to political causes, people have banded together into communities. As the Internet grew in both reach and popularity, virtual communities began to spring up. Suddenly, people could be part of large, diverse communities spread over continents and time zones.

Figure 10-1: Audience engagement through comments.

By bringing the video component to the Internet picture, YouTube made these communities more engaged — and more real. You could actually see your peers. As a result, YouTube communities quickly displayed characteristics important to both creators and companies: They supported and helped their members.

Your community could do much to drive the audience growth for your YouTube channel, but for that to happen you need to be a genuine and active member of the community.

Over time, many members of your community will take that extra step and subscribe to your channel. Subscribers are worth their weight in gold because they watch more and engage more. Clearly that's a good thing, but there's something else: YouTube offers additional features to channels that have a high subscriber count, including fan insights and additional monetization options. (Fan insights provide more detail about who is watching your content, while the additional monetization options enables more ways for you to make money off your channel and content.) As you acquire more subscribers, YouTube gives you more perks.

In the YouTube world, you also hear a lot about fans. Aren't all subscribers fans? Not exactly. Your fans will be that subset of your subscribers who exhibit considerably higher levels of engagement. Take care of your subscribers, but take special care of your fans.

Fans and Insights

If your channel has a large number of subscribers, YouTube provides two interesting options for analyzing your fans in order to learn a bit more about them and (hopefully) communicate with them more effectively. These features — the Fans feature and the Insights feature — are found in the Community section of Creator Studio. Here's how they work:

- **Fans:** This Fans feature shows your top fans based on their subscriber count and their engagement with your channel, including likes, comments, and subscriptions. This feature also highlights recent activity and provides options for communicating directly via Google+.

- **Insights:** With the Insights feature, you're able to put your top fans into a Google+ circle. With that in place, you can look at demographic data — where fans are from, for example — as well as information about their recent activity with your channel.

With the Google+ integration, Insights is a great way to have a "private" discussion with only your fans. You can also share unlisted videos just for them, which is another effective way to engage or to provide a special offer if you're a business.

YouTube can be somewhat vague on how many subscribers you need to access specials feature. That number may also change over time, so be sure to check out `https://support.google.com/youtube` for the latest details. Often, you'll find out that you qualify when you see these new features show up on your channel. If your channel has enough subscribers to warrant access to the Fans and Insights features, you can do so using the following steps:

1. **From the YouTube home screen, click the blue Sign In button in the top-right corner to log in to your YouTube account.**

   If you don't see the blue button, you are likely still logged in. YouTube doesn't log you out when you leave the page.

2. **Click the Channel icon in the top right of the page and then click Creator Studio in the menu that appears.**

3. **Click the Community section of Creator Studio in the menu on the left side of the screen.**

4. **Select either the Fans or the Insights option from the menu that appears.**

   You probably should check out Fans first to get a sense of the community where the Insights are derived.

Fans and Insights are different from the Fan Finder feature, found under the Channel section of Creator Studio, which has more to do with advertising on YouTube. You can find out more about YouTube advertising in Chapter 13.

Understanding Subscribers and Their Value

YouTube allows viewers to connect more deeply with the channels they like by allowing them to become subscribers. To subscribe to a channel, all a viewer needs to do is go to a channel's home page and click either the red Subscribe button or a link to the Subscribe button. (The Subscribe button is shown in Figure 10-2.)

Each Subscribe button also shows the number of current subscriptions to the channel, which is a great way to see how much interest lies in a particular channel.

Understand that your subscribers have both YouTube value — in the sense that more subscribers lets YouTube know that your channel and content are important — and in some cases monetary value. If you make money from YouTube or are planning to, you'll look at audience data and advertising performance to determine what your subscribers are worth. You can read more about these topics in Chapters 11 and 14.

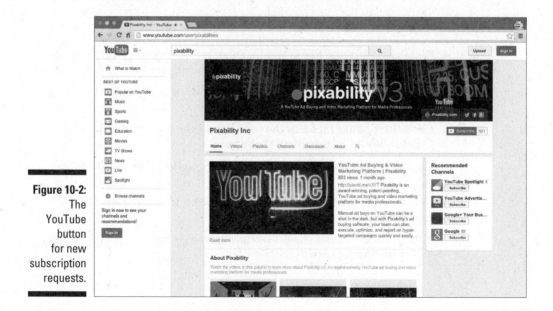

Figure 10-2:
The YouTube button for new subscription requests.

Viewers must be logged in to subscribe to a channel. If they happen to click the Subscribe button when logged out, YouTube simply asks them to log in with their Google credentials.

If a viewer is logged in and visits a channel page that he has subscribed to or visits a video watch page that's part of one of his subscribed channels, he sees a gray Subscribed box with a check mark in it instead, as shown in Figure 10-3. Note that each Subscribed button has the gear icon next to it — click that button and a menu appears, listing options that allow subscribers to control how they receive channel updates.

Figure 10-3:
YouTube
button for
existing
subscribers.

Convincing viewers to subscribe

Channel managers have several options when it comes to getting viewers to subscribe:

- ✔ **Below the channel art:** On every page that has channel art (such as the home page, About page, Watch page, and channel pages) you'll find a Subscribe button, under the right side of the channel art. (Channel art is described in Chapter 2.)

- ✔ **On the Watch page:** Users can subscribe to a channel by viewing a video on the Watch page — the page where viewers watch a video. The Subscribe button is underneath the left side of the video — below the channel name and next to the channel icon. Chapter 2 describes the characteristics of the Watch page.

✔ **Through custom links:** Channel managers can create subscription custom links that will appear on the channel's About page and in the channel art. Start with the following line of code, and add the name of your channel to *yourchannelname:*

```
http://www.youtube.com/subscription_center?add_
        user=yourchannelname
```

✔ **In the channel description:** Subscriber links can be useful in the descriptions uploaded as part of your video metadata. Just use the sub-scriber link code shown in the preceding paragraph. Chapter 9 describes how to modify and optimize (for video SEO) a video description.

Subscriptions links can get long and unsightly. Don't be afraid to sub-stitute a shortlink instead. You also get additional tracking to see which subscription links generate the most clicks. Chapter 9 introduces short-links and the software needed to track them.

✔ **Through annotations:** A video overlay is a great way to add a subscrip-tion link to your channel. YouTube provides all the tools necessary to place these overlays, known as *annotations,* to video without requiring any editing. You can read about annotations later in this chapter.

✔ **Recommendations:** Subscription buttons also show up under the Recommended Videos section of a channel page. The channel manager can hand-select specific channels that may be of interest to the viewer. (Note that, unlike other Subscribe buttons, which are red, these buttons are gray with no subscriber count.)

✔ **With web URLs:** It's easy to get people to subscribe from places not on YouTube; just include a Subscription link like the one shown ear-lier. Clicking the link brings them to a YouTube channel, so determine whether you want the link to open in another tab or window if you don't want the subscriber to exit your site.

Many channel managers put a link to the channel page as the target of the Subscribe link. If you want to bring them to your channel, please let them know that; otherwise, make the Subscribe button trigger a subscription request.

✔ **The old-fashioned way:** Have your video personality look straight into the camera and ask them to subscribe. They can say the name of the Subscribe link. There's no harm in asking! You can even combine an annotation link here to make it even easier.

There are many ways to ask your viewers to subscribe. Don't feel that you have to use only one method. YouTube allows a good deal of flexibility in generating subscription requests, so go ahead and experiment to see what works best for your audience.

Specifying how subscribers get updates

Being a subscriber to a channel is a lot like being a supporter of a local museum: You get notified about things first, and you get to see things before anyone else. Yes, being a subscriber has its benefits. Subscribers can be notified when you

- ✔ Upload a video
- ✔ Add a video to a public playlist
- ✔ Like a video or save a playlist
- ✔ Subscribe to a channel

Subscribers can choose between being notified of all your events or just your uploads. (They do this by clicking the gear icon next to the gray Subscribed button and making their choice from the options that appear.) As a channel manager, you choose how much information you want to share with your subscribers. This is done through the channel feed, which is discussed in some detail in the next section. Don't forget to manage the frequency of communication as well, which is triggered from all the activity discussed earlier.

Your subscribers are your gold, so keeping them happy with your channel and the frequency of your notifications is important. If they receive too many from you, they may unsubscribe; too few and they may forget about you. Moderation is important.

You should understand how your subscribers receive your channel updates:

- ✔ Email
- ✔ Mobile device notification
- ✔ Accounts connected to social media
- ✔ Channel feed

Your channel feed is your richest source of updates. Subscribers receive updates from several areas of the platform:

- ✔ **What to Watch:** When viewers log in to YouTube, click the YouTube button in the top left corner of their browsers, or start the YouTube app on their mobile devices, they land on the What to Watch page.

   This page is customized for each user because YouTube makes video suggestions based on a viewer's subscriptions and recommendations derived from her viewing history.

✔ **My Channel:** This is your channel, not the public view. You can edit your channel page directly here or go into the Video Manager to make individual video-playlist edits or manage your channel settings and analytics. (Details of your YouTube channel are covered in Chapters 2 and 3; additional information on Video manager is also in Chapter 9.)

✔ **My Subscriptions:** When viewers are logged in, they find their subscriptions on their home pages or in the guide. This is where all their subscriptions can be found and sorted by uploads or by all activity. Users can also manage subscriptions and create collections of channels in this section. (For more on subscriptions and guides, see Chapters 2 and 3.)

Setting the channel feed and privacy levels

You can control what your subscribers see by configuring your channel feed, as shown in Figure 10-4.

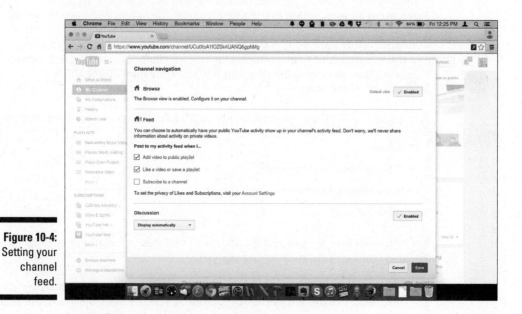

Figure 10-4:
Setting your channel feed.

To configure your channel feed, do the following:

1. Log in to your YouTube account.

2. **Click the guide icon next to the YouTube logo in the top left of the screen and select My Channel from the menu that appears.**

   The My Channel screen appears.

3. **Hover the mouse cursor over the channel name to bring up the Edit button.**

   The channel name sits just below the channel art; the Edit button should appear in the top left, below any links you may have configured.

4. **Click the Edit button and then select Edit Channel Navigation from the menu that appears.**

   Doing so brings up the screen shown earlier, in Figure 10-4.

5. **In the Feed settings section, select the check boxes of those activities you want to share with your subscribers.**

   Your subscribers can be notified when you:

   1. Add a video to a playlist

   2. Like a video or save a playlist

   3. Subscribe to a channel

6. **Click Save.**

You can also set the privacy of your likes and subscriptions under your channel's account settings. To access your account settings, click the Account Settings link from the Edit Channel Navigation screen (refer to Figure 10-4) or by following these steps:

1. **Log in to your YouTube account.**

2. **Click the Channel icon in the top right corner of the YouTube home page.**

3. **Click the gear icon to the right of the Creator Studio button in the menu that appears.**

4. **Select Privacy on the left side of the Account Settings navigation bar.**

5. **Select the check box for the information you want to make private.**

   Your privacy options are:

   1. Keep your liked videos and saved playlists private

   2. Keep your subscriptions private

6. **Click Save.**

You can also go directly to the privacy setting by using yet another method visiting www.youtube.com/account_privacy.

The Google+ dilemma

It's hard to use a product from Google, especially YouTube, without running into Google+, or G+, as it is sometimes known. Launched in 2011, Google+ is the company's fourth attempt to deliver a social media platform designed to counter Facebook.

What made Google+ unique is the concept of *circles,* which allows users to group their social media contacts into distinct groups. Different content could be easily shared with different circles. While on Google+, users could see updates from all their different circles on what was known as the *stream.*

Google+ concurrently evolved into an identity service for other Google properties such as Gmail, Google Maps, Google Play, YouTube, and others. In other words, Google+ made it easy to link many of your online efforts. But there's the rub: Google+ was starting to look like many different things, and the broader user community started to become perplexed.

Making matters worse was the integration of Google+ with YouTube comments in 2013, forcing users to comment with their Google+ profiles exposed and no anonymity. However noble the intent to tame the often-wild YouTube comment jungle, the YouTube nation bit back with a vengeance, including a less-than-flattering response from Jawed Karim, one of YouTube's cofounders. Since then, Google has softened the Google+ stance for many of its products, including YouTube.

Nonetheless, with so much Google+ integration in YouTube, channel managers need to gauge how important Google+ is to their communities. Don't be deceived: There are perks with Google+ integration with YouTube, especially around fan management. In the meantime, YouTube channel managers should stay current on Google+ moves. The YouTube official blog (`http://youtube-global.blogspot.com`) is a great place to start.

Your public channel uploads are automatically part of your feed and can't be set as part of the feed or privacy settings. Only the subscribers can specify whether they want to be notified about your new public videos.

Treating subscribers and nonsubscribers differently

To provide a more customized experience for viewers, YouTube allows you to treat subscribers and nonsubscribers differently when they visit your channel. (Subscribers don't necessarily want to see the same video when they show up at your channel, because they've likely already seen it, so it makes sense to treat them differently than nonsubscribers.)

Working with a channel trailer

The *channel trailer* is a prominent video that's shown whenever viewers first arrive at your channel. It's your chance to convert nonsubscribers, to inform them about what they can expect from your channel, get them excited about you and your content, and give them the details of your programming schedule.

You won't need to change out your channel trailer frequently, because a viewer who subscribes isn't shown this trailer again. Subscribers are greeted by a What to Watch Next page instead of a channel trailer.

Several factors affect what shows up on the What to Watch Next page. If you're live-streaming, that stream shows up first. If you're running a TrueView YouTube advertising campaign (see Chapter 13), your ads will show here. If none of these applies, your related video or most recent uploads will appear to subscribers.

Setting the Channel Browse view

To show a channel trailer, you need to set up Channel Browse view. To do so, do the following:

1. **Log in to your YouTube account.**

2. **Click the guide icon next to the YouTube logo on the top left of the screen and select My Channel from the menu that appears.**

   The My Channel screen appears.

3. **Hover the mouse cursor over the channel name to bring up the Edit button.**

   The channel name sits just below the channel art; the Edit button should appear on the top left, below any links you may have configured.

4. **Hover the mouse cursor over the Edit button and then select Edit Channel Navigation from the menu that appears.**

   The Channel Navigation screen appears (refer to Figure 10-4).

5. **Click the Enable button in the Browse section if it doesn't already show a check mark.**

6. **Click Save.**

Managing Comments

Many people tend to forget that YouTube is also a social media platform. That's a bit odd because it's one of the most heavily trafficked websites on the planet. In fact, one reason YouTube is so effective for creators and companies is precisely because its platform provides a powerful connection not just between a viewer and your brand but also *among* your audience.

Seeing why comments matter

Your interaction with your viewers and channel visitors is an important signal to not just your current subscribers but also potential subscribers. It tells them that your brand and your channel and content are worth their time. Encouraging comments is a great way to grow an audience and feed your community.

Make a concerted effort to add your own follow-ups to comments posted when you upload a video. Channel programming is about regularly scheduling uploads. Channel *manager* programming is about always responding to comments in a timely manner.

Your options for managing any particular comment are listed here:

- ✔ Allow the comment.
- ✔ Allow and respond to the comment.
- ✔ Remove the comment.
- ✔ Report spam or abuse.
- ✔ Ban the commenter from the channel.

You'll typically allow and respond to comments. You'll learn the details of managing comments in the following sections.

Similarly to likes and dislikes on video, viewers can like and dislike comments as well. Pay attention to comments that receive both large numbers of likes and dislikes.

Viewers generally appreciate being recognized by creators and channel managers. You can add the name of a viewer in a comment by typing a plus sign (+) and then their name. YouTube helps by autocompleting the name, so you're assured that the person will be notified of your outreach.

You can respond to comments in one of two ways:

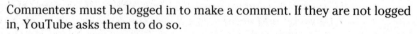

- ✔ **On the Watch page:** Both viewers and channel managers can add comments just below the channel description (refer to Figure 10-1). The Comment field is in the All Comments section; just type right where it says "Share your thoughts."

    Commenters must be logged in to make a comment. If they are not logged in, YouTube asks them to do so.

✔ **Community Comments Section in Creator Studio:** Only channel managers can respond here. The idea is to provide a convenient place for channel managers to respond to comments for all their videos.

Setting up your channel for comments

You may hear some people say not to allow comments on your channel. We're convinced that you'd give up much of the effectiveness of YouTube by following that advice. Much of the concern folks have about comments stems from the fact that some channel managers have done a less-than-stellar job around content moderation, which meant that some channels' Comments sections turned into toxic cesspools. That's a sign of a channel manager falling down on the job, not proof that comments can't work in a YouTube context. In the next section, you can find tips and techniques that you need to keep from falling down on the job.

Enabling channel-level comment controls

As a channel manager, you first have to enable comments for your entire channel; with that out of the way, you can then move on and decide your level of comment control as well.

You control whether comments are posted automatically or only with your approval. In the following steps, we explain how you can screen bad comments before they get posted.

1. **Log in to your YouTube account.**

2. **Click the guide icon next to the YouTube logo on the top left of the screen and select My Channel from the menu that appears.**

   The My Channel screen appears.

3. **Hover the mouse cursor over the channel name to bring up the Edit button.**

   The channel name sits just below the channel art; the Edit button should appear on the top left, below any links you may have configured.

4. **Hover the mouse cursor over the Edit button, click it, and then select Edit Channel Navigation from the menu that appears.**

   The Channel Navigation screen appears (refer to Figure 10-4).

5. **Look at the Discussion section and confirm that the button to the right is selected and labeled Enabled.**

   If it says Enable with no check, simply click the button. Your channel is now enabled for comments.

6. **Determine how you want comments displayed by clicking the button under the Discussion label and choosing the appropriate option.**

   Your choices are

   • *Display Automatically* posts appropriate comments without your approval.

   • *Don't Display Until Approved* requires you to explicitly approve a comment before it is posted.

7. **Click Save.**

In the meantime, you need to enable or confirm that your channel is set up for comments.

Enabling video-level comment controls

With your channel enabled for discussion, your videos can receive comments. You can also control comments on a video-by-video basis. You have three ways to enable comments on individual videos:

✓ **Default:** YouTube allows channel and video comments by default.

✓ **Upload defaults:** In the Creator Studio Channel section, you set the default comment controls for all future uploaded videos. This allows you to set a general policy so you don't have to configure each individual video.

✓ **Advanced settings:** In the Creator Studio Video Manager section, set the comments controls for an individual video and click Save Settings. (We show you how to do this one in a sec.)

For the last two options, you can go with one of these two settings:

✓ **All** will post appropriate comments for the video without your approval.

✓ **Approved** requires you to explicitly approve a comment on the video before it is posted.

To set up video commenting at the individual level, do the following:

1. **Log in to your YouTube account.**

2. **Click the Channel icon in the top right of the page and then click Creator Studio in the menu that appears.**

3. **On the left side of the screen, click the Video Manager heading in Creator Studio's navigation menu.**

4. **Select Videos from the drop-down menu that appears.**

5. **Scroll through your videos to find the one whose Comments feature you want to configure.**

   If you have quite a few videos, you can use the search bar on the Videos page to track down the one you want.

6. **Click the Edit button to the right of the video and then select Advanced Setting under the video.**

7. **Under Comments, check the Allow Comments box to allow comments for this video. (To block comments, uncheck the check box.)**

8. **Click the button to the right of All Comments to select whether you want all comments added automatically or whether they need to be approved first.**

9. **Click the blue Save Changes box on the bottom right to save your changes.**

Moderating comments

As your audience engages more and more with your videos and your channel becomes increasingly successful, comment moderation on a video-by-video basis can become rather tedious. Fortunately, YouTube allows you to moderate comments all in one place — in the Community Comments section of Creator Studio. To access these comments:

1. **Log in to your YouTube account.**

2. **Click the Channel icon in the top right of the page and then click Creator Studio in the menu that appears.**

3. **On the left side of the screen, click the Community heading in Creator Studio's navigation menu.**

4. **Select Comments from the drop-down menu that appears.**

   Doing so brings up the Comments page, as shown in Figure 10-5. By default, clicking on Community should bring you automatically to the Comments section.

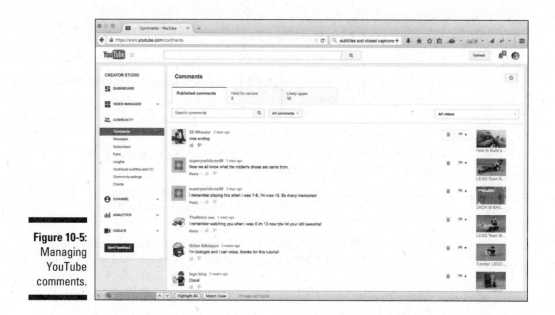

Note the following three tabs:

- *Published Comments:* These are the comments currently posted on your channel. You can do all the standard things with these comments — allow the comment, allow and respond to the comment, remove the comment, report the comment as spam or abusive, or ban the commenter from the channel.

  Whether you're on the Watch page or in the Comments section, you have icons and pull-downs to the right that allow you to remove a comment, block a commenter, or report spam. (You'll probably make much use of the Trash icon, which quickly vaporizes an inappropriate comment.)

- *Held for Review:* Comments are held here when you don't allow automatic posting or when comments are caught by blacklist filters you set in the community guidelines. (For more on blacklist filters, check out the "Configuring Community settings" section, later in this chapter.) If the comment is acceptable, click the Check button; otherwise, click its associated Trash icon to remove it. Review your held comments regularly so the appropriate ones get posted on your channel.

• *Likely Spam:* YouTube, in its efforts to root out spam, places comments here that it regards as likely spam. Ultimately, however,
you are the judge of what's spam and what's not. You should make
sure that YouTube hasn't jumped the gun and mischaracterized a
comment as spam. If it's not spam, just click the check button to
accept; otherwise, click the Trash icon to remove it.

Anything you can do to a single comment on the Comments page — accept,
respond to, delete — can be done to multiple comments in one fell swoop.
Simply check one or more of the comments you're moderating and take bulk
action.

Reacting to inappropriate comments

As a channel manager, you need to draw the line as to what comments are
appropriate to be shown on your channel. Just because someone disagrees
with you doesn't mean you have to call out the military. Some channel managers and creators like a debate, but there are situations where comments
are abusive and inappropriate, while providing no benefit to you, your
viewers, or your community.

With comments, you have the following options:

✔ **Remove.** This will simply delete the comment.

✔ **Report spam or abuse.** Comments and those who comment are subject
to the same community guidelines. (For more on community guidelines,
see Chapter 9.) The Report Spam or Abuse flag is there to report a
guideline violation, not a channel or video comment disagreement. See
the next option if community guidelines are adhered to and yet you still
need to address a situation.

✔ **Ban from channel.** Sometimes you just need to divorce yourself from
certain viewers. This setting prevents them from posting comments.
If circumstance change and you want them back, then you can remove
them from the banned user list in your Community settings. (More about
that later.)

To remove a comment, report spam or abuse, or ban a user from your
channel, channel managers can:

✔ Use the pull-down to the right of the comment that appears on the
Watch page. (See Figure 10-6.)

✔ Manage a comment from the Community Comments section in
Creator Studio. (See Figure 10-7.)

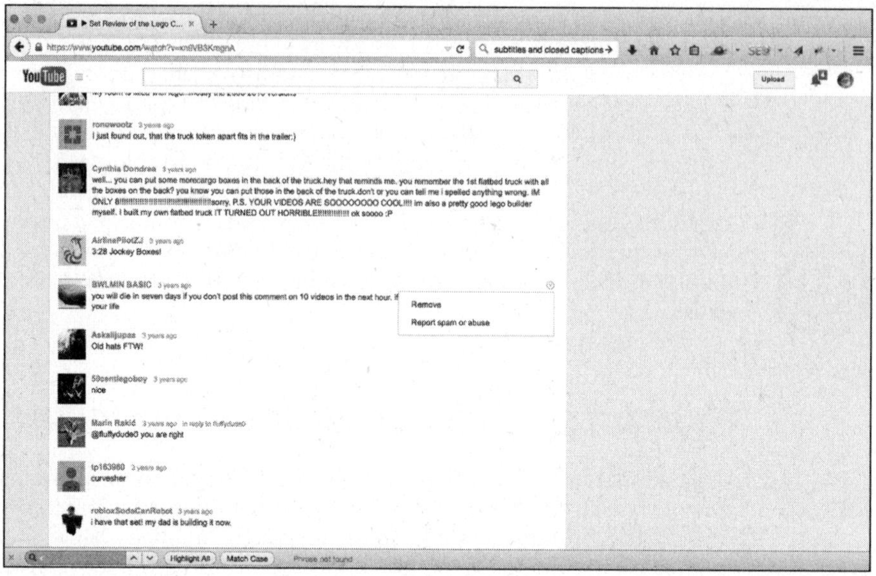

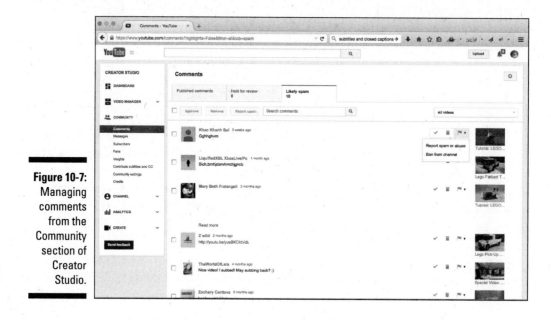

Figure 10-6:
Removing
comments
from the
Watch
page.

Figure 10-7:
Managing
comments
from the
Community
section of
Creator
Studio.

How to kill a troll

User anonymity has been a blessing and a curse since the early days of the Internet. In some instances, it facilitated very honest discussion, and in other cases it provided a cover for bad behavior and malicious intent. This latter group is known as trolls. Popular websites, such as the Huffington Post, decided to forbid anonymous comments because their moderators were too busy filtering out trolls and spam rather than moving the discussion forward. Because YouTube is a social platform with a massive audience, it has attracted more than its fair share of trolls, much to the frustration of channel managers and viewers alike.

Making matters worse, YouTube's platform is decidedly videocentric, which can more easily trigger a response than, say, a three-page blog. YouTube's ease of adding comments didn't help either, because viewers (or malcontents) could add a comment easily, instantaneously, and anonymously. YouTube had a challenge on its hand.

Starting in late 2013, YouTube began putting controls in place to counter trolls as well as spam, because neither serves part of the discussion around a video. It started off by forcing a deeper integration with Google+ to "pierce the veil of anonymity." Though this strategy was well-intentioned, many legitimate viewers cried foul over privacy concerns, with hundreds of thousands of users signing an online petition against what they saw as heavy-handed restrictions.

By 2014, YouTube backed off some of the requirements, but provided channel managers with more tools and controls, such as blacklisting and keyword flagging, to help preserve the integrity of their channels. It's gone a long way toward getting the problem under control, but it will remain an evolving situation for YouTube and many other social platforms.

Using Messaging

Sometimes your audience prefers not to have a discussion in a public forum, so YouTube came up with a messaging system. With it, your viewers can communicate directly with you.

If you've been using YouTube for a while, you may be familiar with the Inbox feature, which has been replaced by Messaging. Be sure to clear out your old Inbox and start using Messages in its place. New users don't have to worry about this.

Messages are an important way to build an audience, but as with comments, managing a large number of messages can be time consuming.

Managing messages follows the same pattern as moderating comments, except that you don't see links to your video content and you have different tabs. To access your messages, do the following:

1. **Log in to your YouTube account.**

2. **Click the Channel icon in the top right of the page and then click Creator Studio in the menu that appears.**

3. **On the left side of the screen, click the Community heading in Creator Studio's navigation menu.**

4. **Select Messages from the drop-down menu that appears.**

   Doing so brings up the Messages page, as shown in Figure 10-8.

   Note that the Messages page has four tabs — not the three you see with Comments:

   • *Approved messages:* These are audience messages that have made their way to you. Feel free to respond to a message, remove it, block it, or report a message as spam.

     Check your messages regularly and respond to important subscribers or audience members in a timely manner.

   • *Filtered Messages:* These are messages caught by the filters you set in the Community Guidelines section. The settings are discussed in the Configuring Community Settings section, later in this chapter.

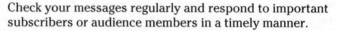

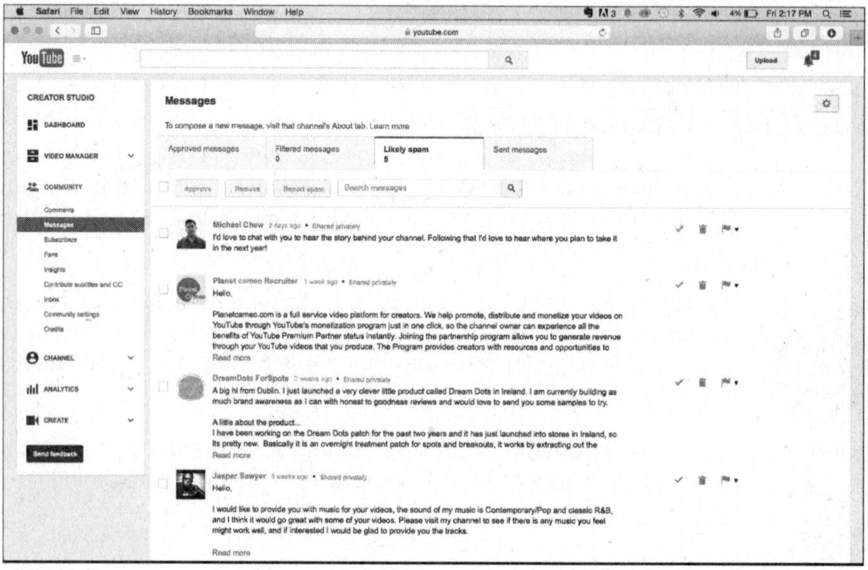

Figure 10-8:
Moderating
YouTube
messages.

- *Likely spam:* As with comments, YouTube wants to do its part when it comes to filtering out spam hiding as messages, but ultimately you have the yea or nay here. Just double-check to make sure YouTube made the right decision when characterizing a message. If a message is not spam, just click the check button; otherwise, click the Trash icon to remove it once and for all.

- *Sent messages:* These are messages that you've sent.

As with comments, anything you can do to a single message on the Messages page can be done to multiple messages in one fell swoop. Simply check one or more of the messages you're moderating and take bulk action.

Configuring Community Settings

You've probably noticed some similarities between comments and messages. Both of these involve the management of users. YouTube makes it easy to manage users from a central location known as Community Settings. To access Community Settings, do the following:

1. **Log in to your YouTube account.**

2. **Click the Channel icon in the top right of the page and then click Creator Studio in the menu that appears.**

3. **On the left side of the screen, click the Community heading in Creator Studio's navigation menu.**

4. **Select Community Settings from the drop-down menu that appears.**

   Doing so brings up the Community Settings page, as shown in Figure 10-9.

Community settings consist of three sections:

1. **Automated filters:** There will be viewers who are constructive and viewers who are not. That's just the nature of YouTube. This is where you manage:

   1. *Approved users:* Enables automated posting of comments and messages from identified users.

   2. *Banned users:* Block comments and messages from identified users.

      Both approved and banned users can be managed using their Google IDs, Google+ profiles, or Google+ circles.

   3. *Blacklist:* Comments and messages that match phrases or words in this list will be held for review. This also applies to live chats and the content will be blocked.

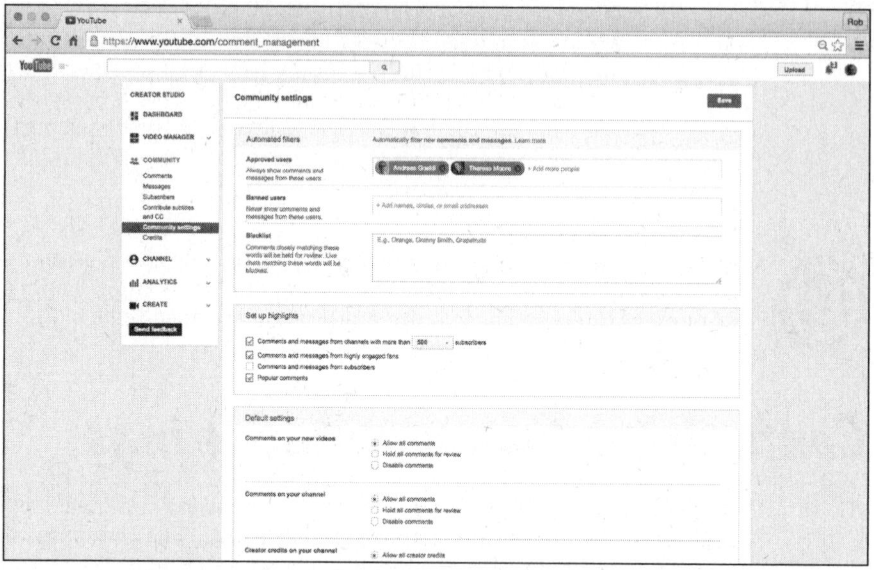

Figure 10-9:
YouTube
Community
settings.

✔ **Set up highlights:** This helps you limit what comments you see in order to help you identify the most relevant ones. This is important because you may want to respond to specific community members. If you have tons of comments, this will prevent you from seeing all of them. Approved comments will still end up on your channel, but you may not see them all.

✔ **Default settings:** This is your overall comment management. You can:

- Allow all comments

- Hold all comments for review

- Disable comments

Think hard before disabling comments. It's tough to develop a community when you've taken away a key engagement component of YouTube.

Getting Viewers to Engage

After you have a solid channel and an active audience commenting, messaging, and sharing your content, you have to ask whether they're doing everything you expected. In Chapter 5, we talk about establishing the goals for your channel. Some of those goals may be YouTube related, such as getting more views and subscribers, or they could be more commerce-oriented, such as influencing a brand decision and driving a product purchase from a website. Either way, you need to get your audience to click on the video and take the next action.

It's all about the click, and YouTube has some tools to make that click happen.

Working with annotations

Annotations are overlay elements that you can add to your existing videos. They allow a viewer to do something when they click on the annotations, such as subscribe, get more information about you, or view more content. (An annotation also happens to be one of the best ways out there to get your audience to engage with your channel, just in case you were curious.)

For channel managers, annotations are editable fields that can be added to videos after they're uploaded. Annotations can be modified and updated at any time. In other words, you're not stuck with an annotation once you've created it; you can change it, delete it, move it, and so on. Annotations can just be plain text or links back to other content on YouTube, or off YouTube, such as specific social networks, nonprofits, fundraising, retails accounts, and other associated websites.

Use annotations to create what are called *custom end-cards* — a collection of one or more annotations at the end of a video that help instruct viewers in what to do when the video is completed. This can also include subscription requests. Custom end-cards are good for branding consistency, and they always helps your audience identify with your content. Figure 10-10 shows what an end-card could look like.

Exploring the annotation types

YouTube would seem to subscribe to the notion that variety is the spice of life, given the number of annotation options it offers. The following list gives you an overview:

- **Speech bubble:** This annotation is a lot like the clouds you see in newspaper comics. Use it whenever you want to visually express thoughts or spoken words.

- **Note:** This annotation is similar to a speech bubble, except that the text is enclosed in a box.

Figure 10-10:
Use of an
end-card.

✔ **Title:** An overlay name for your video, like one you might add during the editing process. Doing it as an annotation lets you be more flexible later on if you decide to change the title. Titles are non-clickable.

✔ **Spotlight:** Use this annotation to create custom end-cards or to highlight an element in the video. Spotlight annotations are different from other types of annotation because they only appear when the viewer moves the mouse over the section of the video that has the annotation. It minimizes viewers distraction while still provide a path for engagement.

✔ **Label:** When a viewer hovers the cursor over the annotation, your label appears. This is commonly used for videos featuring multiple products at a time on the screen. Viewers can choose what interests them most and interact with only that item. Labels prevent the video from getting cluttered and does not take away from the viewing experience.

Specifying an annotation target

Though coming up with a cool annotation design can be a lot of fun, never lose sight of your end goal. Annotations are meant to point your viewer to some new place on the Internet — another video, a playlist, an associated website, you name it. Above all, this new place — the target of your annotation — has to relate to the video that was viewed.

Viewers need be directed to targets that make sense based on the context of the video. If they feel misled or sent to a confusing target, chances are good that they won't click on another annotation. Even worse, they may unsubscribe from your channel.

Your site must be in good standing to use annotations. See Chapter 9 for more information to learn more about keeping your channel in good standing.

Setting up annotations

To create annotations, follow the same path you'd use when working with any video on your channel — in other words, you need to pay another visit to the Video Manager. To set up annotations, do the following:

1. **Log in to your YouTube account.**

2. **Click the Channel icon in the top right of the page and then click Creator Studio in the menu that appears.**

3. **On the left side of the screen, click the Video Manager heading in Creator Studio's navigation menu.**

4. **Select Videos from the drop-down menu that appears.**

5. **Scroll through your videos to find the one you want to annotate.**

   If you have quite a few videos, you can use the search bar on the Videos page to track down the one you want.

6. **Click the Edit button to the right of the video.**

   Doing so brings you to the Video Editing page; the Info & Settings tab is shown by default.

7. **Select the Annotations tab above the video.**

   The Annotations tab of the Videos page appears.

   You can alternatively select the down arrow next to Edit, which provides a drop-down where you can select Annotations that will drive you to the Annotations section in the Video Editing page. The first way, you have to take two steps, the second way you only take one step to get to the Annotations tab.

8. **Click the + Add Annotation button on the right side of the video.**

9. **Choose an annotation type from the menu that appears.**

   Your choices are Speech Bubble, Note, Title, Spotlight, and Label.

10. **Choose when the annotation runs by either dragging the mouse cursor over the Play bar to the point where you want the annotation to show or manually entering the times in the Start and End boxes.**

11. **Add text to the annotation text box and customize the font size, font color, and background color by using the editing toolbox that's provided.**

12. **To make your annotation a clickable link, select the Link check box.**

13. **Paste the URL into the field under the Link check box.**

14. **Click the Video button to the right of the Link check box and select the link type.**

    You must use YouTube-accepted links, which include the following targets:

    - Another video
    - A playlist
    - Another channel
    - A Google+ profile page
    - A Subscribe prompt
    - A fundraising project
    - An associated website
    - A merch (an approved retail site)

15. **If you've chosen a linked video, set the start time.**

16. **Click the Open Link in a New Window button if you want the clicked link to open in a new window.**

17. **On the Annotations tab, preview the newly annotated video, as shown in Figure 10-11, and be sure to play and pause the video when the annotation appears.**

18. **Using the sizing handles, change the annotation size and location, if necessary.**

    Do not put annotations at the top of a video or in the lower third, because they can be obstructed by overlay ads.

19. **Click the Apply button to save your work.**

Getting creative with annotations

Want to take annotations even further and provide an even more interactive experience for your audience? Use annotations to offer surveys your viewers can then use as an easy way to decide what they most want to view from you.

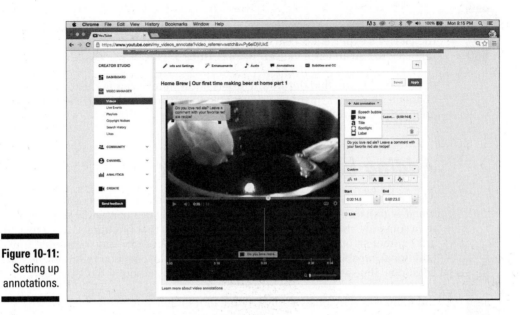

Figure 10-11:
Setting up
annotations.

In Figure 10-12, you can see how British Airways does a great job of helping
its audience choose what adventure video to watch next. (To see this nice
bit of annotation work in the context of YouTube, check out `https://www.`
`youtube.com/watch?v=d6VdAR3-O1U`.)

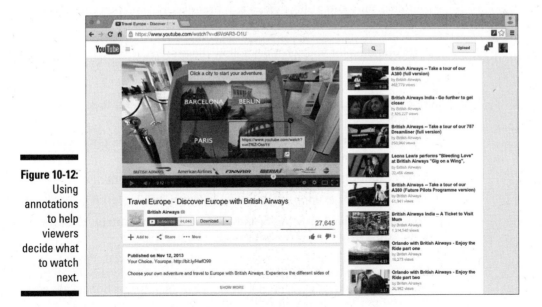

Figure 10-12:
Using
annotations
to help
viewers
decide what
to watch
next.

Be sensible about annotations. They should complement, not detract from, the viewer's experience. Don't be shy, either. The end of a video is a wonderful place to use an ask a viewer to subscribe.

In Chapter 11, you find out how to assess how much your audience likes your channel. That assessment should be able to tell you how much they like your annotations as well.

Adding branding to the mix

Audiences engage with your channel, but they also come to recognize your *brand* — those unique elements that tell the world your content is *yours* rather than someone else's content. YouTube recognizes that branding is a big deal in our content-saturated world. That's why it goes out of its way to provide some additional capabilities to apply branding without forcing you to invest the additional time and effort that always comes with an additional video edit.

Branding was previously known by the more confusing name: *InVideo programming.*

When it comes to branding, YouTube allows channel managers to do the following:

- ✓ Add a brand watermark to the top left corner of each video on the channel.
- ✓ Automatically add a short video as a branded introduction to each of your channel's videos.

To set up branding for your channel, follow these steps:

1. **Log in to your YouTube account.**

2. **Click the Channel icon in the top right of the page and then click Creator Studio in the menu that appears.**

3. **On the left side of the screen, click the Channel heading in Creator Studio's navigation menu.**

4. **Select Branding from the drop-down menu that appears.**

    The Branding page appears, as shown in Figure 10-13.

5. **To add a standard opening branded video to your content, click the blue Add a Branding Intro button. (See Figure 10-14.)**

    You can upload a video that's three seconds or less as your intro. This branding video must already be on your channel and you should set its privacy to unpublished. Refrain from making the introduction an advertisement per YouTube policy. You can subsequently change branded intros, but do so sparingly so you don't alienate your audience. You can also remove a branded intro by simply clicking the Remove button.

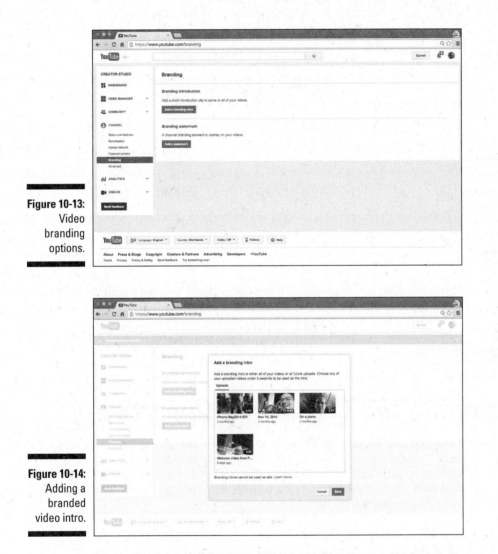

Figure 10-13:
Video branding options.

Figure 10-14:
Adding a branded video intro.

6. **To add an overlay brand watermark, click the blue Add a Watermark button. (See Figure 10-15.)**

   Upload a PNG or GIF file less than 1MB in size. After you've saved the branded watermark, choose the duration for when you want it to show:

   • For the entire video.

   • At end of the video.

   • At a custom time within the video.

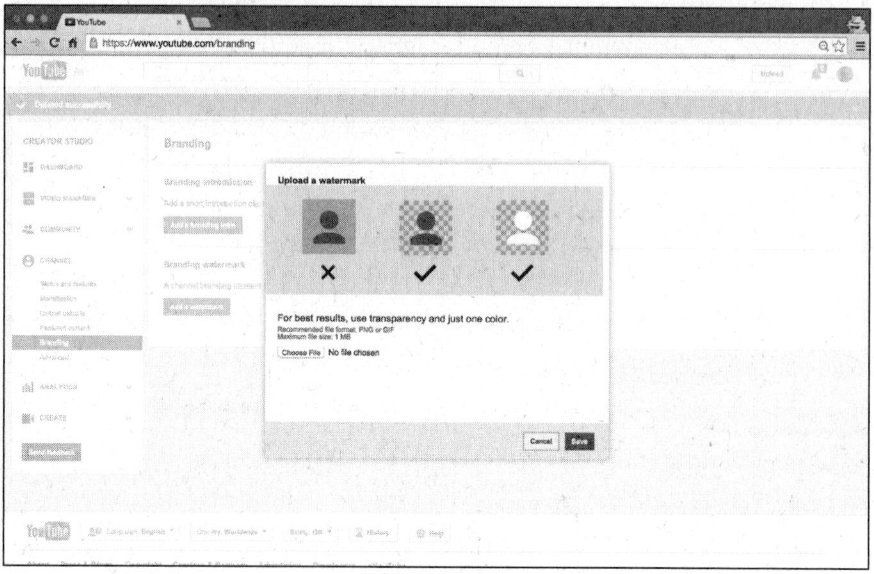

Figure 10-15:
Adding
a brand
overlay
watermark.

Like a branded video intro, you can subsequently remove a watermark by clicking the Remove button.

The full branding experience may not be fully integrated into all mobile devices.

Capturing the Captioning Opportunity

Language and sound should not be barriers to connecting with your audience. YouTube provides tools for subtitles and closed captions. Subtitles and closed captions allow viewers who don't speak your language to watch and understand your video. Even viewers with hearing disabilities can enjoy watching your content, too.

Adding subtitles and closed captions

Don't let the thought of dealing with closed captions and subtitles scare you. Working with these elements is similar to working with any other video element on your channel — in this, as in all things, Video Manager is your friend. Use the following steps to create subtitles and closed captions:

1. **Log in to your YouTube account.**

2. **Click the Channel icon in the top right of the page and then click Creator Studio in the menu that appears.**

3. **On the left side of the screen, click the Video Manager heading in Creator Studio's navigation menu.**

4. **Select Videos from the drop-down menu that appears.**

   By default, clicking on Video Manager should bring you automatically to the Videos section.

5. **Scroll through your videos to find the one you want to work with.**

   If you have quite a few videos, you can use the search bar on the Videos page to track down the one you want.

6. **Click the Edit button to the right of the video and select the Subtitles and CC tab from the menu that appears above the video.**

   Doing so brings up the Subtitles and CC tab of the Videos page, as shown in Figure 10-16.

   You can also click the down arrow to the right of Edit button and select Subtitles and CC directly.

7. **Click the Add subtitles and CC drop-down menu to the left of the video to view your language choices.**

8. **Choose your language or search for it in the search box.**

   After your language is selected, you'll be prompted with how you'd like to add your subtitles or closed captions.

Figure 10-16: Subtitles and captions.

9. **Select your method:**

- *Upload a file.* Add a text transcript or timed subtitles in the form of an uploadable file.

- *Transcribe and set timing.* Type or paste a transcript into the video transcript box that comes up on the right of the video. YouTube autoconfigures the timing.

- *Create new subtitles or CC.* Add captions as you watch the video either by uploading a transcript file or by entering the text directly into a transcript box. You can pause and play while doing this.

Having viewers contribute subtitles and closed captions

Some channels, known as *participating channels,* allow their own viewers to submit subtitles and closed captions. Expect this limited function to be more broadly available in the future, representing a great way to get your audience to help out.

For more information on subtitles, closed captions, and participating channels, see `https://support.google.com/youtube`.

Giving Credit Where It's Due

YouTube videos frequently represent the work of many people. Some of the more elaborate content on YouTube could easily rival a small Hollywood movie. Recognizing the people who work with you on YouTube productions has been a bit of a challenge. More creative channel managers have sometimes called out collaborators in the video description field.

YouTube has formalized the attribution of key contributors with a new functionality called creator credits.

Receiving credit

In the YouTube world, channels with higher subscriber counts gain certain benefits. Being able to assign credits is limited to channels with 10,000 or more subscribers. (Note that YouTube may lower thresholds over time.) However, you don't need that many subscribers to have someone else credit you.

If you're just dying to know where you've been credited, do the following:

1. **Log in to your YouTube account.**

2. **Click the Channel icon in the top right of the page and then click Creator Studio in the menu that appears.**

3. **On the left side of the screen, click the Community heading in Creator Studio's navigation menu.**

4. **Select Credits from the menu that appears.**

   Doing so brings up the Credits page. Note the four tabs where your collaboration work could (potentially) be recognized: Pending, Published, Removed, or Spam.

5. **Approve or remove credits.**

   You have control over were you've been credited, so you can remove the attribution if you want.

People who receive credit always receive an email notification. Credit settings can also be configured in the community guidelines.

Assigning credit

When you reach 10,000 subscribers, you can assign credit to your production partners. Creator credits are shown on the Watch page, as shown in Figure 10-17. Viewers need to click Show More to reveal more.

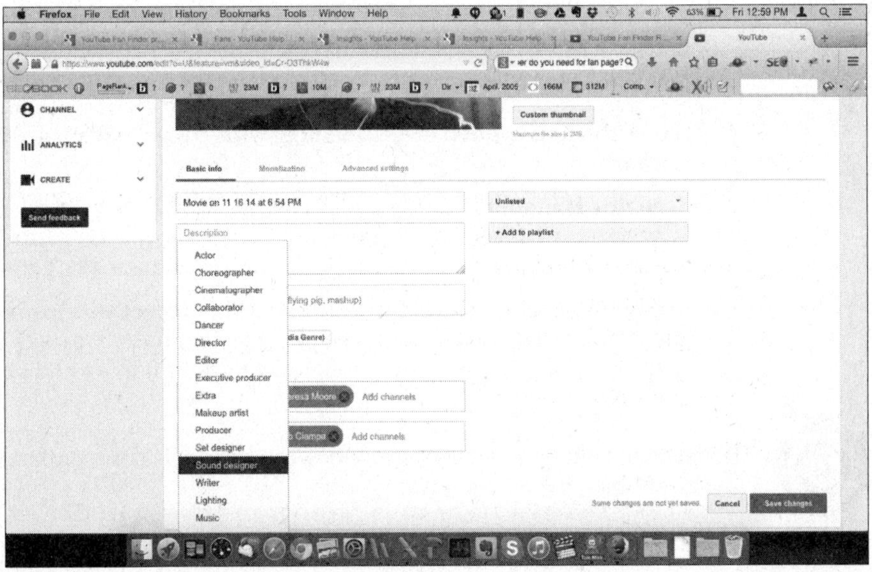

Figure 10-17: Creator credits.

To add creator credits to your video, do the following:

1. **Log in to your YouTube account.**

2. **Click the Channel icon in the top right of the page and then click Creator Studio in the menu that appears.**

3. **On the left side of the screen, click the Video Manager heading on Creator Studio's navigation menu.**

   By default, clicking on Video Manager should bring you automatically to the Videos section.

4. **Use the search bar on the video screen or scroll through your videos to find the one you want to work with.**

5. **Click the Edit button next to the video thumbnail. It should come up in the Basic info setting be default. If not, select the Basic Info tab.**

6. **Scroll down to the Video Credits section at the bottom.**

7. **Click the + Add Role button to bring up a list of available roles.**

8. **Hover over the appropriate role and click it. The role will be added.**

9. **Type in their YouTube channel user name or channel URL until YouTube shows a match.**

10. **Click the blue Save Changes button on the bottom right.**

Producing Live Events

Putting together live events on YouTube is a great way to build an audience and drive engagement. You have several options for managing live content on YouTube:

- ✔ **YouTube live events:** Live-streaming with active management of the comments.

- ✔ **Google+ Hangouts On Air:** This is a great way to have a video-based discussion with your fans. Hangouts On Air allows you to stream live events or online discussions from either Google+ or YouTube.

- ✔ **Off-platform events:** Grab the opportunity to meet with your fans in real life. Many YouTube creators use physical community events such as VidCon (www.vidcon.com) to meet with their fans — and shoot some live content with them.

Repurpose your live event content for your channel. Your audience will love the attention.

Chapter 11

Knowing Your Audience

*I*magine driving along in your car and suddenly your dashboard goes out: no lights, no gauges, and no navigation. You can either pull over to the side of the road and call a tow truck, or just keep driving. Whatever the decision, you'll have a tougher time making it to your destination. As a YouTube channel manager driving down the video highway, you need a dashboard, too: That dashboard is YouTube Analytics.

YouTube Analytics is all about getting meaningful information about how your channel is doing. If you're working with YouTube creators and other online video personalities, chances are good that you'll be prompted to provide some interesting reports about all the wonderful things happening with the YouTube channel. In some cases, though, you may have to deliver some not-so-good news: Maybe your audience and fan base just aren't liking the new videos that are being uploaded to the channel. YouTube Analytics is there to help you figure out what may have gone wrong — and a whole lot more.

YouTube Analytics is where you find the details about your audience: where they're finding you, what they like, where they're watching, and so on. After a while, YouTube Analytics will likely be your first YouTube stop every day. Spend time mastering the analytics process and extracting the key insights it contains because it will help you craft a more robust channel — and significantly better video content. If you're making money from your channel, YouTube Analytics can help you earn even more.

YouTube Analytics isn't just for new channels. If you already have a channel and it's not performing to your satisfaction, YouTube Analytics is a valuable resource for diagnosing and subsequently fixing problems.

Getting Started with YouTube Analytics

It's tough to talk about analytics with YouTubers without hearing supporting terms like metrics and insights. Don't be put off by all the geeky terms. In Chapter 5, you can find out all about setting goals for your channel. This chapter, however, is all about determining whether you're meeting your goals; to able to do that, you need to work with metrics and insights.

Here's the skinny: Metrics are *quantitative* things you measure, such as the number of views and percentage click-through rates on your channel. Metrics gauge your goal attainment against your plan. Insights are *qualitative* and *actionable* things you learn and do from analyzing metrics, including whether your content is working for you or your annotations are well placed in your video.

YouTube Analytics shows you how you're tracking against your goals and also where you may need to make adjustments. Understanding metrics and insights is relatively straightforward, but you need to know where to look in YouTube Analytics to get the data you need.

As a channel manager, always think in terms of metrics and insights. You must *act* on those insights, though. For example, if the view count and number of likes (metrics) for your new video are 25 percent of your target, it may indicate that your video isn't resonating with your audience or that you released it at the wrong time (insights). Take the time to fix what may be immediately wrong (such as poor metadata) or change future content or programming. You should verify the video metrics again over time.

As you become more sophisticated in your use of YouTube Analytics, you'll realize that certain metrics may depend on other metrics. For example, your earnings metrics may be impacted by view metrics, which may be impacted by engagement metrics. Don't sweat the details — the relationship among all metrics comes together quickly.

Chapter 5 covers two important metrics — views and subscribers — in some detail. Make sure that you understand what other metrics impact these two.

Reading YouTube Analytics reports

Your go-to place for all aspects of YouTube Analytics is the Analytics section of Creator Studio. To make your way there, do the following:

1. **In your web browser, go to** www.youtube.com.

2. **Log on to your YouTube account.**

   If you see a blue Sign In button in the top right corner of the YouTube home page, enter your email address and password.

3. **Click on the logged-in icon and choose Creator Studio from the menu that appears.**

   The Creator Studio navigation menu should appear on the left side of your browser.

4. **Click the Analytics section of Creator Studio.**

   By default, it should go directly to the Overview submenu, as shown in Figure 11-1.

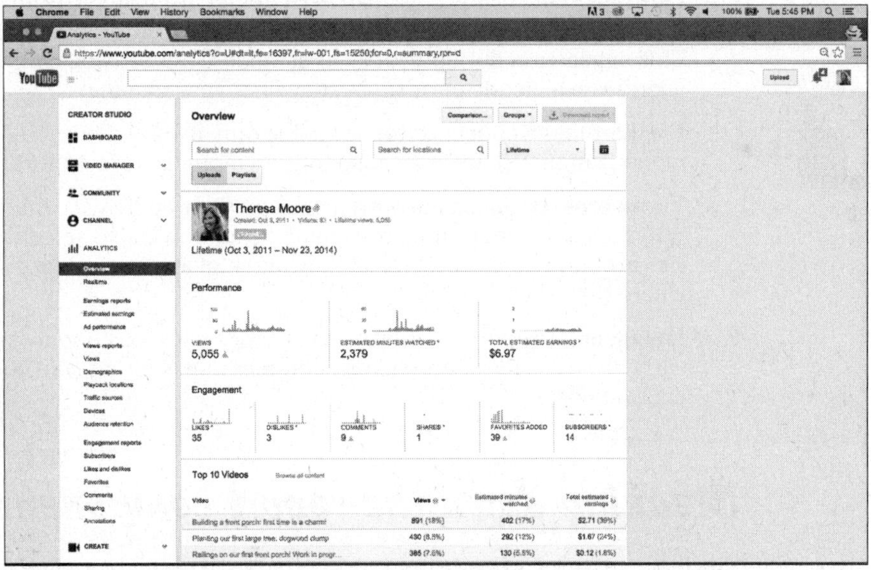

Figure 11-1: YouTube Analytics overview.

You can also bypass these steps by going to www.youtube.com/analytics.

When you look at the Analytics section on Creator Studio's navigation menu, you can see that YouTube Analytics is divided into five subsections. They're described, from top to bottom, in this list:

- **Overview:** Presents a high-level view of your channel's overall performance. It includes these five subsections:

  - *Performance:* Data on views, watch time, and earnings.

  - *Engagement:* Includes likes, comments, social shares, and subscriber action.

  - *Top 10 Videos:* Lists your most popular videos along with their views, estimated watch times, and estimated per-video earnings.

  - *Demographics:* Includes viewer geography and gender.

  - *Discovery:* Specifies top playback locations and leading traffic sources.

- **Realtime:** Displays a two-column comparative report on the five newest videos on your channel. Column 1 looks at the last 48 hours, and Column 2 measures the past 60 minutes.

- **Earnings reports:** Partners can earn money from advertising with Google, along with YouTube Rentals, which are like online movie rentals. This subsection not only looks at estimated advertising revenue but also analyzes which ads perform best against your channel.

  The Earnings Report section is visible only if you have enabled channel monetization. (Chapter 14 has more on monetization opportunities.)

- **Views reports:** Spells out who makes up your audience, what they're watching, and where they're coming from. You'll also see critical metrics around *retention,* which is how much of a video viewers watch and where they stop viewing.

- **Engagement reports:** Analyzes subscriber additions and losses, along with whether viewers are liking, commenting, sharing, and clicking annotations.

Breaking down the report components

YouTube provides a rich set of reports that may seem overwhelming at first, but you'll quickly discover that navigating the reports is quite easy because they have a similar structure that consists of these three distinct sections:

✔ **Filter:** Over time, you'll add video content, construct playlists, build annotations, engage subscribers, and do so much more. You'll definitely want to set up dynamic filters that are meant to show you only the information you're looking for. The Analytics Filter section is shown in Figure 11-2.

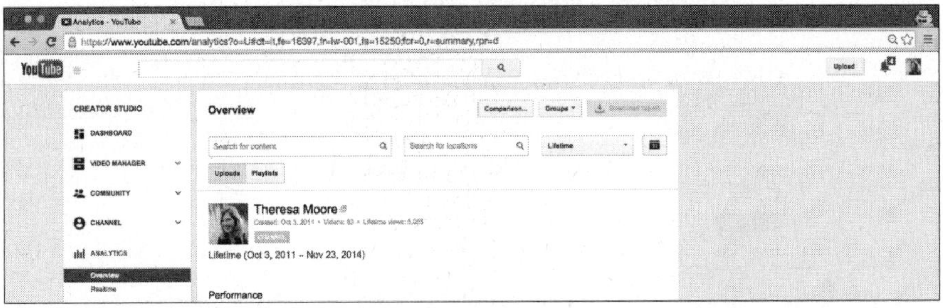

Figure 11-2: An analytics filter.

✔ **Chart:** After you've determined what you want to analyze, you can get lots of information with some fairly flexible graphical representations (charts, in other words) to guide your understanding. These will help you assess the performance of your channel, your content, and your community. (You can see an example in Figure 11-3 of a YouTube Analytics chart showing views over a multiyear period.)

Figure 11-3: An analytics chart.

✔ **Details:** Shows itemized details that correspond to the particular YouTube Analytics report. For example, in the Views report, you can get a detailed list of your top 200 videos, including name, views, percentage growth in view, estimated minutes watched, and average view duration. You have similar access to geographical, date, and language data. Figure 11-4 shows what the Details section of a YouTube Analytics report might look like.

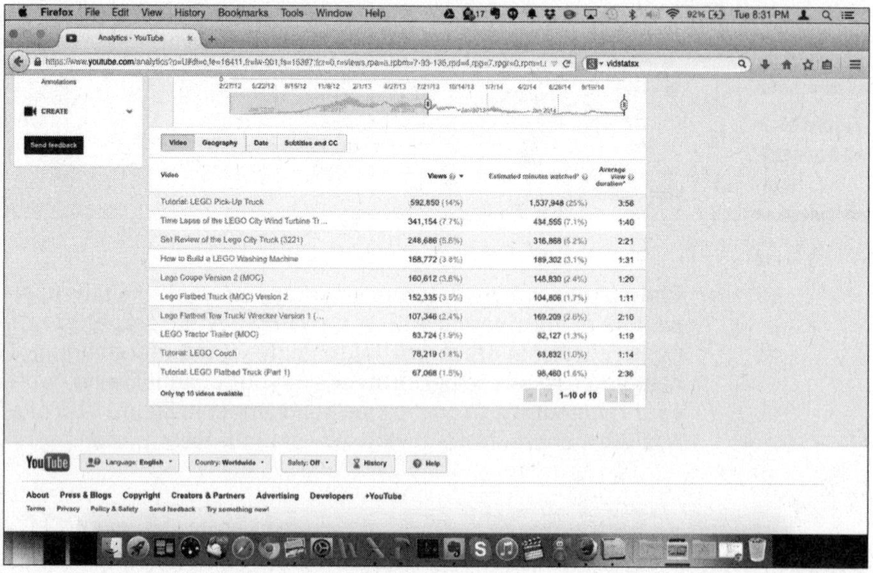

Figure 11-4:
The Details section of a YouTube Analytics report.

Grouping information

To simplify some of your channel analysis, you can create custom groups of videos or playlists for analysis. If you manage a baking channel, you may want to create one group for all your bread videos and playlists and another for your cake baking videos and playlists. (To create a group, simply click the Group button, give the group a name, select the videos or playlists you want in the group, and then click Save.)

A group is used for your analysis work; it lets you aggregate related content. It's different from a playlist, which is meant for audience viewing. Yes, YouTube even lets you group playlists for analysis!

Comparing data

In the earlier (hypothetical) example of a baking channel, wouldn't it be great if you could compare how your bread-baking videos or playlists are performing against your cake-baking videos or playlists? Well, with YouTube Analytics, you can do precisely that. You can even make comparisons by country and date. (To compare videos, groups, or playlist, click the Comparison button and enter the names of the items you want to compare. YouTube Analytics will pull the data together for you.)

If you're running a YouTube advertising campaign (see Chapter 13), groups and comparisons are effective ways to determine which channel videos may be the best one to advertise with.

Setting up report filters

Creating truly informational reports is easy: Just figure out which data you want to include and which data you don't. The Analytics Filter section not only makes this task possible but also lets you see the results of what you're doing *immediately,* which lets you fine-tune the filter so that the data is exactly what you want.

By using the following text fields and drop-down menus, found in the Analytics Filter, you can ensure that you're looking at only the data you need:

- ✔ **Search for Content field:** Include only a specific video, playlist, or group for analysis.

  If you want to include more than one video, group the videos first. This feature doesn't let you filter for multiple individual videos unless they're part of a group or playlist.

- ✔ **Search for Locations field:** Select video data that is gathered worldwide, by continent, or by country. You may want to do this, for example, to determine how many viewers you get from Europe, Asia, South America, and so on.

  You cannot currently group countries or continents.

- ✔ **Preconfigured Date drop-down menu:** The default value is Last 28 Days. Click the button to the right of the Location section to choose common date criteria, such as this year, last year, or this quarter.

- ✔ **Custom date range:** If a preconfigured date doesn't work, you can pick a more suitable and customizable date range by clicking the Calendar button to the right of the Preconfigured Date menu.

- **Uploads/Playlists:** By default, YouTube Analytics looks at the performance of the videos on your channel. Playlists, however, can be as important an asset as videos. This button, which sits below the Search for Content field, lets you toggle between video uploads and playlists.

- **Show Only Subscriber Views:** Your analytics reporting looks at the behavior of your entire audience. For certain reports, such as Demographics and Traffic sources, you can look at behavior by only your subscribers. Simply click the Show Only Subscriber Views checkbox, if it's present, to the right of the Uploads/Playlists.

- **Groups:** Add a custom video and playlist groups to your filter criteria by clicking the Groups button. You can also modify existing groups.

- **Comparisons:** Clicking the Comparisons button brings up a second filter section immediately under the first. Currently, YouTube allows only two comparisons. When you're finished with the analysis, merely click the Cancel Comparison button that appears to the left of the Groups button, initially where the Comparison button was when you started.

You need to set up a filter only once in the Analytics section of Creator Studio. You can move among all report types, and your filters will remain in place. However, after you leave the Analytics section and move over to the Video Manager or Community sections, for example, you have to reenter the filter information whenever you return to Analytics.

Understanding visual charts

Moving from report to report in the Analytics section, you're sure to see both the graphs and the data changing in the Chart section below the filter criteria. Though the reports are similar, each may have specific metrics based on the report type. For example, you'll find subtitles and captions in a Views report, but such items would make no sense in an Engagement report.

YouTube Analytics always presents data relevant to the particular report type.

In the Chart section, you generally see the following elements:

- **Key Metrics:** A banner below the filter criteria indicates the major metrics associated with the report. Clicking on a major metric immediately graphs it on the chart. If you're looking at a Subscriber report, you can choose among subscribers, subscribers gained, and subscribers lost.

- **Comparative Metrics and More Metrics:** Charting different metrics against one another can provide insight into what channel actions influence another. On a Views report, you may find that charting views and total estimated earnings show similar and aligned graphs. You can use this information to formulate the actions needed to drive views and accelerate earnings. To add metrics, click the Comparative Metric or More Metrics button, whichever shows up under the Key Metrics banner on the left. A complete list of your choices is shown in Figure 11-5.

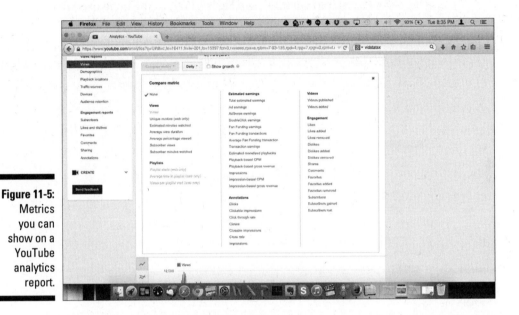

Figure 11-5:
Metrics you can show on a YouTube analytics report.

✔ **Graphing controls:** You can find additional graphing controls under the Key Metrics banner. Look for the Charting Granularity control just to the right of the Comparative Metrics or More Metrics button. You can graph using daily, weekly, or monthly spans. Depending on the chart, you can also add totals and percentages to see how your data compares with your totals.

✔ **Chart type:** YouTube Analytics has six chart types, as indicated by the six icons down the left side of the Chart screen:

- *Line:* Shows one key metric and a comparative metric over a period that you select. This is effective for showing trends or viewing patterns. For a View report, it would show total view counts for your channel over time. (Figure 11-6 shows a sample line chart.)

- *Multi-line:* Graphs the side-by-side details of the components of a major metric. For a Views report, it can show the side-by-side graphing of your top videos. (You can customize to show any 25 of your top 200 videos, if you were curious.) This is effective not only for observing the increase in the number of video views but also seeing whether views trend together. (Figure 11-7 shows a multi-line chart.)

- *Stacked:* Like its multi-line cousin, a stacked chart shows the relative portion attributed to each component while showing the total number of videos compared. (Figure 11-8 highlights a stacked-chart example.)

- *Pie:* An old standby (see Figure 11-9) that can be used to display how items are distributed over a particular period.

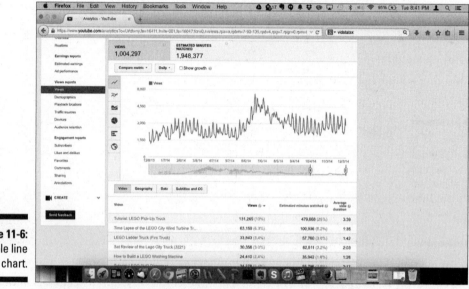

Figure 11-6: Sample line chart.

Figure 11-7: Multi-line chart.

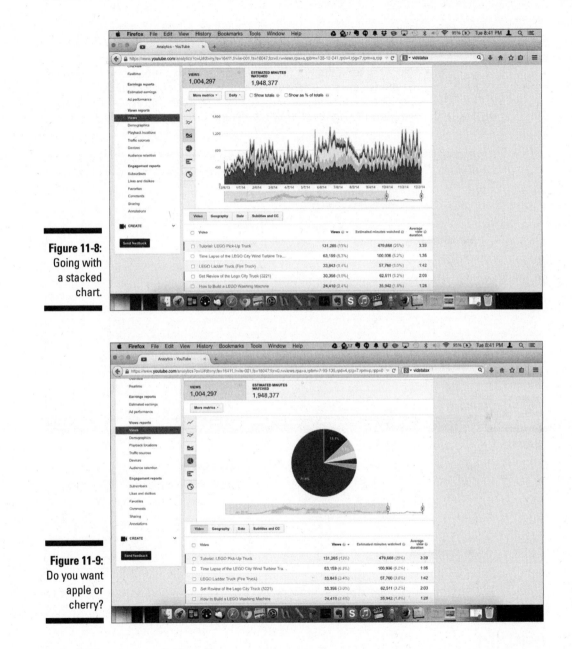

Figure 11-8:
Going with
a stacked
chart.

Figure 11-9:
Do you want
apple or
cherry?

- *Bar:* Illustrates relative proportions of a selected metric as horizontal bars, as shown in Figure 11-10.

- *Map:* Reveals a map of the world that displays metrics as you hover the mouse cursor over each country. More active countries for a specified item — views, subscribers, likes, and more — are shown with darker shades so that they stand out, as shown in Figure 11-11.

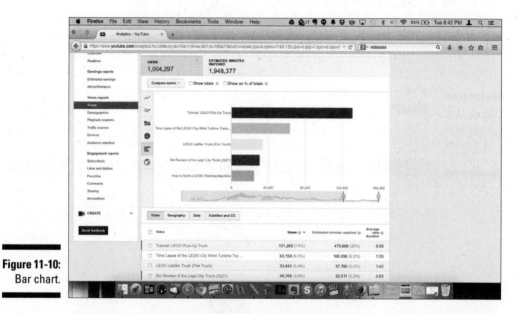

Figure 11-10:
Bar chart.

Figure 11-11:
An interactive map lets you explore each country.

Pick the chart type and graphing items that best reflect what you're trying to analyze. If you want to see trends, a pie chart or bar chart may not be the best choice. Instead, pick a graph with a strong time axis, such as line, multi-line, or stacked.

Just because YouTube Analytics lets you graph as many as 25 items doesn't mean that you should do so. In fact, a complicated graph may hide the exact nuggets you're trying to find.

Managing report details

For each chart, YouTube lets you see the detailed information that supports the graph. Just remember that every chart is different and that its features depend on the metrics used. If the chart you're working with has modifiable details, you can find a banner under the graph that you can use to manipulate the chart. Figure 11-12 shows the choices for the Views report, which let you look at details based on the following categories:

- ✔ **Video:** List the top videos for views.
- ✔ **Geography:** Order the top countries that generated the views.
- ✔ **Date:** Show when the views were generated.
- ✔ **Subtitles and CC:** Itemize the viewing language.

Figure 11-12: Specifying details for a Views report.

Sometimes you want to customize your own charts or combine details of your YouTube Analytics data with other information. You can download your data into a comma-separated values (CSV) file and import it into Microsoft Excel or another common spreadsheet program. To do so, just click the Download Report button on the top right part of the filter section associated with your report.

Learning about Views

YouTube Analytics provides plenty of insights, but you still have to come up with the final answers. To be effective, put on your proverbial Sherlock Holmes hat and pick up a magnifying glass as you sift through all the YouTube metrics clues. To see how that could work, let's look more closely at a specific report type: the Views report.

Seeing which content is the most popular

Like most YouTube channel managers, you want to know which videos are attracting the most views. Getting that info is simple:

1. **In your web browser, go to** www.youtube.com.

2. **Log on to your YouTube account.**

   If you see a blue Sign In button in the top right corner of the YouTube home page, enter your email address and password.

3. **Click on the logged-in icon and choose Creator Studio from the menu that appears.**

   The Creator Studio navigation menu should appear on the left side of the browser.

4. **Click the Analytics section of Creator Studio.**

   By default, it should go directly to the Overview submenu (refer to Figure 11-1).

5. **In the Analytics Navigation pane, click Views under the Views Report heading.**

   Doing so brings up a line chart that shows your total views over the last 28 days. (*Note:* You can change the analysis period by changing the time from the filter section that sits above the graph.)

6. **Examine the line.**

   Is it moving up and to the right? Do you see peaks during certain days? Look for patterns and look for spikes, both high and low.

   If you see consistent peaks, that means your audience is viewing your content on a regular basis. Think about the programming schedule from Chapter 5, and align it with your audience's viewing patterns.

7. **From the listing running down the left side of the chart area, click the Multi-line Chart icon.**

   Doing so brings up a chart showing your top five videos, graphed by color. In the Details section, you see a color key matched to each video so that it's clear how one video is performing compared to the others. Select the Video Details button next to the listed video to add and remove videos from the chart.

You won't break anything by looking at the different chart type or changing the analysis timeframe. You should become comfortable navigating and modifying your analysis.

Determining whether viewers are watching or leaving

One of the truly great aspects of YouTube is the detail it can provide about how much of your videos your audiences actually watch. If you're thinking about the view duration, that's partially correct: If you have a 4-minute video and viewers watch only about half the video, you have a 2-minute (or 50 percent) view duration.

View duration, though important, tells only part of the story. A channel manager needs to know more, including the answers to these questions:

✔ Where is my audience dropping off?

✔ How does the audience attraction compare with similar videos?

Audience retention — determining the steps you need to take to hold on to your audience — should be a critical part of the analytics process. The Audience Retention report generated by YouTube Analytics allows channel managers to see these two factors:

✔ **Absolute audience retention:** You're greeted by a timeline that displays what percentage of your audience views your video. If you have a 3-minute video, you see a retention graph for the entire three minutes aligned with the player for the entire video. You can see exactly where an audience watches and where they drop off.

> Don't become upset when you discover that your audience is not watching 100 percent of your videos for their entire duration. Drop-offs are perfectly normal — think about your own viewing patterns on YouTube.

> ✔ **Relative audience retention:** After you realize that you won't have 100 percent audience retention, you need to determine how your retention rates compare with similar content from other channels. Relative retention rates displayed in the Audience Retention report show how your video compares over time and display whether parts are average, above average, or below average.

You can also look at audience retention by playlist; just click the Playlists button in the Filter section of the YouTube Analytics page.

So, does an audience retention report sound intriguing? Here's how to carry one out:

1. **In your web browser, go to** www.youtube.com.

2. **Log on to your YouTube account.**

   If you see the blue Sign In button in the top right corner of the YouTube home page, enter your email address and password.

3. **Click on the logged-in icon to and choose Creator Studio from the menu that appears.**

   The Creator Studio navigation menu should appear on the left side of your browser.

4. **Click the Analytics section of Creator Studio.**

5. **In the Analytics Navigation pane, click Audience Retention under the Views Reports heading.**

   By default, a line chart appears, displaying the average duration of all your channel videos. The Absolute Audience Retention chart is also shown by default.

6. **In the report's Details section on the bottom part of the page, click on the name of a particular video you want to analyze.**

   Doing so automatically fills in the video name in the filter section and brings up the audience retention graph.

   If you don't see the video you want to analyze for retention, simply use the Filter menu to search for it.

7. **Search for peaks and valleys in the graph.** You may be scratching your head and trying to figure out why a peak is showing up on a viewing graph. Your audience may be choosing to *rewatch* a segment, signaling vital content. The valley represents viewer loss, so look at what's

happening at that point in the video below the graph. The cause might be boring or overly long content, which is something that you should consider when editing upcoming content.

8. **Click the Relative Audience retention button just above the retention graph.**

    You should determine how your content is performing against comparable videos. If it's consistently below average, look at other content to understand how it's different and why it may be more interesting to the audience than yours.

The watch time plays a crucial role in increasing your video's profile in YouTube search results (as we talk about in Chapter 5). Audience retention provides you with insight you need in order to keep viewers watching.

A retention drop always occurs at the beginning of a video because that's when viewers decide if they've chosen the right video to watch. However, if the drop seems rather precipitous at the beginning, it may be a sign that the title, metadata, or thumbnail is out of sync with what viewers expected when they found the video. Never mislead viewers, and fix any concerns based on what your retention reports indicate.

Understanding Your Audience

View reports and Audience Retention reports are designed to help you understand how well your viewers are responding to your channel content. To find out who's watching your videos, you have to try a different tack: the Demographics report.

Diving into demographics

It helps to know who's watching your content so that you can make important content-planning decisions. The Demographics report in YouTube Analytics is a fascinating way to analyze your audience, because you can get concrete information about your audience members' genders, ages, and countries of residence.

Demographics is a vital chart area that lets you apply a Subscriber Only filter. Sometimes it's interesting to see whether your subscriber demographics mirror your general audience demographics.

To access your demographics, follow these steps:

1. **In your web browser, go to** www.youtube.com.

2. **Log on to your YouTube account.**

   If you see the blue Sign In button in the top right corner of the YouTube home page, enter your email address and password.

3. **Click on the logged-in icon and choose Creator Studio from the menu that appears.**

   The Creator Studio navigation menu should appear on the left side of your browser.

4. **Click the Analytics section of Creator Studio.**

5. **In the Analytics Navigation pane, click Demographics under the Views Reports heading.**

   Gender is the major metric, and both Male and Female are shown by default, as shown in Figure 11-13.

   You can focus on only one gender by clicking Male or Female in the banner above the chart. The chart shows a breakout by age bracket and a pie chart split by gender.

6. **Examine the charts and their accompanying details.**

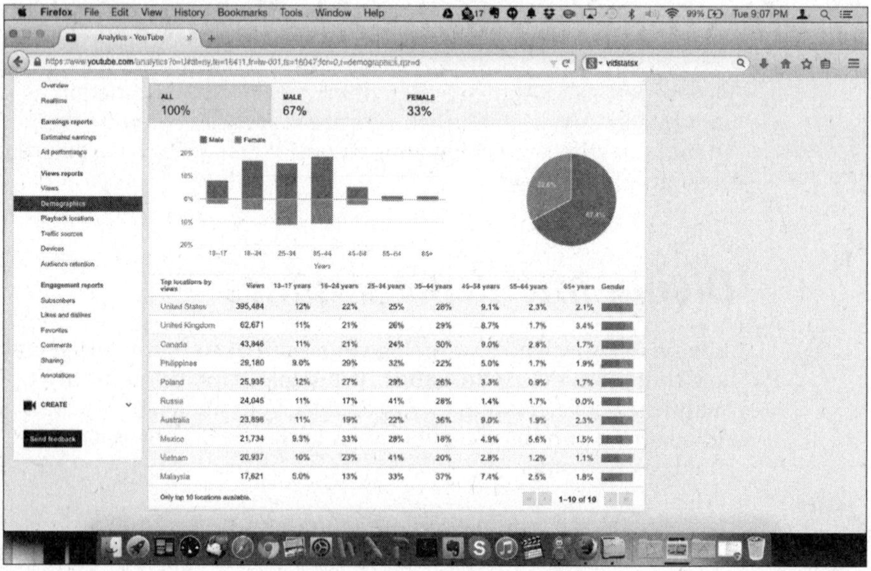

Figure 11-13:
YouTube
Analytics
demograph-
ics report.

Top locations by views	Views	13–17 years	18–24 years	25–34 years	35–44 years	45–54 years	55–64 years	65+ years	Gender
United States	395,484	12%	22%	25%	28%	9.1%	2.3%	2.1%	
United Kingdom	62,671	11%	21%	26%	29%	8.7%	1.7%	3.4%	
Canada	43,846	11%	21%	24%	30%	9.0%	2.6%	1.7%	
Philippines	26,180	9.0%	29%	32%	22%	5.0%	1.7%	1.9%	
Poland	25,936	12%	27%	29%	26%	3.3%	0.9%	1.7%	
Russia	24,045	11%	17%	41%	28%	1.4%	1.7%	0.0%	
Australia	23,898	11%	19%	22%	36%	9.0%	1.9%	2.3%	
Mexico	21,734	9.3%	33%	28%	18%	4.9%	5.6%	1.5%	
Vietnam	20,937	10%	23%	41%	20%	2.8%	1.2%	1.1%	
Malaysia	17,621	5.0%	13%	33%	37%	7.4%	2.5%	1.8%	

Only top 10 locations available.   1–10 of 10

It's terrific if your audience is exactly what you thought it would be. If it isn't, revisit your assumptions. You may find that your content is having wider interest, which may be a good thing. Conversely, if you're not seeing enough traction, perhaps you're not engaging enough with key creators and fans in your core demographic to help you get the word out.

7. **Click Show Only Subscriber Views in the Filter section.**

   Look at how the graphs change. If you see a big difference, determine whether subscription requests are working more broadly than expected, because your content certainly is appealing to others.

Make it a habit to compare your demographic information over time to detect any shifts in your audience.

Diving into subscribers

Knowing your subscribers' patterns and where they subscribe is an important part of your channel management responsibilities. YouTube is well aware of that, which is why it offers a Subscriber report as part of YouTube Analytics. Here's how to access it:

1. **In your web browser, go to** www.youtube.com.

2. **Log on to your YouTube account.**

   If you see the blue Sign In button in the top right corner of the YouTube home page, enter your email address and password.

3. **Click on the logged-in icon and choose Creator Studio from the menu that appears.**

   The Creator Studio navigation menu should appear on the left side of your browser.

4. **Bring up the Analytics section of Creator Studio.**

5. **In the Analytics Navigation pane, click Subscribers under the Engagement Reports heading.**

   You see a line chart with subscription patterns, similar to the one shown in Figure 11-14.

6. **Look at the report's Details section to see the most popular subscription locations. (You may need to click the Geography tab to see locations.)**

   You see the number of subscribers lost, too, which is a normal part of channel activity.

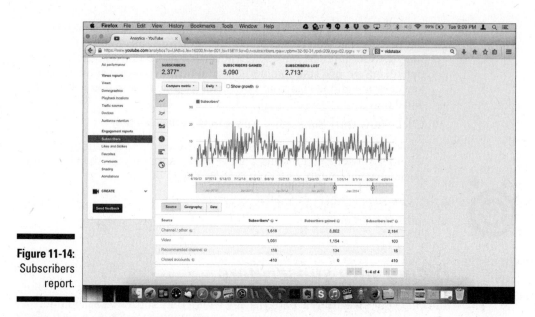

Figure 11-14:
Subscribers
report.

On some of your reports, you see the label Closed Account, which happens when YouTube purges accounts every so often. You lose subscribers whenever their accounts are closed.

Optimizing Discoverability

YouTube is a huge place, and it's growing every day. YouTube, Google, Bing, and Yahoo! visitors are presented with many options as they search for videos that interest them. In Chapter 5, you find out about the importance of discoverability and its importance for helping YouTube get your content in front of the right viewers so they can watch. Ideally, you want your content offered up first, but that takes some time. (Rome wasn't built in a day, you know.) As a channel manager, you use analytics to figure out whether your quest for discoverability is moving in the right direction.

Seeing where viewers find your content

As your content becomes more popular and relevant for specific viewers, YouTube will offer up your videos as Recommended videos and as part of their search results. These are important ingredients in your overall channel performance. So, too, is community engagement, which helps your content show up on playlists, on websites, in social media, and more. YouTube Analytics can help you determine where your audience is discovering your content.

The Traffic Sources report from YouTube Analytics is designed to show you how viewers discover your content. It includes not only sources within YouTube but also external sites and social media. To see how your viewers find you, do the following:

1. **In your web browser, go to** www.youtube.com.

2. **Log on to your YouTube account.**

   If you see the blue Sign In button in the top right corner of the YouTube home page, enter your email address and password.

3. **Click on the logged-in icon to and choose Creator Studio from the menu that appears.**

   The Creator Studio navigation menu should appear on the left side of your browser.

4. **Bring up the Analytics section of Creator Studio.**

5. **In the Analytics Navigation pane, click Traffic Sources under Views Reports.**

   By default, you see a line chart with aggregate channel views, which is not terribly interesting, so you should change to a more meaningful view.

6. **In the row running down the left side of the Chart area, click on the Bar Chart icon.**

   Doing so changes the view into something a bit more interesting — your top five YouTube channel traffic sources. (Figure 11-15 gives you an idea of what such a view looks like.)

7. **Modify the graph by using the Filter section, or select sources in the Detail section.**

8. **Review your traffic sources.**

   Sources here might include

   - YouTube advertising

   - YouTube channel page

   - YouTube Guide (YouTube homepage and subscription screen)

- YouTube partner promotion
- YouTube playlists
- YouTube Search
- YouTube Suggested Videos
- YouTube video annotation
- Unknown — direct (mobile apps and external website)
- Unknown — embedded player (views from external websites)
- External app
- External website
- YouTube — other features (analytics, editing screen, and other random stuff)

9. Click YouTube Playlists in the Details section.

Doing so brings up all the playlists — yours and others — that include your videos.

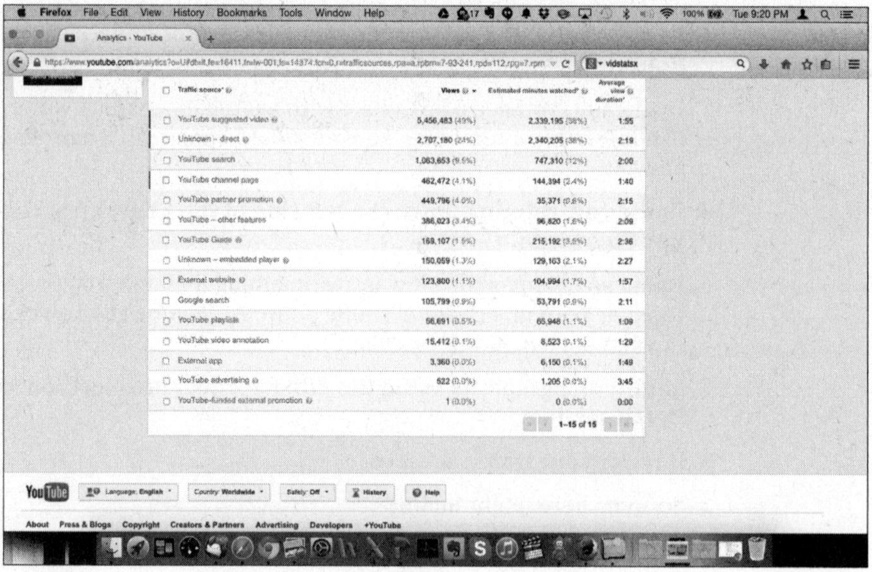

Figure 11-15:
Viewing your YouTube channel traffic sources.

Finding out where (and how) viewers watch your content

Channel managers also need to know where their video content was watched and on what kind of devices, including computers and mobile devices. You can get that information with the help of two specific reports:

- ✔ **Playback Locations:** Shows whether the video was viewed from YouTube or an external website or device.
- ✔ **Devices:** Specifies the device format and the operating system used to view video content.

Don't underestimate the importance of how your audience consumes your content. If mobile devices dominate, be sure that your videos don't require a 55-inch plasma display to get your point across.

To determine where your audience is viewing:

1. **In your web browser, go to** www.youtube.com.

2. **Log on to your YouTube account.**

   If you see the blue Sign In button in the top right corner of the YouTube home page, enter your email address and password.

3. **Click on the logged-in icon and choose Creator Studio from the menu that appears.**

   The Creator Studio navigation menu should appear on the left side of your browser.

4. **Bring up the Analytics section of Creator Studio.**

5. **In the Analytics Navigation pane, click Playback Locations under the Views Reports heading.**

   By default, you see a stacked chart with aggregate channel views.

6. **Modify the chart by using the Filter section or selecting Sources in the Details section.**

7. **Click on the Embedded Player on Other Websites link in the Details section.**

   The report highlighting embedded players appears, as shown in Figure 11-16.

   YouTube allows websites to embed your video, which is one of the highest forms of engagement.

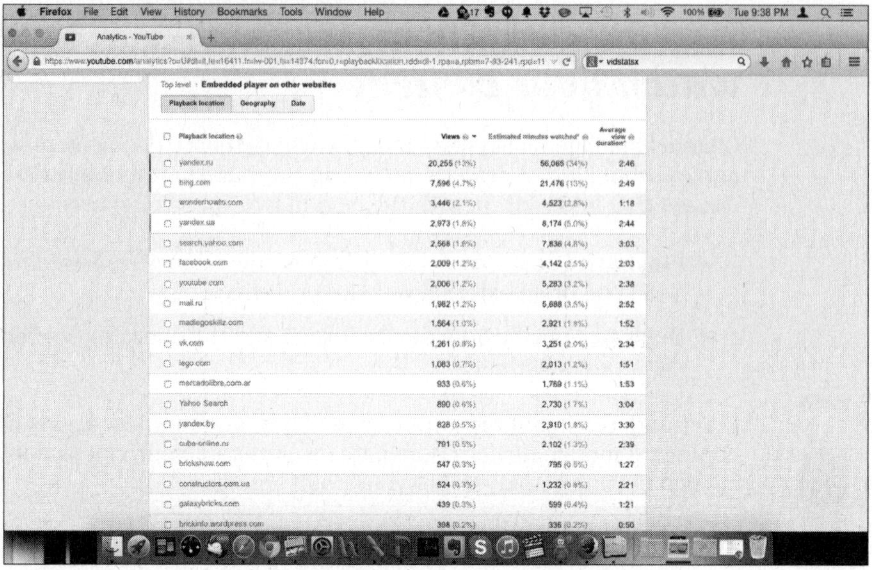

Figure 11-16:
Reporting your embedded-player locations.

You always get full view credit for embedded videos. If you have a website, feel free to embed videos from your YouTube community and your subscribers as well. It's good practice because it highlights how you interact with your subscribers.

8. **To probe a bit deeper, go back and click Devices under the Views Reports heading.**

   Under the graph, you can toggle between the device type and the operating system. Here are some popular devices:

   - Computer
   - Game console
   - Mobile
   - Tablet
   - TV
   - Unknown

9. **To see even more information, click a specific device type or operating system in the Details field.**

   If you find certain types to be the most popular, you can test your channel by using those particular devices and operating systems. That way, you can ensure that your audience has the best viewing experience possible.

Google Analytics and YouTube

If you're setting up a YouTube channel, chances are good that you have a website. And if you have a website, you're likely to have one or more analytics packages integrated into it, including the most popular one: Google Analytics. The good news here is that you can use Google Analytics for your YouTube channel.

Rather than use your existing Google Analytics tracking ID, create a new property only for your YouTube channel under your existing Google Analytics account. This new tracking ID must then be added to Creator Studio's Channel section under the Advanced tab.

After the new tracking ID is in place, you can follow many of the interactions that visitors are specifically having on your YouTube channel page rather than on your Watch pages or playlists. Google Analytics helps show you what YouTube Analytics doesn't: how viewers discover your *channel*. Remember that YouTube Analytics shows only how viewers are discovering your content, not your channel as such. With Google Analytics, you can figure out which videos drive the most viewers to your channel.

Making Sure Your Audience Is Engaged

Engagement is all about your viewers going beyond just watching a video. You want them to comment, share, and interact with you. The Engagement report offered by YouTube Analytics lets you look at several types of engagement:

Subscriptions: This feature displays information on subscriber gains and losses, along with specific info about where in the process they are choosing to subscribe.

Like and dislikes: This feature captures details around view sentiment about your content. This category also includes geographical information, which would let you know if some of your content is resonating better in some countries than others.

Favorites: This feature shows which videos are being added to viewers' Favorites playlists.

Comments: This feature highlights those videos that receive viewer comments. Don't forget the date dimension here to find out when most of the comments are posted.

If comments are made in the first few hours after you post a video, you may want to make sure you're always available after posting for immediate engagement.

Sharing: This feature itemizes which videos are shared and shows you which social media service they were shared on. (You might use this latter bit of information to find out whether your community prefers a particular service, such as Twitter or Facebook.)

Annotations: This feature helps analyze the performance of your annotations, showing which ones generate the most clicks.

Getting Engagement Reports

If Engagement reports sound like a good deal, start cranking them out. Here's how to do that:

1. **In your web browser, go to** www.youtube.com.

2. **Log on to your YouTube account.**

   If you see the blue Sign In button in the top right corner of the YouTube home page, enter your email address and password.

3. **Click on the logged-in icon and choose Creator Studio from the menu that appears.**

   The Creator Studio navigation menu should appear on the left side of your browser.

4. **Bring up the Analytics section of Creator Studio.**

5. **In the Analytics Navigation pane, click any of the reports under the Engagement Reports heading.**

   For the purposes of this example, say that you want to see where your viewers chose to subscribe and which countries they came from.

6. **In the Analytics Navigation pane, click Subscribers under the Engagement Reports heading.**

   You're presented with a line chart.

7. **Click Source in the Details section below the chart.**

   Doing so brings up a list of locations where your subscription activity happened.

8. **Click Video in the Details section.**

   Look for particular videos that drove the most subscriptions.

9. **To discover which countries your subscribers come from, click Geography in the Details section.**

   You see all the countries where you added and lost subscribers.

You always lose subscribers, no matter how great your channel and content. Why? Often because viewer interests change. You should, however, make sure that the subscribers you gain outnumber the subscribers you lose.

10. **If you prefer a pretty picture, click the Map icon to the left of the chart to graphically show where your subscribers come from. Then click the Geography button under the map.**

    Figure 11-17 shows your subscriber detail by country.

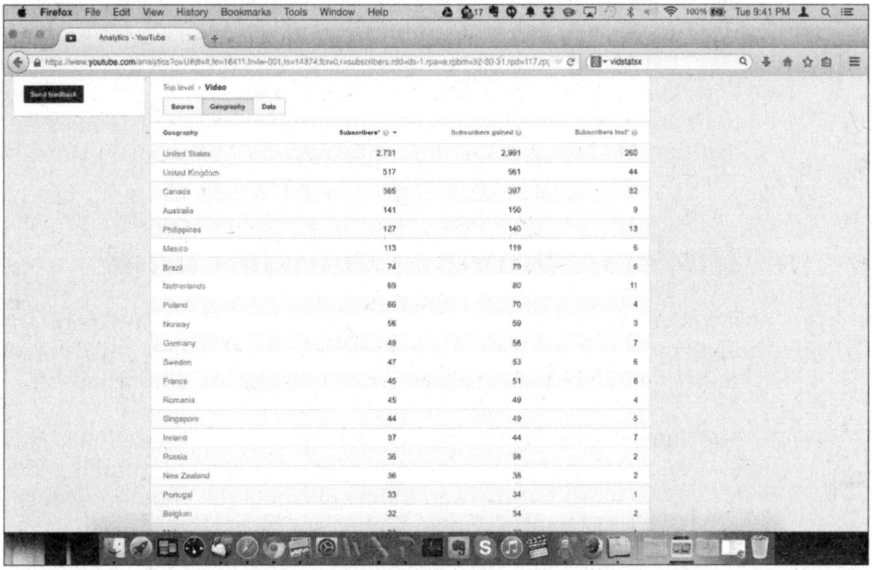

Figure 11-17: Subscriber interactive map with accompanying details.

Analytics and language

You may have discovered that many of your viewers don't come from your own country or speak your language natively. Unfortunately, with your busy schedule as channel manager, creator, or digital brand video guru, you probably don't have time learn a new language — even though you'd love to.

Luckily for you, you can provide captions in a different language — see Chapter 10 for all the details. Use YouTube Analytics to discover what language and countries are most important to your channel. You may be able to collaborate with your fans who are native speakers or with services such as the Google Translator Toolkit (`https://translate.google.com/toolkit`).

After you have a general idea how to access the Subscribers report, you should be able to apply that knowledge to accessing the other Engagement reports. Drill down into the details to understand exactly what your audience is doing with your content.

Going In-Depth on Annotation Analytics

Regardless of whether you're an independent creator or a business, you often want your audience to do *something*. Annotations — the clickable elements you can add to a video — can be quite an effective way to help the audience take that action. (If annotations don't ring a bell, check out Chapter 10.) Fortunately, YouTube Analytics helps you determine whether your annotations are effective, which is often important to not only you as a channel manager but also your viewers, who may be looking to do something.

Understanding annotation lingo

If you've ever dealt with any type of web commerce, you'll find the metrics and nomenclature around annotations familiar. If not, you can pick it up rather fast. Here are some key terms to know for annotations:

- **Impression:** This is the number of times an annotation is shown. If an annotation appears once in a video, for example, and the video is shown 1,000 times but the watch time presents the annotation only 572 times, that's 572 impressions.

- **Click:** If the viewer clicks on the annotation, that's a click. Note that not all annotations are clickable.

- **Click-through rate:** This percentage shows the number of clicks divided by the number of impressions. If a video received three clicks for 88 impressions, that would be $\frac{3}{88}$, or a 3.4 percent click-through rate.

- **Closes:** If the viewer closes the annotation, it's a close. Note that not all annotations can be closed.

- **Close-rate:** This percentage shows the number of closes divided by the number of impressions. If a video receives four clicks for 40 impressions, that's $\frac{4}{40}$, or a 10.0 percent close rate.

You see all these metrics in Annotation reports prepared by YouTube Analytics.

Getting your annotation metrics

After you all the "vocab" out of the way, it's time to generate some Annotation reports. Here's how it's done:

1. **In your web browser, go to** www.youtube.com.

2. **Log on to your YouTube account.**

   If you see the blue Sign In button in the top right corner of the YouTube home page, enter your email address and password.

3. **Click on the logged-in icon and choose Creator Studio from the menu that appears.**

   The Creator Studio navigation menu should appear on the left side of your browser.

4. **Bring up the Analytics section of Creator Studio.**

5. **In the Analytics Navigation pane, click Annotations under the Engagement Reports heading.**

   You see a line chart that shows annotation clicks for the last 28 days.

6. **Use the Report filter to change the timeframe or to select particular content that you want to analyze.**

7. **Click on the major annotation metrics shown in the banner above the chart: Clicks, Click Through Rate, Closes, and Close Rate.**

   Look for any trends, peaks, or valleys in the graph.

   Repeatable patterns, trends, and chart anomalies are your analytics friends. Be on the lookout for them and try to understand why they're occurring. Use chart comparatives and other analytics reports to probe deeper.

8. **Click the Annotation Type tab in the Details section.**

   This step helps you determine whether your audience prefers a particular type of engagement. Figure 11-18 shows an annotation report with itemized annotation types.

9. **Click on Video tab in the Details section.**

   Your top-performing videos, ranked by annotation click, are listed.

   If you're not seeing a particular video, go to the Filter section and reset your choices.

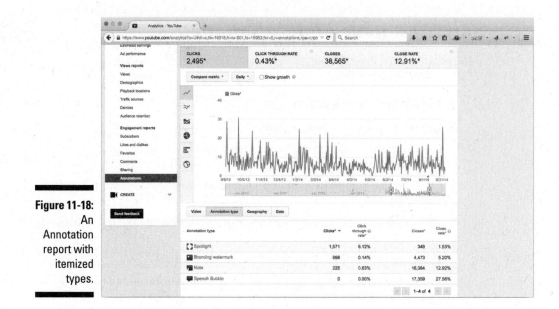

Figure 11-18:
An
Annotation
report with
itemized
types.

10. **Click on the video name to see the annotation performance for a particular video.**

    You see a list of all annotations, ranked by click frequency.

    Clicks tends to attract all the attention, but also pay particular attention to annotations that are closed. A high close rate may be a sign that you're annoying your viewers and risking watch time, unsubscribes, and dislikes.

11. **Click the Video Manager section of Creator Studio to modify or remove annotations.**

    Analytics gave you the insights, so be sure to take action. Chapter 10 has all the details on annotations.

As a channel manager, you'll continually look at your metrics and make adjustments. That's perfectly normal. There's never one fix, so just keep repeating the process (within reason) until you get it right.

Seeing whether your annotation are working

After you see all these interesting metrics — such as click-through rate (CTR), subscriber growth, favorite additions, and more — you may wonder how your metrics compare. Though you'd probably like to hear that a click-through rate of 3.1345 percent is the norm, you'll quickly see that there really is no single "good" value for a metric. Establish the norm, and continually compare performance among all components of your channel.

A good end-card (see Chapter 10) may have several side-by-side annotations with associated thumbnails. YouTube Analytics is a goldmine in this example because it shows not only the clicks; it also provides insights into what viewers watch next, which thumbnails are drawing attention, and how the thumbnail orientation affects the number of clicks.

Beyond YouTube Analytics

If you have only a few channels and limited programming skills, and you aren't doing any advertising, YouTube Analytics will do a fine job for you. If you want to analyze broader markets on YouTube for competitive reasons or you are interested in selecting places to advertise on YouTube, you need different tools and analytics. The same holds true if you're only looking to see lists of trending videos.

Analytics on YouTube isn't restricted to YouTube Analytics in Creator Studio. There are third-party solutions, such as VidStatsX (www.vidstatsx.com) and Pixability (www.pixability.com), that provide creators, channel managers, and brand marketers with the tools necessary to analyze industry trends, manage multiple channels, and run advertising campaigns. Figure 11-19 gives you a taste of what VidStatsX can offer, in the form of a nice Top 100 list, and Figure 11-20 shows Pixability's analytics for the most influential creators in the beauty industry on YouTube.

Using the YouTube Analytics API

It's quite easy to access YouTube Analytics from your laptop, your tablet, or even your mobile phone. You get some nifty graphs from which you can make some rather powerful decisions about your channel and your audience. But that's not the only way to get the metrics and insights you need in order to run your channel.

You can also access YouTube Analytics via an application programming interface (API). That's tech-speak for having your computer programs talk directly to YouTube and do all sorts of tasks, such as upload videos, grab analytics data, and so much more. A number of powerful video marketing and advertising platforms from companies such as Pixability make extensive use of YouTube APIs.

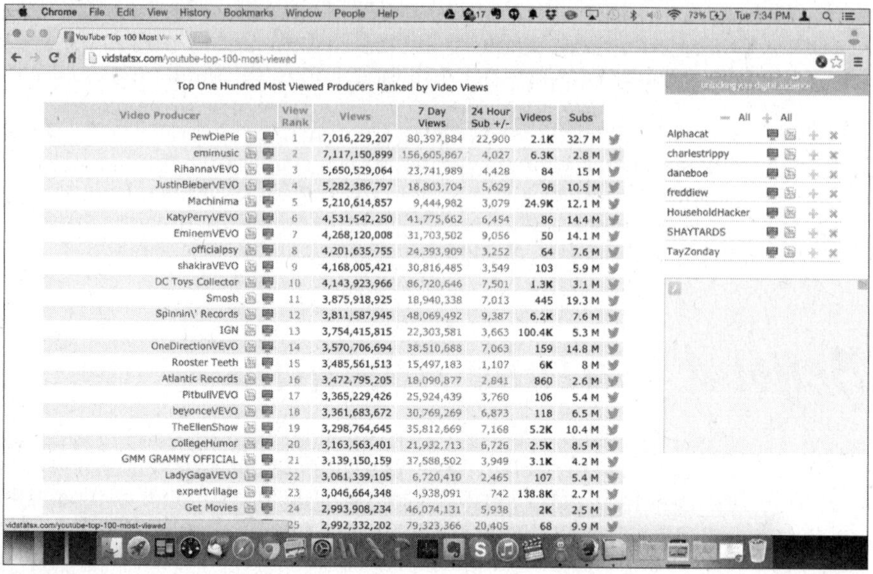

Figure 11-19:
Seeing what
VidStatsX
analytics
has to offer.

Figure 11-20:
Pixability
analytics
crunches
the beauty
numbers.

Only you have access to your YouTube Analytics data. Other analytics tools use public information only, often combining data from several different sources to come up with a much broader analytics view beyond just your channel.

Part IV

YouTube Channels Are Serious Business

Find out more about how a YouTube channel can supercharge your business at www.dummies.com/extras/youtubechannels.

In this part . . .

- See why businesses bother with YouTube.
- Look at your YouTube advertising options.
- Explore the earning potential of YouTube.

Chapter 12

How and Why Businesses Use YouTube

*U*rban legend has it that when asked why he robbed banks, famed criminal Willie Sutton responded, "Because that's where the money is." You won't learn much about bank robbery in this chapter, but you will understand why doing business on YouTube is a big deal: *because that's where your customers are.* In fact, that's where nearly everyone who's doing business today is.

YouTube now reports that it receives over 1 billion unique visitors *per month* who watch over 6 billion hours of video during that period. They're watching from desktops, laptops, tablets, smartphones, smart TVs, game consoles — and pretty soon, from intelligent watches. They're watching around the world from over 60 countries. (In fact, 80 percent of YouTube views occur from outside the United States.) Wherever a YouTube video is played lies a potential opportunity to help your business.

If you're serious about taking your business to the next level, YouTube can provide you with some rich capabilities designed to help you reach that goal. In later chapters, you find out how to work as an *advertiser* (someone who buys ad space) or as a *creator* (someone who sells ad space). Fortunately for you, Google and YouTube take care of most of the messy work for you while helping you integrate YouTube into your paid marketing initiatives, such as your display and search campaigns.

Understanding Video and Business

Before you think about YouTube for business, you may want to think about video for business. It doesn't matter whether you're part of a Fortune 500 multinational corporation or running a one-person community nonprofit: Your business will benefit greatly by bringing video into your marketing efforts. YouTube helps you make that happen easily while also giving you the tools to help you reach your business goals.

If you're a business, the audience you're trying to reach also includes those viewers who can help you sell more. They're your prospective — or existing — customers, other businesses that can help you sell, or potential advocates who may become your brand champions. Your challenge is to get their attention, which is especially difficult these days because they're getting bombarded with digital media from so many different sides. That's why video is vital: It helps you cut through all your audience's distractions and deliver your value proposition fast and effectively. The good part, according to market research company eMarketer, is that online video not only is the fastest-growing type of media but will also be the largest, as shown in Figure 12-1. YouTube is a great place to be.

It's all about video marketing

Because the focus of this book is on YouTube, you've probably already embraced the broader concept of video marketing and advertising. If not, check out the book referenced in Chapter 5, *Video Marketing for Dummies*, by Kevin Daum, Bettina Hein, Matt Scott, and Andreas Goeldi (Wiley). It deals with the broader concept of video as an effective medium for helping your business. In this chapter and the following, you'll learn about how YouTube fits into the business equation.

Figure 12-1: Media consumption by type for all U.S. adults.

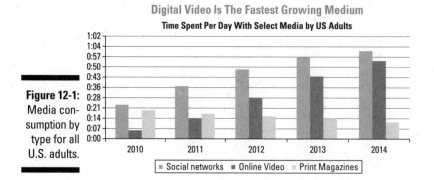

Digital Video Is The Fastest Growing Medium
Time Spent Per Day With Select Media by US Adults

■ Social networks ■ Online Video ▪ Print Magazines

Using video for marketing and advertising is nothing new, especially for larger companies that have spent fortunes on television advertising and paid infomercials. Lots of cutting-edge organizations alternatively jumped onto the web-based, online video bandwagon, but many became frustrated because it was difficult to gauge whether video advertising actually helped their businesses. They couldn't determine who was watching, they were unable to engage their audience, and they were at a loss to explain to their bosses how well their fancy video campaigns worked. Too bad their leaders were often asking about viral videos rather than business results.

Betting your business on viral video is like betting your retirement on lottery tickets: It's just not a sound strategy. You'll end up investing all your money and time in something that has little or no chance of succeeding. A much better strategy is to make great content regularly and add a dash of paid advertising to build your business the right way.

Most folks are well aware that a revolution has occurred in video capture, production, and editing over the past decade. We're at the point where someone using the smartphone in their pocket can shoot, edit, and upload a high-quality video, all within minutes. The thing is, the revolution didn't stop there. It happened in distribution and social media, too. With YouTube, you can also reach millions of viewers, all within a matter of minutes. Keep that point in mind as you make your way through this chapter.

Brand decisions are made on YouTube

YouTube is now where consumers frequently turn to make decisions about what products to buy. Because of the rich engagement capabilities that YouTube provides, the site is far more than just a place you go to when you want to watch a few videos — it has become a gathering place, a true community, a powerful social platform. By combining the social aspect with video (both branded video and video that's independently produced), YouTube now hosts its fair share of trusted advisors who act as product experts and influencers who are in a position to guide consumers on their journey to making a decision about a product or service.

Figure 12-2 shows consumer search patterns around tablets in the consumer electronics industry. What's most striking is the amount of ongoing YouTube search traffic that's shown. Compare that with the corresponding Google search graph, which shows only seasonal search spikes — a sure sign that consumers are looking for the big sales after having already selected their products. The implications of Figure 12-2 are profound, especially for business: Brand and product decisions are being made on YouTube, and purchase decisions are being made on Google.

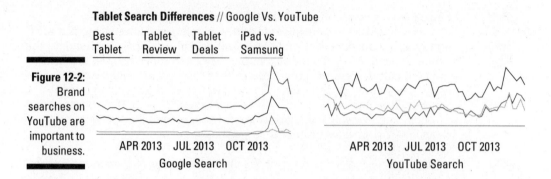

Tablet Search Differences // Google Vs. YouTube

Figure 12-2:
Brand
searches on
YouTube are
important to
business.

Being on YouTube is no longer just an advantage; it's a necessity for business. If you've doubted where YouTube fits into your business cycle, think again. YouTube now represents the first few steps in your customers' journey with you.

Understanding Your YouTube Business Components

If you have a business, more likely than not you also have a *business model* — a plan that sets down how you intend to make money, to put not too fine a point on it. This chapter is designed to help you find a place for YouTube in your business model. (You may want to read this chapter in combination with Chapter 5, where we talk a bit more about how you can ensure that your YouTube channel objectives and video content align with your business goals.)

Don't be rigid about your YouTube business model. Ultimately, your audience is the judge. Relevant content, engagement, and collaboration may all be important factors to consider. YouTube Analytics — and your sales performance — are your guides, so be sure to scrutinize your channel's numbers. (See Chapter 11 for more on YouTube Analytics.)

Content matters

No ifs, ands, or buts — content is critical to business on YouTube. If you come from the TV world, your first instinct may be to drop the standard 15- or 30-second commercial on YouTube. Your first instinct would be wrong. YouTube viewers don't want commercials; they want authenticity. They don't want glitz; they want reality.

If you have a product to sell, picture your viewer's journey with you and with your brand as a series of steps that viewer must take. Each step represents a stage where your viewer, who may now be a bona fide business prospect, is looking for more — yet different and increasingly detailed — information. These steps are shown in Figure 12-3.

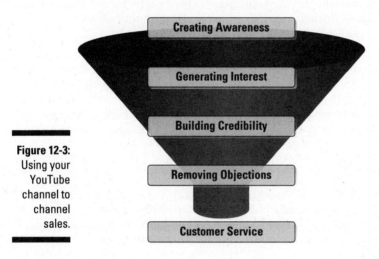

Figure 12-3:
Using your
YouTube
channel to
channel
sales.

You may believe that these steps look and sound a lot like the proverbial sales funnel. You'd be right to think so. Viewers frequently complete a series of distinct phases before they make a product decision. The reason it's called a *funnel* is that it's wider at that top than at the bottom because not everyone who looks at your products (or terrific videos) will buy something. Your business goal is to use YouTube to help them pick you when they make a purchase decision.

With these steps in mind, your YouTube content should align with the stages of your customer's journey. Here are some phases to consider as you try to help viewers make a decision:

✓ **Create awareness.** Initially, viewers likely have no idea who you are or what you offer as a product or service. You want to elevate their knowledge of you in the fastest way possible. Think of the video content at this stage as a short YouTube commercial. It's different from regular ads and TV commercials because it may provide annotations and web links for viewers seeking more information. In other words, you won't leave them hanging. If you're going to advertise on YouTube, content at this stage may be perfect for your campaign.

Don't make viewers think too hard! Make it ridiculously easy for them to find more information about what is shown in the video. Use all the tools in your toolbox — annotations, metadata, and shortlinks, for example — to keep them engaged. (For more on the tools you can use to keep viewers engaged, see Chapter 11.)

✔ **Generate interest.** Think of endorsements or partnerships. If you're big enough — or rich enough — you're talking about *celebrity* endorsements.

Aside from being expensive, celebrity endorsements often come with severe licensing restrictions. If you end up getting a million views — and lots of business — from a celebrity endorsement, that's great, until you're forced to pull the video after licensing rights expire. Be sure to create licensing contracts that do not require you to remove the video from your YouTube channel. After you delete a video or list it as private on your channel, your channel won't be able to show those video views on your About page as views and your channel won't be rewarded for them in YouTube search.

✔ **Build credibility.** Building credibility usually necessitates adding tutorials and longer videos that take the time to describe product details. Don't be surprised to see a 30-minute longer-form video at this stage perform as well as shorter-form content at an earlier stage.

Content curation (or playlisting videos you haven't produced) is often as important as content creation. If your raving fans are making awesome videos about your products, don't hesitate to include them in your playlists. There's probably no better way to establish credibility with sales prospects than to show the enthusiasm of your fans. Don't forget that including your community on your channel is a great community high-five as well.

✔ **Remove objections.** Having collaborators producing tutorials are great for not only building trustworthiness but also removing potential objections. Sometimes, though, you need something different from a tutorial, perhaps videos that describe how your product or service benefited the customer. This is where you make the sale happen, so make sure it counts.

✔ **Provide a service.** After your prospective channel viewer has turned into a paying customer, you may think that your YouTube work is done. Not exactly. Remember that if customers love their experience with you and your business, they'll likely buy from you again, and again, and again. One way to ensure this level of loyalty is to make the experience they have with you and your brand *after the sale* a rewarding one. We're talking about customer support and service. This is where YouTube can truly shine. Your customer will no doubt have questions about your product, application scenarios, maintenance, and so much more. That's okay and perfectly normal, so help them out. For example, the auto manufacturer Audi does a great job with customer service on YouTube, as shown in Figure 12-4. As car electronics became more advanced and sophisticated, Audi stepped up as one of the first companies to offer tutorial videos. Check out the tutorial videos at www.youtube.com/AudiofAmerica.

When your customers visit your YouTube channel for product support, they also see your new product offerings — which is an excellent upsell or referral opportunity.

Rob and Theresa spend much of their time working with brands and agencies on YouTube for business. One of the top challenges they face is getting companies to move beyond producing content for only the top of the funnel (refer to Figure 12-3). Creating awareness is a necessary marketing function and has well served brand advertisers targeting television audiences for many years. The digital world, however, expects something more from the content on your YouTube channel. Give them an authentic video experience, not an isolated 15-second ad. Moving beyond dumping repurposed one-off commercials on YouTube to a more holistic, funnel-based approach is the most important way to help your business.

Effective content doesn't have to be all about products, either. American Express (www.youtube.com/AmericanExpress) does an outstanding job of producing channel content that provides important advice for small businesses, as shown in Figure 12-5. Doing so isn't the core business of a credit

Figure 12-4:
Audi uses YouTube for customer service and support.

Figure 12-5:
American
Express
delivers
audience-
centric
content on
YouTube.

card company such as American Express, but it's obviously quite important to its target audience. Always remember that your best content aligns with your audience's needs.

Video optimization and effective channel management are essential to effective business on YouTube. For more on these topics, check out Chapter 9, where you can find out all about the importance of video thumbnails, metadata, playlists, and more.

Community and content creators

If you have an interesting product or service that people are passionate about, there's likely to be a conversation about it on YouTube. Chances are good that there will be *many* conversations and they'll be happening whether or not you're involved. This situation often comes across as quite strange to companies that are accustomed to controlling the business conversation around their brands and products. Though YouTube shatters that notion of control, don't be afraid of having others talk about you: They may be your army of brand champions — and the best salespeople you've ever had.

One of the most interesting business segments found on YouTube is the beauty industry. Now, before you roll your eyes and close this book because your business has nothing to do with mascara and eyeliner, take a moment to reconsider the implications. The dynamics of the beauty industry show where the future of YouTube is for business: independent creators producing fantastic content for a passionate and purchase-motivated fan base. These creators, or beauty vloggers, also know the importance of subscribers. Figure 12-6 shows the number of subscribers for the top beauty brands versus the top independent beauty vloggers. It's not even close: The audience often prefers authentic, independent voices.

In many industries, you'll find a strong, independent, and creative force where YouTube creators are crafting content in your topic space. Don't fear that force. In fact, you can embrace the representatives of that force by doing the following:

- ✔ **Include their content in your playlists.** This is the ultimate tip of the hat to independent creators.

- ✔ **Comment on their channel.** Add to their conversation in a meaningful way.

- ✔ **Respect their independence.** They may show your products and your competitors' *in the same video*. Don't ask them to do otherwise. Creators do what is best for their audience.

- ✔ **Consider sponsorship or another type of promotion.** Whether you are the creator or the brand, only enter into partnerships that support your channel objectives and provide your audience with an experience that will keep them coming back for more. (See Bonus Chapter 1 for more information on sponsorships.)

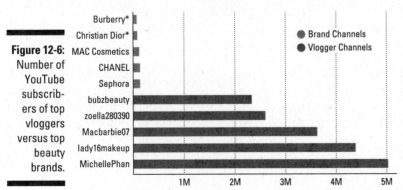

Figure 12-6: Number of YouTube subscribers of top vloggers versus top beauty brands.

Number of YouTube Subscribers of Top Vloggers vs. Beauty Brands

If you're in independent creator in your own right, keep in mind that brands and larger companies may not be in a position to work like you do because they have neither the content production flexibility nor the means to engage with subscribers at the same level of intimacy you may have.

Brands steer clear of vloggers who want something — whether it's product bling or cold, hard cash — in exchange for a favorable review. You may not get the audience engagement if the vlogger isn't really into your product or services because the audience can tell when it is not authentic content.

Brands versus vloggers

Recently, Pixability conducted a comprehensive study of the beauty industry, one of the most active and leading-edge industries in the digital video marketplace. The report, titled *Beauty on YouTube: How YouTube Is Radically Transforming the Beauty Industry and What That Means for Brands*, identified and analyzed how 168 major beauty brands and 45,000 YouTube beauty-focused personalities manage, produce, and socialize more than 877,000 makeup videos and hair, skin, and nail care videos. (See the blurb about the report in the sidebar figure.) The report highlights striking differences in impact between those who manufacture products and those who manufacture videos about products. Some of the findings are listed here:

Beauty brands own a surprisingly small share of YouTube's audience.

✔ Beauty brands on YouTube typically get far less views and engagement compared to vloggers talking about beauty, thus making the brands' impact on the space smaller than the independent creators.

✔ Beauty brands control only 3 percent of YouTube's 14.9 billion beauty-related video views.

✔ YouTube vloggers and other beauty content creators control 97 percent of conversations around beauty and brands on YouTube.

✔ Top beauty brands partner with key YouTube content creators in addition to running YouTube advertising campaigns to increase their YouTube brand footprints by way of organic views and user-generated content.

Beauty brands need to consistently create a wider variety of YouTube content — and more of it.

✔ YouTube's top beauty vloggers have ten times more videos on their channels than beauty brands manage to place on their channels.

✔ Top beauty vloggers publish new YouTube content seven times more frequently than beauty brands do.

✔ Beauty brands are underinvesting in YouTube's popular long-format beauty tutorials and seasonal events and are overinvesting in publishing less popular commercials.

✔ YouTube's top quartile of beauty brands vary video lengths five times more than the bottom quartile of beauty brands.

Beauty brands aren't being found on YouTube.

✔ Beauty brands show up only 2.5 percent of the time in YouTube search results for popular beauty keywords.

✔ YouTube's top beauty-brand creators use seven times more playlists and 170 percent more metadata tags than the bottom quartile of beauty brands, to ensure that video content is discoverable on YouTube.

Audience engagement is the key to beauty-brand marketing success on YouTube.

✔ YouTube's top 25 beauty vloggers possess 115 times more subscribers and receive 2,600 percent more comments on average than beauty brand channels.

✔ YouTube's top beauty-brand quartile successfully engages with target audiences to receive 16 times more views per video than the bottom quartile.

✔ Top-performing beauty brands focus on converting YouTube views into sales by including conversion links 260 percent more often than less successful beauty brand performers on YouTube.

Advertising

Discoverability — the ease with which potential viewers can find your content — is crucial on YouTube. Your content needs to be easy to find if you want to capture the most engaged target audience. You can let discoverability grow *organically* over time on its own by way of community, engagement, watch time, and more. Sometimes, though, the business world doesn't work at that organic speed, so you may need to add a bit of "fertilizer" to help the process move a little faster. That's what YouTube advertising is all about: Apply some cash to help get your content in front of viewers who may turn into customers or avid viewers.

As a YouTube channel manager, you need to decide whether advertising will work for you and figure out which side of the business ad equation you're on:

✔ **Publisher:** You're a content creator looking to monetize your YouTube channel by having appropriate ads placed against it.

✔ **Advertiser:** You want people to become aware of your channel and consume more of your content, perhaps even subscribe. Maybe you have a product and you want viewers to buy something — at a store, online, or via a business partner.

Paid, owned, earned

If you hang out around marketers often enough, you'll hear them talk about paid, owned, and earned media. Each of these three categories plays an important but related role in your business strategy, so this is as good a time as any to figure out exactly what the terms mean. They're easier to understand if you change the order a bit, though:

✔ **Owned** consists of the web properties and resources you control, which includes your website and your YouTube channel.

✔ **Earned** is what your customers are saying about you and how they engage with your channel. From the YouTube perspective, this one includes videos about your

products that are produced by independent creators.

✔ **Paid here means "paid advertising."** The good part about the paid category is that you can experiment and discover audiences that may not find your channel and content organically. Paid works well on YouTube because it can drive meaningful views, help add subscribers, and increase sales.

All three media — paid, owned, and earned — feed off one another, so your YouTube strategy and your business strategy should always take all of them into account.

Chapters 13 and 14 have lots more detail about YouTube advertising from both sides, but for now just remember that there are no hard-and-fast rules or thick walls between publishers and advertisers. You may find your business is okay doing a little of both.

Effective advertising is all about measurement, so you'll use YouTube Analytics extensively to make sure you're getting the most out of your ad dollars or maximizing your monetization potential. (For more on YouTube Analytics, check out Chapter 11.)

Don't view YouTube advertising as an isolated activity. Done correctly, an outstanding ad campaign not only moves the sales meter in the right direction but also generates important free follow-on channel activities, like additional playlist views and subscriptions from engaged viewers, which are critical to increasing discoverability. Unlike other paid media, YouTube advertising helps organic growth.

If you're a creator who's working with a brand or another type of sponsor, *be transparent about it.* Your success on YouTube is closely tied to your authenticity and openness. Getting a sponsorship deal and placing products in your videos is fine, as long as your audience knows what's going on. You'll find your YouTube audience extremely loyal — but unforgiving (and unsubscribing) if they feel misled in any way. If you're a brand or sponsor, your brand reputation on YouTube should be treated with the same care you'd expend anywhere else. Be conscious of your YouTube partners.

Integrating YouTube with Other Campaigns

Broadcast television, cable, newspapers, magazines, and direct mail may not have the same impact they once did, but they're not going away anytime soon, either. And don't forget your email and display campaigns: They're probably an important part of your business strategy, so you should nurture them. If you're holding special events and conferences, keep them coming, too. The point is that YouTube is a great way to not only integrate all your diverse business campaigns but also make them more effective and memorable.

Cross-media integration

To see what an effective integrated business campaign might look like on YouTube, look no further than the campaign put together by the NBA (`www.youtube.com/nba`), one of the better sports leagues on YouTube. The NBA does many things well for its business, including

- **Content generation:** The NBA updates its YouTube content quite frequently, often releasing custom highlights just for its YouTube audience. It's a useful example of how to repurpose TV content for a YouTube audience.

- **Promotion integration:** The NBA's YouTube channel sections are always up to date with the newest content, *tentpole* events — seasonal or timely content releases around an event, playoffs for example — and more. If the NBA is doing something on court or off court, it's guaranteed to be on YouTube.

- **Video optimization:** Well-chosen, accurate, custom thumbnails entice viewers to click and watch. Many of the NBA's videos also have other interactive elements, such as annotations and end-cards.

- **Channel monetization:** The NBA knows how to make money, and it has taken that formula to YouTube. You'll see extensive use of pre-roll ads against its channel content. (The idea behind pre-roll video ads is that they play before the NBA video assets, and the channel then earns earns money from each view of an ad.)

Figure 12-7 shows the highly engaging NBA YouTube channel.

Figure 12-7:
The NBA uses YouTube to integrate many of its highlights and activities.

YouTube isn't television (or cable)

Business professionals who treat their YouTube channels as though they're television channels are the ones who complain most loudly about the results. The truth is that television commercials just don't perform well in terms of both views and engagement on YouTube. Rather than do what the NBA has been doing — repurposing great content specifically for its fan base on YouTube — many brands simply plop down their TV ad product on YouTube and expect miracles to happen. It just doesn't work that way. If you're coming from the world of television advertising and programming, look through the YouTube lens, not the TV camera. Figure 12-8 highlights some big differences between YouTube and television.

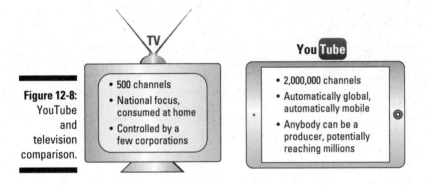

Figure 12-8:
YouTube
and
television
comparison.

TV
- 500 channels
- National focus, consumed at home
- Controlled by a few corporations

You Tube
- 2,000,000 channels
- Automatically global, automatically mobile
- Anybody can be a producer, potentially reaching millions

According to Nielsen, one of the major media-measurement companies, YouTube reaches more 18-to-34-year-olds than any cable network. This shows something important: Younger audiences aren't consuming traditional media in the same old way. Many people, affectionately known as *cord cutters,* no longer even subscribe to cable. They are, however, watching a good deal of video by way of YouTube, Hulu, Vimeo, Facebook, and other online video providers.

But don't assume that people outside this age bracket aren't consuming online video. Remember to use demographics as a guide, not as a rule. If your content is relevant and your target audience is online, you'll get the business results you want.

Keep in mind as well, when migrating from television to YouTube, that many of the traditional metrics associated with performance, especially those around viewership and advertising, differ radically between the two platforms. TV tends to focus on impressions, which measures how many people may have been exposed to a program or an ad. The dominant metrics on YouTube are how many people actually watched your content and your ads.

You don't measure distance with your bathroom scale, so don't measure your media the wrong way, either. Use the proper measurement in the digital world. Use television metrics for TV, and YouTube metrics for your channel. For more on YouTube metrics, see Chapter 11.

YouTube isn't Google, either

It's a fact: How a viewer searches on YouTube is different from how a viewer searches on Google. (Don't believe us? Take another look at Figure 12-2.) Google is indeed the number one search engine and YouTube is the number two, but it's *how* viewers search that makes them so vastly different.

It's worth repeating: Brand and product decisions are being made on YouTube, and purchase decisions are being made on Google.

From an advertising perspective, YouTube advertising — specifically, TrueView by way of AdWords for Video — behaves much differently from traditional AdWords. You get all the details in Chapter 13. It's important to note, though, that effective business management requires understanding the difference between traditional search and display for business, compared with YouTube search, display, engagement, subscriptions, and views.

Chapter 13

Expanding Your Audience through YouTube Advertising

*M*any channel managers often believe that after their channels are set up, their view counts are increasing, their subscriptions are growing, and engagement is up, they can then sit back and focus on making some content. Well, that's not exactly the case. You have another powerful resource in your tool chest that can potentially take your channel to the next level: It's *advertising*.

Now, before you close this book with a sigh, sure as sure can be that advertising is nothing more than a fancy way of throwing away money and annoying people, you'd better think again. YouTube advertising is highly effective because it allows you to reach a large part of your target audience who may not have discovered your channel and your content *organically* — without the help of advertising, in other words.

Unlike many types of advertising, well-run YouTube ad campaigns end up delivering not only views but also increased watch time and additional subscriber growth, both of which are great for your channel in YouTube's eyes. Why? Because effective YouTube advertising can help with discoverability, creating a virtuous cycle for your channel. A well-targeted ad campaign lets the right kind of viewers discover your channel — those you really want to reach. Once they subscribe and watch other videos on your channel after seeing your ads, your channel's search ranking will improve, which in turn will let other viewers with similar interests discover your content.

YouTube advertising builds on Google's successful AdWords product — one of the world's most popular advertising platforms. The part that ties into YouTube is AdWords for Video. As you can probably imagine, many ad types can be used with YouTube. Chances are good that you've seen the video masthead ad on YouTube's home page or animated ad overlays over the lower center area of YouTube videos. This chapter focuses on the specific ad types you configure via AdWords for Video. They're called YouTube *TrueView* ads.

YouTube TrueView ads are different from many other types of ads because you as the advertiser pay only if the viewer does something concrete, such as watch a video ad or click on a display ad. TrueView ads include both video and display ad formats. In other words, some ads use videos, and others use regular display ads, with just a static image and some text. A *pre-roll* ad is a video ad that is shown immediately before displaying the video that the viewer clicked to see. If you've been on YouTube, you've seen them. They're the ones that let you skip off after 5 seconds. Concerned that tons of people are sure to skip off after the first 5 seconds? Don't be. The good part is that you pay only for the viewers who choose to watch rather than those who skip off. In other words, you pay only for viewers who have a strong interest in the ad you've put in front of them.

Most channel managers should have no problem setting up an ad campaign for YouTube. Though you have to complete quite a few steps to set up an ad, most of the time you can simply use the default values for each step. Over time, you tweak the settings to produce even better results, but for your first campaign, we recommend sticking with the defaults.

Google Display Network

You're not restricted to YouTube for your TrueView ads. Google also has the Google Display Network (GDN), a massive, worldwide collection of more than 2 million websites that allow display and video advertising. Ads on the GDN can support all screen types, including desktop computers, laptops, tablets, and smartphones. A majority of the world's most heavily trafficked websites are part of the GDN, but that doesn't ensure that you'll be able to run placements on only the best sites.

You have the option during the YouTube ad campaign setup to include the GDN for placement of your ads. When setting up targeting groups for your ads, you can also itemize specific placement within YouTube and within the GDN. The GDN supports all types TrueView ads.

Understanding YouTube Advertising

To understand YouTube advertising, you need to know a little bit about Google advertising. You may believe that Google is simply a big search engine company, but it's really a big *advertising* company — that's where it makes its money. The same logic holds true for YouTube. People think of it as an amazing video site, but at its core, it's really a major advertising platform.

A fortune is being spent and made on YouTube. You know all those YouTube stars like PewDiePie, Jenna Marbles, and Ray William Johnson? They're earning the lion's share of their money from advertising. Granted, they're also now signing other types of lucrative endorsement deals, but their YouTube fame led to their first fortune — and that came from advertising.

There are two sides to the advertising equation:

- **Advertiser:** The person or organization paying for and placing the ads
- **Publisher:** The person or organization whose property has the ad placed on it and who receives a cut of revenue from the ad

On YouTube, you can be an advertiser or a publisher, or both. In this chapter, you can read about the advertiser side. Chapter 14 tells you all about the publisher side.

Other YouTube ad formats and pricing models

TrueView in-stream and in-display aren't the only ad types available on YouTube, but they're highly effective for many advertisers because they are charged only when a viewer watches the whole ad or — for longer ads — at least the first 30 seconds. There are other types of ads, however, such as a *masthead* (the big ad that shows up on the YouTube home page) or an *in-video overlay* (an ad that appears in the lower center of a video and acts like an annotation). For more on these (and other) ad types, go to www.youtube.com/yt/advertise/.

You may also want to check out *Google AdWords For Dummies*, by Howie Jacobson, Joel McDonald, and Kristie McDonald (John Wiley & Sons, Inc.). It provides all the details you need to become an AdWords guru.

TrueView ads' claim to fame is that they use cost per view (CPV) pricing. Other ad types may have different pricing methods, including cost per thousand impressions, also known as CPM. As you advertise more, it's worth your time to explore all ad types available via Google for YouTube.

Google and YouTube help on both sides of the advertising equation and have product offerings for both. On the advertiser side, you use Google AdWords for Video, which we cover later in this chapter. On the publisher side, you use Google AdSense to manage how your YouTube channel receives ads. (For more on Google AdSense in a YouTube context, check out Chapter 14.) Don't assume that you have to connect with publishers directly. Google acts as an intermediary — for a share of your profits, of course. (It's more proof that nothing in this life is ever free.)

Recognizing the importance of ad policy

If you're new to YouTube advertising, take a few minutes to understand ad policy, which basically states that advertising should conform to certain behavioral standards. (Go to `http://support.google.com/adword spolicy` for details.) Better yet, check out Chapter 9, which talks in some detail about the YouTube community guidelines — rules for everything from obscene material to copyright infringement and privacy controls. Google does its utmost to ensure that appropriate and relevant ads are placed, but both advertisers and publishers have further control as well.

Community guidelines are upheld nonstop, all day and all year. Violations not only jeopardize your ability to advertise, but you also risk your channel being taken down.

In addition to being in line with the YouTube community guidelines, ads must conform to technical guidelines and specification. This helps ensure both consistency and fairness across the YouTube platform; it also lowers the likelihood that you'll annoy viewers. Ad format details can be found at `http://support.google.com/displayspecs`.

Looking at YouTube ad types

This chapter concentrates on YouTube TrueView ads. These formats work well for many advertisers because charges occur only when a viewer watches an ad or clicks on a video thumbnail. This is a signal of a higher degree of audience interest, making those viewers much better targets for your ads.

YouTube TrueView ads come in two flavors: in-stream ads and in-display ads. In-stream ads work a bit like TV commercials. Before users can see the video they want to watch, they have to watch your video ad first. This is known as a *pre-roll* ad. YouTube lets users skip an in-stream ad after 5 seconds, but they can also click on the call to action banner to go directly to your website or YouTube channel.

As for the in-display ads, they appear on search results pages and on YouTube Watch pages and are marked with a gold AD icon. (Figure 13-1 shows a typical example of an in-display ad above the organic search results.)

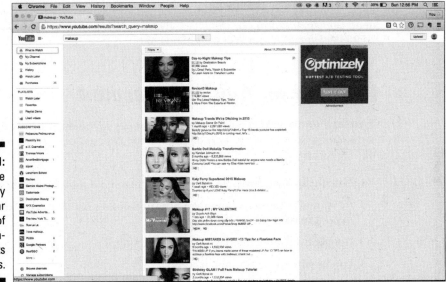

Figure 13-1:
YouTube
in-display
ads appear
on top of
search-
results
pages.

Since YouTube prioritizes videos with longer viewer session watch times and high engagement rates in its search results, highly engaged viewers from paid ads can support your SEO efforts.

You can go to `http://support.google.com/youtube` to learn all about the other ad types. Remember that YouTube TrueView ads are a great way to start your advertising work. To learn more about all the YouTube ad types, check out the YouTube media guidebook from Pixability, a company that specializes in YouTube marketing and advertising: `www.pixability.com/industry-studies/mediaguidebook/`.

Planning for Advertising

Advertising on YouTube requires some familiarity with Google AdWords. (Luckily for you, you can achieve the necessary level of familiarity simply by reading this chapter.) First and foremost, you need a Google AdWords account, which you can easily access via your regular Google account.

Note, however, that you need to explicitly tie your AdWords account to your YouTube account. (Don't worry: We show you how to do that as well.)

You don't need to learn all about AdWords to work your YouTube advertising magic. However, if you have a commerce website and need to drive more traffic, you may want to consider learning a lot more. In that case, we recommend *Google AdWords For Dummies*, by Howie Jacobson, Joel McDonald, and Kristie McDonald (John Wiley and Sons, Inc.).

Creating an AdWords account

Creating an AdWords account used to be pretty involved, but that was then. Fortunately, Google has greatly simplified the process of opening a new AdWords account:

1. **Point your web browser to** `http://adwords.google.com/video`.

2. **(Optional) Choose a language other than English (US) from the drop-down on the bottom right.**

   Google translates the page into that language.

3. **Log in with your Google account.**

   Normally you'd use the same Google account you'd use to manage your YouTube channel.

   If you already have a Google account for Gmail, YouTube, or another Google service, you can use it for your AdWords account. If you're a Gmail junkie, for example, connect the accounts so that you don't sign yourself out of AdWords every time you check your mail. If you already have a Google Analytics account (a free service that measures what visitors do on your website), the email address of your AdWords account must be the same as your Analytics admin user email.

4. **Click the Skip the Guided Setup link.**

   This setup process is designed for search advertising, not video ads, so you don't need to go through it.

5. **In the new screen that appears, select your time zone and currency from the drop-down lists and then click the Save and Continue button. (See Figure 13-2.)**

   Google might change the sign-up process and its billing practices at any time, so take the preceding instructions with a grain of salt. They may be accurate for years — or they may be out of date one week after this book shows up in the bookstore.

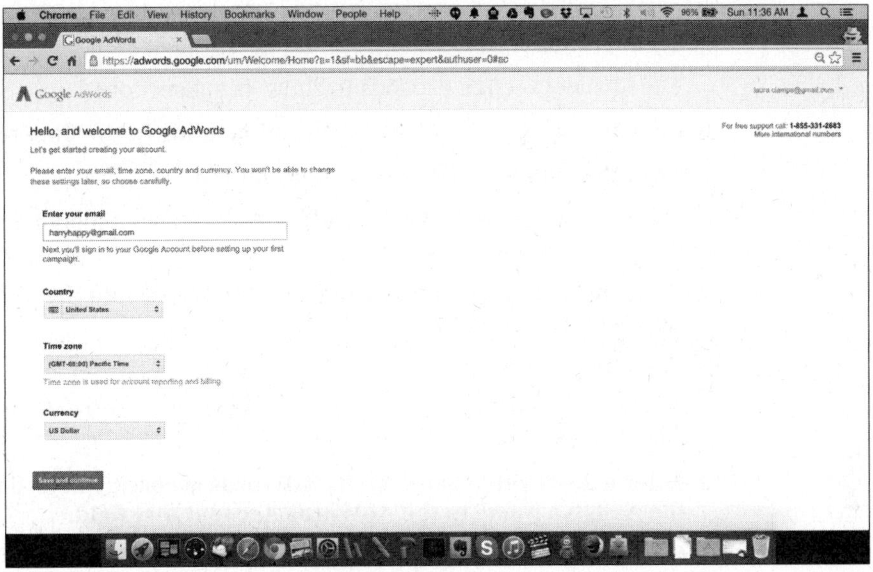

Figure 13-2:
Setting up
an AdWords
for Video
account.

Linking your AdWords account and YouTube channel

For your YouTube advertising project, you should link your AdWords account with your YouTube channel to access deeper ad analytics. A well-run YouTube ad campaign produces lots of views, subscriptions, engagements, and clicks. By linking your accounts, you have access to much deeper statistics.

To link your accounts, follow these steps:

1. **Log in to your AdWords account.**

2. **Copy your customer ID.**

   An AdWords customer ID is a three-part number that uniquely identifies your AdWords account. You'll find it in the top right corner of your AdWords page, right above your email address and to the left of the account settings icon.

3. **Log on to your YouTube account.**

4. **On your YouTube page, click your channel's icon and then choose Creator Studio from the menu that appears.**

   Doing so brings up the Creator Studio dashboard.

5. **In the Navigation menu on the left, click the Channel section of Creator Studio.**

   The Channel section expands to show its subsections.

6. **Click the (newly revealed) Advanced heading in the Channel section.**

7. **Click the Link an AdWords account button.**

   Doing so brings up the Link an AdWords for Video Account dialog box, as shown in Figure 13-3.

8. **Paste the customer ID that you copied in Step 2 into the dialog box's Customer ID text field.**

9. **Click the Next button.**

   A new dialog box with all the linkage details appears, as shown in Figure 13-4.

10. **Enter a descriptive name of the AdWords account you're linking into the Assign a Name to the AdWords Account text field.**

11. **Select the account permissions.**

    Linking your AdWords and YouTube accounts gives you access to additional capabilities. These include

    - *View counts and call-to-action,* which will provide you with more detailed information about video views and will let you add a clickable call-to-action button to your video ads.

    - *Remarket,* which will enable you to show your ad to viewers who previously visited your channel.

    - *Engagement,* which shows you what viewers do after seeing your ad

    We recommend checking all options as part of your initial campaigns.

12. **Click Finish.**

    Your AdWords account is now linked with your YouTube channel, and your permissions settings are saved.

You can unlink the AdWords account that you associated with your YouTube channel at any point, if you feel so inclined. Just remember that, by unlinking your accounts, you lose access to earned metrics, which measure the impact your advertising has had on important channel metrics such as views and subscriptions. You can find out more about earned metrics later in this chapter.

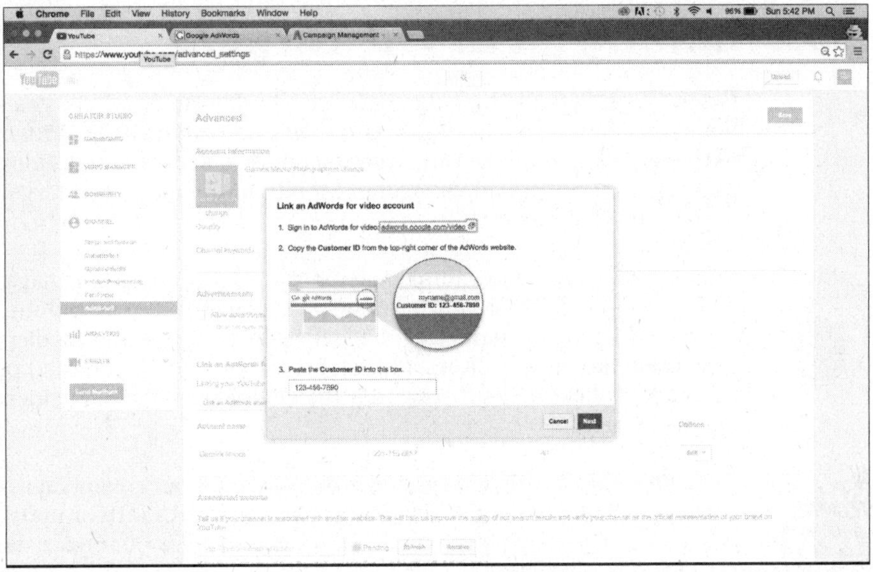

Figure 13-3:
Moving your
AdWords
customer
ID into
YouTube.

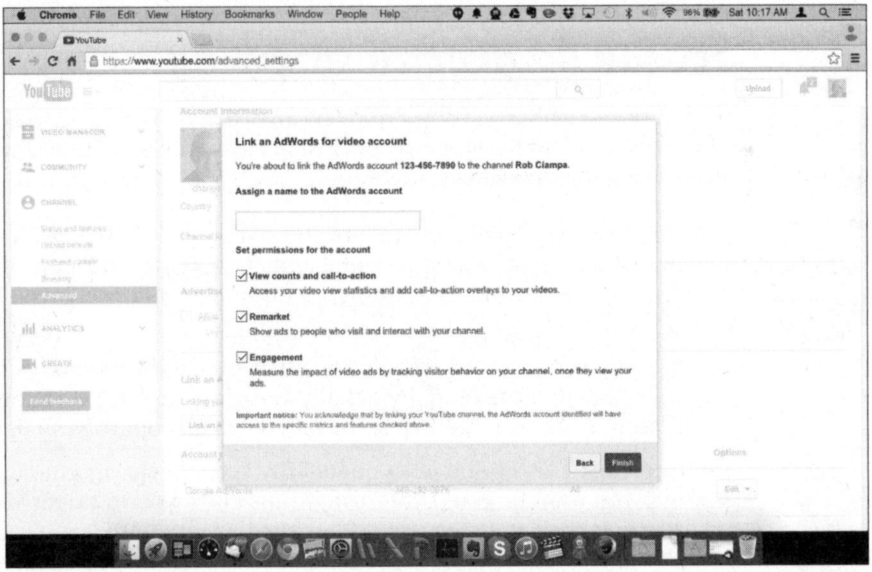

Figure 13-4:
Linking your
AdWords
account and
YouTube
channel.

Determining Your Ad Targets

Before starting your campaign, you have to determine where you want your ads placed. This is known as *ad targeting*. AdWords for Video provides extremely rich and powerful targeting options. Each set of options is known as a *targeting group,* and you can use multiple, simultaneous targeting groups in the same campaign.

Running a YouTube ad campaign isn't like placing an ad in a magazine or a commercial on television, where the ad is placed and you're done. Effective digital marketing — marketing that relies on YouTube and on display and search advertising — allows advertisers to constantly "tune" ad performance by making adjustments throughout the campaign, which may include changing the targets.

You can set up multiple targeting groups throughout a campaign, so don't try to be exhaustive out of the chute. You can even share or update target groups among campaigns, which allows you to streamline your campaign setup and management.

Setting up general targeting

To get started with YouTube TrueView advertising, you need to get a handle on the basics of ad targeting. Your default AdWords for Video setup lets you target using the following criteria:

- **Demographics:** This option lets you select your audience characteristics by age, gender, and parental status, as shown in Figure 13-5. Always choose the age and gender of your targeting audience, if you know it.

  YouTube does not let you target viewers under the age 18. You can, however, make some assumptions that parents with young children will share devices (and, by default, Google accounts) with their kids. (Parental status targeting isn't available in all countries.)

- **Interests:** This option lets you identify specific viewer characteristics that you want targeted. Interest groups allow you to target viewers who are interested in that topic even when they are not viewing content about that topic. Google determines viewers' interests by analyzing the type of videos they're watching and by the websites they're visiting.

- **Keywords:** This option lets you target videos that are relevant to the keywords you itemize. For example, if you have a video ad for your pottery product, *pottery* would then be a good keyword to add to your campaign.

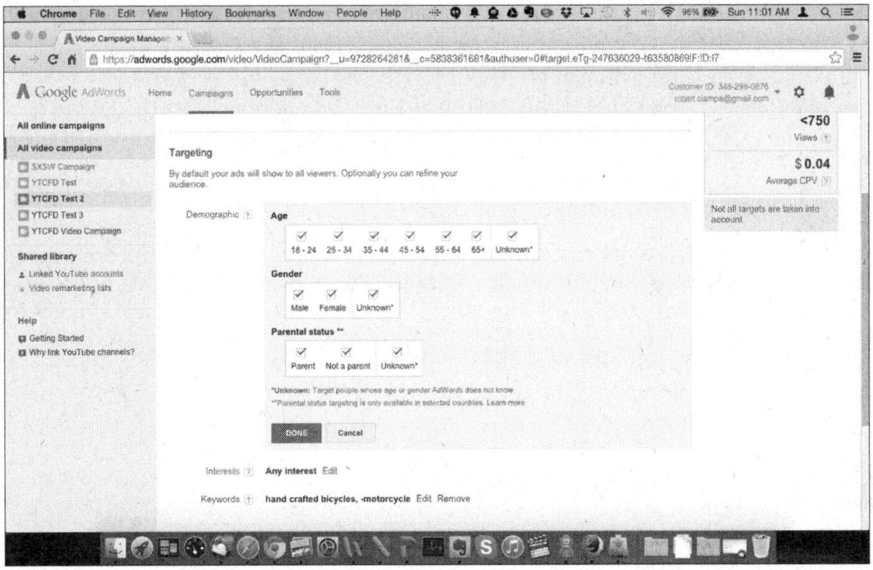

Figure 13-5:
Your
AdWords
for Video
demo-
graphic
targeting
options.

Start off with broad keywords, you can always add in more niche terms after testing. Keywords are used to deliver ads for both YouTube search and watch, along with the Google Display Network.

Adding a minus sign (–) in front a keyword ensures that your ad won't show against content that matches this keyword. If you don't want your audience to be reminded of the fact that pottery might break, you might enter –glue as a keyword to filter out any videos dealing with glue.

We're giving you the lay of the land right now when it comes to preparing for your YouTube ad campaign. As for the nuts and bolts of setting up a YouTube ad campaign, we cover that topic a bit later in this chapter (in the section that just happens to be entitled "Setting Up a YouTube Ad Campaign").

Configuring more narrow targeting

Even though general targeting may work for your campaign, you'll probably get better results by using more narrow targeting. AdWords for Video lets you get more detailed and select your targets by letting you focus on the following categories.

✔ **Topics:** You can target specific content on either YouTube or the GDN corresponding to the selected topic. When configuring topic-based targeting, you can go broadly, such as Home & Garden, or be more specific in the category by selecting Rugs & Carpets under the Home Furnishings subcategory. (Note that you can select different topics in the same group.)

Topic-based targeting applies only to *video* content on YouTube and the GDN, not to display ads.

✔ **Remarketing:** You can target viewers who have interacted with your channel, videos, or website. That means they have done one of the following:

- Viewed your content
- Looked at your ads
- Engaged with your videos
- Visited your channel
- Subscribed (or unsubscribed) from your channel

By linking your AdWords for Video and YouTube accounts, you can remarket to these viewers or visitors. You target with remarketing by creating a remarketing list, which you can find out about in the next section. You can use several different remarketing lists in the same advertising campaign.

Remarketing is just a fancy term for targeting users who have already interacted with you. Google and YouTube privacy rules prevent you from knowing who they specifically are, but that shouldn't prevent you from giving those remarketed viewers a more customized ad experience. For example, if viewers have watched a particular video, you can serve them a different video ad next, rather than the same one.

You can also remarket to viewers who have watched videos similar to the ones on your channel. This strategy significantly increases the reach of your ads.

AdWords for Video treats remarketing lists and interest groups together, so have an interest group set up if you're using remarketing.

✔ **Placements:** You can create a list of YouTube channels, specific videos, exact websites, or itemized pages in the GDN where you want your ad served. This is an excellent way to ensure that your content is appearing in the right places next to videos about specific topics. (Placements apply only to YouTube videos and to the GDN, not to YouTube Search.)

To access your more advanced targeting options, click on the Narrow Your Targeting (Optional) drop-down menu, as shown in Figure 13-6.

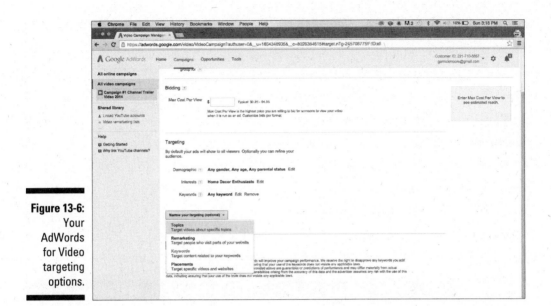

Figure 13-6:
Your
AdWords
for Video
targeting
options.

Navigating the AdWords for Video Page

AdWords for Video has a powerful interface that lets you set up and check the status of your campaigns. Using this single interface, you can look at the performance of all your campaigns (see Figure 13-7) or dive into a particular campaign.

Exploring the Campaign navigation menu

The Campaign navigation menu appears on the left side of the page (refer to Figure 13-7) and consists of these sections:

- ✔ **All online campaigns:** This one shows all your AdWords campaigns, including display campaigns.

- ✔ **All video campaigns:** This option limits the view to just your AdWords for Video campaigns. By default, you see all your video campaigns. If you want the details about a specific campaign, simply click on the campaign name.

- ✔ **Shared libraries:** Here you'll find a list of YouTube accounts and video remarketing lists. If you haven't linked your AdWords account with your YouTube account yet, you can start that process by selecting the Linked YouTube Accounts option. If your campaigns will include remarketing, you can set that up by clicking the Video Remarketing Lists option.

- ✔ **Help:** This option offers additional help for AdWords for video.

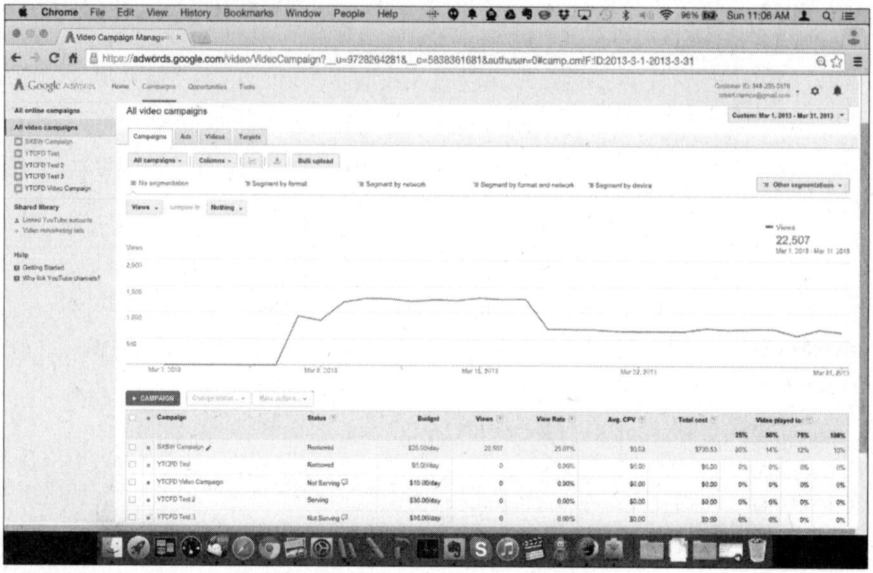

Figure 13-7:
The
Campaigns
tab for
all video
campaigns
in an
AdWords
account.

TIP

If you're familiar with the YouTube Analytics interface, you may see some similarities. For example, you can filter your results using the date pull-down in the top right corner, just as you would with YouTube Analytics.

Looking at your campaign details

If you've clicked on All Video Campaigns or on a specific campaign, you see some (or all) of the following tabs appear in the Details section in the main pane of the interface window:

- ✔ **Campaigns:** This tab shows up only when you choose All Video Campaigns. You use this tab to set up a campaign.

- ✔ **Ads:** This tab displays your actual ads. You can have multiple ads running in a campaign.

- ✔ **Videos:** This tab lists the videos that are used as your ads.

- ✔ **Targets:** This tab lists your targeting groups.

- ✔ **Settings:** This tab shows up only when you click a specific campaign; it details such areas as budget and scheduling.

TIP

If you have many more tabs showing than what we list here, you've likely clicked All Online Campaigns. Simply click All Video Campaigns in the Navigation menu on the left side to get to the right place.

Other important parts of the AdWords for Video interface include information around reporting, metrics, and ad performance. Key areas include

- **Details buttons:** These are found under the main tabs and allow you to

  - View specific campaign, ad, and targeting information

  - Control chart visibility

  - Upload campaign configuration data (for power users who enjoy using spreadsheets)

  - Download campaign reporting metrics to a spreadsheet

  Depending on which tabs or Details button you select, you may (or may not) see the following interface details.

- **Chart:** After you've determined what to analyze, you can get lots of information with some fairly flexible graphical representations of your campaign performance — your views, for example, cost per views, impressions, and more. (An Analytics Chart section is shown in Figure 13-8.)

- **Details section:** This section appears when you scroll down on the page. It shows itemized details that correspond to the campaign details, such as lists of campaigns that are running or stopped, ads, videos, and target groups.

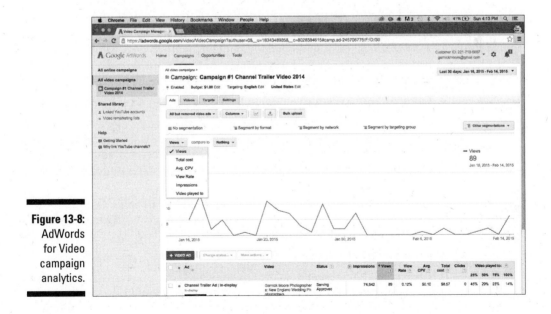

Figure 13-8: AdWords for Video campaign analytics.

Setting Up a YouTube Ad Campaign

So you've informed yourself about the costs and benefits of YouTube advertising and decided to give it a shot. We can only say, "Smart move." Now it's time to get your hands dirty and set up your first YouTube ad campaign.

Going with a general campaign

Unfortunately, no one has yet invented a robot that sets up YouTube video ads for you. The process might sound a bit complicated at first because AdWords for Video is quite powerful, but it's fairly easy to start your first campaign. To set up a new YouTube ad, follow these steps:

1. **Log in to** `https://adwords.google.com/video`.

   If you haven't created an AdWords account yet, do so by following the instructions in the "Creating an AdWords account" section, earlier in this chapter.

2. **Click the + Campaign button at the top of the Details section.**

   A Create New Video Campaign page appears onscreen.

3. **(Optional) Click the Load Settings button if you have an earlier campaign and you want to reuse some of its configuration data.**

   As you become more proficient in running campaigns, you can save time and automatically populate new campaign fields by reusing older content. You can also change the settings for the campaign even after you've autoloaded it.

4. **Enter a name for your campaign in the Campaign Name field.**

   Choose a relevant and informative name such as Acme Electric Z500 Product Launch as opposed to Campaign #1. If you have special targeting, add words such as *mobile* or *desktop* to the campaign name. This will make it easier to identify and manage these particular campaigns later in the list of all your campaigns.

   Don't rush through the naming process; you want to be as descriptive as possible. Trust us: You're sure to forget important campaign details even if you have only a few campaigns.

5. **Enter your daily budget in the Budget field.**

   This is the amount you're willing to spend per day on your ads. You can increase or decrease the budget at any time, so enter an amount that you feel comfortable to experiment with. Start with a small amount, such as $50, and increase it gradually as you start seeing the results you want.

6. **Pick your ad delivery method.**

   You set the rate at which your ads are served over the course of a day. Click Standard if you want them spread evenly over your ad day. Select Accelerated to deliver your ads rapidly.

   Your ad budget is daily. If you run an accelerated campaign and max out your daily budget, your ads stop for the day and start up again during the next day you're serving ads.

7. **Select your networks.**

   These are the types of places where your ads will appear.

   As a YouTube advertiser, you have three choices for where your ads are shown:

   1. *YouTube Search:* You get to post your TrueView ads in search queries. The only allowed ad type is TrueView in-display.

   2. *YouTube Videos:* You run either in-stream video ads against YouTube videos or in-display ads on the YouTube Watch page.

   3. *Google Display Network:* You have to also select the YouTube Video network option above. The GDN supports both in-stream and in-display ad formats.

8. **Pick your locations.**

   Don't let the simple interface fool you. You have the option to pick world-wide, United States, or Canada, but when you click Let Me Choose, you're presented with a powerful interface that lets you do precision location targeting of your ads, down to the city or area level. (To see how specific geo location targeting can get, check out Figure 13-9.) You can mix and match locations, but you also have the option to exclude certain areas.

   You can not only run ads on a specific region but also put together simultaneous campaigns with region-specific offers.

9. **Choose the language of the viewers who will see your ads.**

   This step ensures that your ad appears only in places where the language of the ad matches the language of the targeted audience — an important consideration when you're dealing with GDN targeting.

10. **(Optional) Enter the video ad you want to use.**

    If you already know which of your existing videos you want to use for your campaign, select it here. The easiest way is to copy the URL of your video (`https://www.youtube.com/watch?v=0XiC830EhHQ`, for example) and paste it into this field.

    Any video that you want to use for your ad campaign has to be previously uploaded to your YouTube channel. If you haven't done this yet or if you want to decide later which video to use, you can leave this field empty for now.

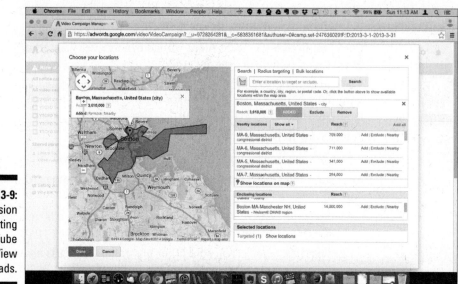

Figure 13-9:
Precision
targeting
for YouTube
TrueView
ads.

You can always enter a video later or add more than one video to an existing campaign. See the "Placing and Managing Your Ads" section, later in this chapter, for all the details on ad configuration.

11. Select the platform and carrier on which the ad can appear.

Your target audience may prefer one platform or carrier over another. AdWords for Video therefore lets you specify desktops, smartphones, or tablets as targets and choose to place ads only on specific mobile providers by country, such as AT&T, Verizon, or others in the United States.

12. Configure mobile bid adjustments.

Always strive to get the best mix of ads for your ad campaign. If you discover that mobile ads are your least successful ad type, you can use mobile bid adjustments to change the ratio of mobile ads all the way down to 0 percent so that none of your ads shows on mobile. (Just set your mobile bid adjustment to –100 percent.) If mobile ads end up being quite successful, you may want to adjust the bid +20 percent; this number allows your maximum bid to raise by 20 percent for mobile.

13. Schedule when your ad runs.

You get to pick when your ad campaign starts and ends, along with the days and times you want it to run. You can leave this option empty and manually start and end campaigns as needed.

Ad scheduling is helpful if you know when your viewers are watching and would likely see your ads. For example, if you're in the beauty or fashion business and you want to target women getting ready for work, you'd likely schedule your ads for weekday mornings. This strategy is especially helpful if you accelerate your ads; you don't want to burn up all your budget before your core target audience is even awake.

14. **Manage your ad delivery.**

   This step is advanced stuff, so you may want to leave the default settings for your initial campaign. Here's what's involved:

   • *Ad rotation:* This feature determines how often your ad is served in relation to the other video ads in the same campaign. Note that you can optimize for views or conversions; the default ad rotation optimizes for views. The best ads get more budget and views naturally with this default.

   If you want all your ads to get equal play, you can choose to rotate them evenly. This is one method that can be used to determine which videos hit your goals best upon campaign start without click-through and conversion rates impacting the results. However, if click-through or conversion rates are your primary goals, this option may not be the right one for you.

   • *Frequency capping:* This feature sets the average number of times a unique user will view your ad over a given period, unless the viewer sees your in-search ad on YouTube. In-search ads are not affected by frequency capping.

Selecting bidding and your target audience

After your general settings are in place, you need to determine who will get the ad and what you're willing to spend for each ad action.

With all types of TrueView ads, you pay only if the viewer *does* something, such as watch an in-stream ad or click on an in-display ad.

To specify the audience for targeting and establish the price for each ad action, take the following steps:

1. **In your Campaigns screen, click the Targets tab.**

2. **Click the + Targeting Group button.**

   A Create New Targeting Group page appears onscreen.

3. **Give the target group a name in the Name field.**

Choose a relevant and informative name such as Atlanta Area Acme Users as opposed to Targeting Group #1, as shown in Figure 13-10.

4. **Set the bidding amount.**

This is the maximum amount you're willing to pay each time a viewer watches your video or clicks on your display ad. A good amount to start with is 20 cents. You can optimize the amount later.

TrueView ads are sold on an auction basis. You are competing with other advertisers who want to reach a similar target audience and are willing to bid a certain amount per view. If your bid is too low, your ad won't get many views and you'll need to adjust your bid. If you leave a campaign running year-round, take seasonality into account and understand that you may need to raise your maximum bid to get enough views during high-volume ad buying seasons, like the beginning of December.

For in-display ads, you pay only if people click on an ad, not for the ad just showing up. In the case of in-stream ads, you're charged only when the viewer watches at least 30 seconds of your video ad. This *pay per view* method makes YouTube ads highly cost effective.

Click the Customize Bids per Format link in the Bidding section if you want to establish different bidding for in-stream versus in-display.

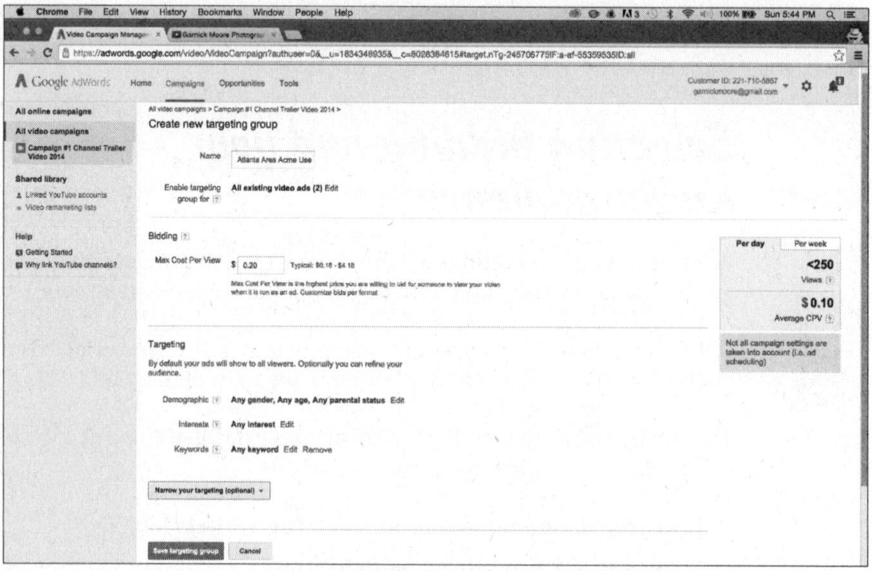

Figure 13-10:
Adding a
new target
group.

5. **In the Demographic section, click the Edit link and select the demographic groups you want to reach.**

   You can select any combination of age, gender and parental status by checking or unchecking the respective categories. When you're happy with your selection, click the Done button.

6. **In the Interests section, click the Edit link and choose the interest profiles that you want to reach.**

   Interest groups come in three flavors:

   - *Affinity audiences* are groups of viewers who are particularly enthusiastic about certain topics, such as fashion, comics, or home décor. If you're marketing to enthusiasts, this is your best bet.

   - *In-market audiences* are viewers who are currently shopping for a particular type of product. For example, you can reach viewers who are evaluating a new computer in the Computer & Peripherals category.

   - *Other audiences* groups viewers who are have demonstrated a general interest in certain topics. For example, people who occasionally visit websites about cars can be reached in the Autos & Vehicles category.

   Explore these categories using the + sign buttons in front of every category. You can drill down over several levels to find very specific interest groups that match your marketing goals, as shown in Figure 13-11. Click the Add link next to a group to add it to your targeting set. When you're done with your selection, click the Done button.

7. **If you want to refine your targeting even further, click the Narrow Your Targeting drop-down box and among between Topics, Remarketing, Keywords, and Placements.**

   We explain the purpose of these targeting types earlier in this chapter in the "Configure more narrow targeting" section. Each of these targeting types works in the same way: Click the Edit link to make modifications, then explore the list of options to find the ones that match your goals, then click the Add link to include them in your targeting. When you're happy with your selection, click the Done button.

8. **Click the Save Targeting Group button.**

   This will create your new targeting group. You will see it in the list of targeting groups on the Targets tab.

With the campaign and targets set up, you must now associate one or more ads with the campaign. You can find out how to do that in later sections, but first we take care of one last side issue — your remarketing list.

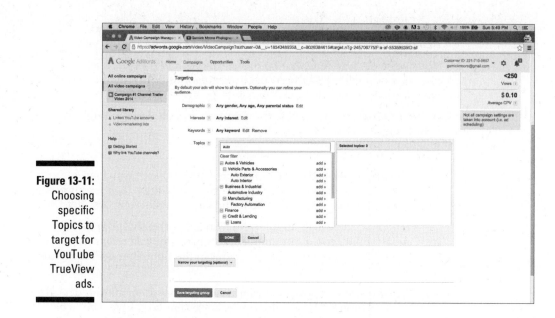

Figure 13-11:
Choosing
specific
Topics to
target for
YouTube
TrueView
ads.

Sharing your remarketing list

Remarketing is all about targeting viewers who have already interacted with your channel, videos, or website, by either viewing your content, seeing your ads, visiting your channel, or subscribing to your channel. You can set up remarketing when you build an individual campaign, or you can set it up separately so that your remarketing lists can be shared among different campaigns. If you want to share remarketing lists, follow these steps:

1. **Log in to** `https://adwords.google.com/video`.

   The home page for Google AdWords for Video appears.

2. **On the Navigation menu on the left, click Video Remarketing Lists under the Shared Library heading.**

   This step brings up the Video Remarketing page.

3. **Click the red + Remarketing List button.**

   You see the Create Remarketing List dialog box.

4. **Select the remarketing items you want to use from the dialog box's List Type drop-down menu.**

   The List Type drop-down menu (see Figure 13-12) shows all actions a viewer could have made in order to make them eligible for retargeting options. Select the most relevant actions for this particular remarketing list.

5. **Click the Create List button.**

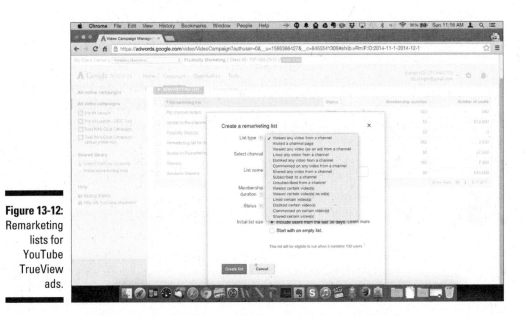

TIP

You can also remarket to viewers who have watched content similar to yours — just select that option in the Details section of the Video Remarketing page. (Note that YouTube decides what content is "similar" — you have to take its choice or leave it.)

You can find more in-depth details about remarketing with YouTube by making your way to `https://support.google.com/adwords`.

Placing and Managing Your Ads

Lots of people set up their video and display ads when they configure their general campaign settings. Just remember that you can also add ads to an existing campaign. No matter where you are in your ad campaign, here's how to get that scintillating ad of yours in front of your viewers:

1. **Log in to** `https://adwords.google.com/video`.

   The home page for Google AdWords for Video appears.

2. **Click the name of the campaign you want to work with.**

   It should be listed under the All Video Campaigns section of the Navigation menu on the left side of the page.

3. **Click the red + Video Ad button in the Campaign Details section of the AdWords page.**

   Doing so opens a Create New Ad page.

4. **Paste the YouTube video URL of your ad into the Your Video field.**

   The video has to be uploaded to your YouTube channel before you do this. Videos that are to be used as ads need to be either public or unlisted. Check Chapter 9 for details on how to upload a video.

   As soon as you paste a correct video URL, you will see your video with its thumbnail picture, and several additional options will appear.

   Your YouTube ad might be the first thing that people see about your company, so use a video that is short, catchy, and to the point.

5. **Select the ad format you want to use.**

   Select or deselect the check boxes in from of the In-stream and In-display formats, depending on which one you want to use for this ad. It's best to use only one format per ad because it gives you the best control over your bidding and targeting strategy. If you want to use the same video in different formats, create separate video ads for each.

6. **If you've chosen an in-stream ad, use the In-stream section of the new page that appears to configure your in-stream ad.**

   Figure 13-13 shows you the in-stream configuration options of the ad creation page. (Note that you have an input panel and preview pane that shows what your ad will look like for both types of TrueView ads — in-stream and in-display.)

   Here's a rundown of the in-stream settings:

   • *Display URL:* This is the website link that is shown on your video ad.

     This isn't the destination that the user goes to when the ad is clicked, so keep this one short, sweet, and informative. Viewers need some sense of where they'll end up, so be sure to get that information across.

   • *Destination URL:* This is the actual web location where viewers end up after they click.

     Do not indulge in bait-and-switch tactics. Always send viewers to a web page that clearly has something to do with the ad. If you try to trick your viewers, you'll only end up wasting your ad budget and alienating viewers who may be interested in your channel, product, or services.

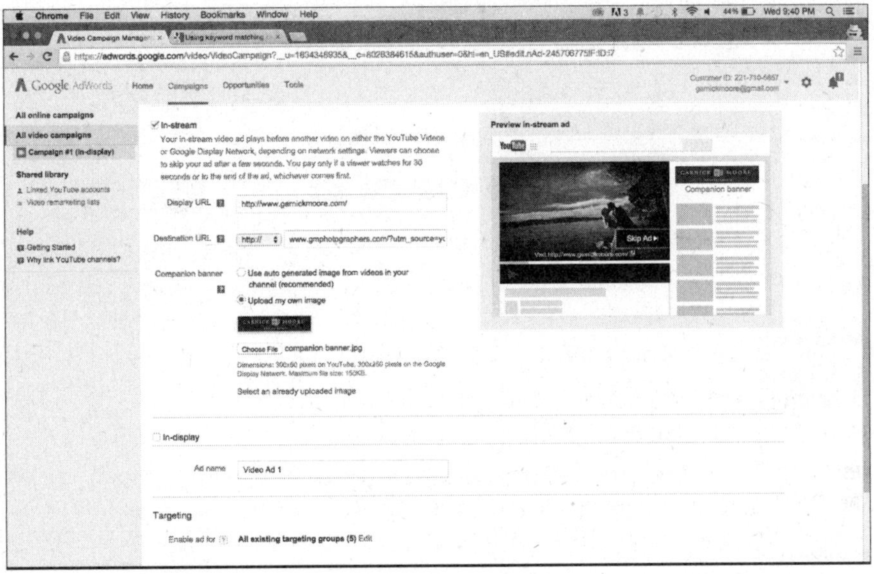

Figure 13-13:
YouTube
TrueView
in-stream ad
configura-
tion.

- *Companion banner:* This is a 300 x 60 pixel companion banner for YouTube display or a 300 x 250 pixel companion banner for the GDN. The companion banner should have a strong call to action so that viewers are more likely to click. Note that the companion banner is the only element that remains up after your video ad has finished playing or has been skipped by the user. We recommend the YouTube default banner if you have a several videos on your channel or if you are looking to gain subscribers with your ad. It gives the viewer three options: Subscribe, watch more content, or visit your destination URL.

7. **If you've chosen an in-display ad, take the following steps to configure your in-display ad:**

    a. *Write the ad text.* This short bit of text appears next to the video thumbnail in your ads. (See Figure 13-14.) You get one headline with a maximum length of 25 characters and two lines of description text with 35 characters apiece.

    Attach a catchy title, and be sure to tell people why they should watch this video. You can test ad copy by creating multiple versions of the in-display ad.

    b. *Choose the thumbnail picture that you want to use.* YouTube gives you only four predefined options. See the "Thumbnails" section in Chapter 9 for tips on how to select an effective one.

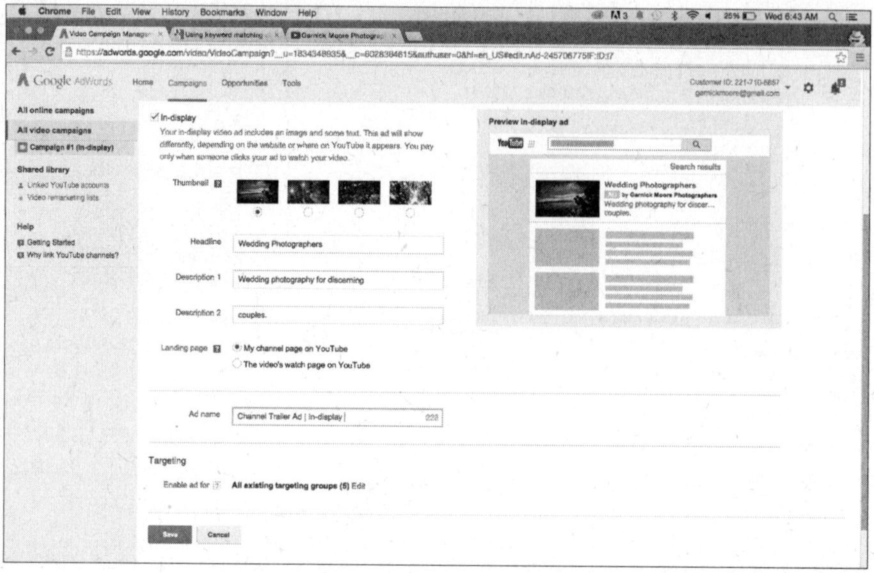

Figure 13-14:
YouTube
TrueView
in-display
ad con-
figuration.

c. *Enter your website address in the Display URL field.* This is the web address that appears in the ad for viewers to see.

d. *If you want to direct viewers to a particular page other than your website's home page, enter a web address in the Destination URL field.* For example, you could use a landing page that promotes a specific product. When users click on your video ad, they're sent to this page.

8. Enter the ad name.

Use a descriptive name that makes it easy for you to find the ad later.

9. Select the targeting groups for the ad.

By default, all existing targeting groups are selected.

You can set up multiple targeting groups for your ads to optimize the results. For example, you can set up one target group only for search keywords, another one for topics, and a third one for specific channel placements. To add a targeting group, go to https://adwords.google.com/video, select the campaign you want to change, and click the Target tab. Then click the New Targeting Group button and follow the steps in the "Selecting bidding and your target audience" section, earlier in this chapter.

10. Click Save.

11. **If this is the first time you've bought ads on Google or YouTube, you're asked for your billing information.**

Follow the simple process on the screen to provide your credit card information.

You're billed for your AdWords account only after you start your ad campaign.

12. **Verify the status of your ad.**

If your money's good, you should see your new ad listed in the Details section of the AdWords for Video home page. Looking at the Status category, you should see the text *Not yet serving/Under review.* That's a good sign. It's proof that your ad is complete — you just need to wait on final approval from Google. Usually, that takes no more than 24 hours. If it's taking any longer, call AdWords Google support at 866-246-6453 to see whether there's a problem.

Be sure to check out how your ads are performing after your ads are approved by Google. (You can find out more on how you can actually do that in the next section.) Monitor your campaigns regularly to find the most effective videos, targeting groups, and ads. Always test different versions of your ads, and make changes, if necessary.

If you need to modify an ad name or ad copy after the ad has been saved, you lose all the performance data associated with that ad. Click the little arrow next to the title of the ad in the Details section to make any edits. (If you want to keep your performance data, we recommend duplicating the ad and then making changes to the new version of the ad.)

You can always pause an ad campaign from the All Video Campaigns view by highlighting the check box next to the campaign name and clicking the Change Status drop-down menu so that it shows Paused. We recommend that you never remove an ad because you can't get it back in case you change your mind.

Measuring Clicks and Results

Tracking the success of your campaign regularly is essential. If you don't pay attention, you may be spending ad dollars for ineffective views, or you might miss out on interesting opportunities to reach your audience. Fortunately, the YouTube ad management tool gives you all the important numbers you need in order to manage your campaign.

When you analyze your campaign results, it's important to understand the following distinction:

- ✓ **Paid metrics:** These represent the direct results of your ads, such as ad views and the average cost per view.

- ✓ **Earned metrics:** Think of these as the follow-on activities that occur as a result of your ads, including new subscribers and additional channel views.

Both sets of metrics are important to advertisers and YouTube channel managers because they tell them whether their ad money is being spent effectively.

You're charged for paid metrics, not for earned metrics. If your video ad results in a viewer going to your channel and watching ten more videos, you paid for 1 view and received 10 for free. In other words, that's 11 views for the price of 1.

Looking at campaign information

The YouTube ad management tool is your friend. To gain the full benefit of this friendship, you need to visit (you guessed it) `https://adwords.google.com/video` and click the All Video Campaigns link to see the most important performance numbers. You also see the details for every video campaign.

These are your *paid metrics*. This list describes what the numbers mean:

- ✓ **Impressions:** These figures represent how many times your ad was shown to a user (irrespective of whether the user clicked on it). *Thumb* impressions refer to the little picture-and-text in-display ads in search results and next to videos, whereas *Video* impressions count how many times your video was shown as an in-stream ad just before another video.

- ✓ **Views:** This number shows how many views your videos got by way of paid ads. For in-display ads, a view is counted when a viewer clicks on an ad and starts watching the video. For in-stream ads, a view means the user watched at least 30 seconds of the ad (or the whole ad if it's shorter).

- ✓ **View rate:** This represents the percentage of people who saw your ad and either clicked on it (for in-display) or chose not to skip it (for in-stream). Don't be disappointed if this number seems low. Typical rates are well under 1 percent for in-display and around 15-20 percent for in-stream ads. The higher the number, the more effective your ad.

> ✓ **Average cost per view (CPV):** This figure tells you how much you spent for one person to watch your video. This value can differ depending on the topic and the amount of competition you face, but ranges between 4 cents and 40 cents are typical.
>
> ✓ **Total cost:** This is the total amount you spent on all your YouTube ads.

Successful campaigns have a high view rate and a low CPV. But what the numbers should be depends strongly on your industry. Some industries, such as financial services, are highly competitive in their online marketing efforts, so expect a high CPV amount. In other industries, you may be able to draw viewers for only a few cents a pop.

Watch how your campaign performs over time. When the view rate value drops and your CPV rises, it's time to optimize.

Getting earned metrics

The great part about YouTube advertising is that it can lead to increased viewer activity with your channel. These are *earned metrics,* and they include:

> ✓ **Earned views:** The number of new video views that occur within seven days from viewers who've seen an ad from your channel
>
> ✓ **Earned subscribers:** The number of new subscriptions that occur within seven days from unsubscribed viewers who've seen an ad from your channel
>
> ✓ **Earned playlist additions:** The number of playlist additions that occur within seven days from viewers who've seen an ad from your channel
>
> ✓ **Earned likes:** The number of video likes that occur within seven days from viewers who've seen an ad from your channel
>
> ✓ **Earned shares:** The number of video shares that occur within seven days from viewers who've seen an ad from your channel

Earned metrics are not displayed by default, so you have to set them up through AdWords for Video:

1. **Log in to your AdWords for Video account.**

   The home page for Google AdWords for Video appears.

2. **Click All Video Campaigns in the Navigation menu on the left.**

3. **Click the Campaigns tab.**

4. **Click the Columns button and select Customize Columns from the menu that appears.**

   You're presented with a Customized Columns configurator, like the one shown in Figure 13-15.

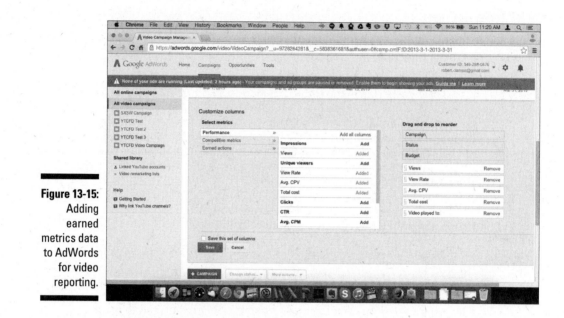

Figure 13-15:
Adding
earned
metrics data
to AdWords
for video
reporting.

5. **Click Earned Actions.**

6. **Select each of the earned metrics you want to add by clicking the Add link next to each earned metric.**

7. **Click the Save button.**

   You now have full access to your earned campaign metrics.

This technique can be used for customizing all reporting, including adding and removing other paid metrics as well as competitive metrics around impressions.

Optimizing Your Campaign

Because you pay for every click on your YouTube ads, you must choose highly effective keywords and placements for your campaign. When you initially create your campaign, you make certain assumptions about which targets will deliver results. Some assumptions may turn out to be wrong, and you may want to try other options over time.

Fortunately, YouTube offers a powerful way to manage targets for every video ad. Follow this step-by-step approach:

1. **Log in to your AdWords for Video account.**

   The home page for Google AdWords for Video appears.

2. **Click All Video Campaigns in the Navigation menu on the left.**

3. **Click on the campaign you want to optimize, and then click the Segment by Targeting Group link.**

4. **Look at the campaign details.**

   You see the number of views you've received and the amount of money you've spent for each ad. Below these numbers, you see a list of the targeting groups that have contributed to these results.

5. **Review the list of targeting groups to determine which ones are effective.**

   The most important number is the *cost per view,* or *CPV* — the amount you pay for every viewer who sees your video because of that particular keyword. Low CPVs are attractive, but sometimes you may want to spend more on targeted keywords.

6. **To optimize a targeting group, click the Targets tag and then click the name of the targeting group you want to change.**

7. **Click on each category link under the Targeting heading to look at the details of how your keywords and placements perform.**

   You can look at detailed information for YouTube search keywords, display network keywords, topics, and placements.

8. **Remove the nonperforming keywords and placements by clicking the green button next to them and selecting Paused from the menu that appears.**

   Pause keywords and placements, rather than delete them, because the performance information for paused targets is retained by the system.

9. **If you have ideas for additional keywords, click the Add Keywords button or Add Placements button to add them.**

   If you aren't drawing enough views, consider increasing your bid on the targets that you particularly like. Click the Targets tab and then the Edit link next to the name of the targeting group you want to change. Increase the value of maximum CPV and click the Save and Enable Targeting button.

Creating a Call-to-Action Overlay

After you draw viewers to your video, you want them to then take action — by coming to your website, for example, or by signing up for your newsletter or even buying your product online.

YouTube advertisers use an attractive feature that lets you place a call-to-action message on top of your videos. This call-to-action overlay consists of a small picture, three lines of text, and a link to your website, and it starts up immediately when your video plays.

It's an effective way to draw YouTube viewers to visit your site.

Follow these steps to create a call-to-action overlay:

1. **Log in to your YouTube account.**

2. **On your YouTube page, click your channel's icon and then choose Creator Studio from the menu that appears.**

   Doing so brings up the Creator Studio dashboard.

3. **Click the Video Manger heading in the Navigation menu on the left.**

4. **Click Video under the Video Manager heading.**

   Doing so brings up the Video page.

5. **Find the video you're using for advertising and click the Edit button.**

   If your video is public, you see a call-to-action overlay link under the video on the same level as Basic Info and Advanced Settings.

6. **Click the Call-to-Action Overlay link.**

   You're prompted for overlay information, as shown in Figure 13-16.

7. **Add a headline and two lines of description text for your overlay.**

   This should be a strong call to action that entices people to click on it.

   Special offers always work well.

8. **Enter the display URL and the destination URL that you want to use.**

   The display URL is the web address that people see in the overlay (www.acmeelectric.com, for example). The destination URL is the link to the page that opens when someone clicks on the overlay. It can be a product-specific page, as in this example:

   ```
   www.acmeelectric.com/products/z500.
   ```

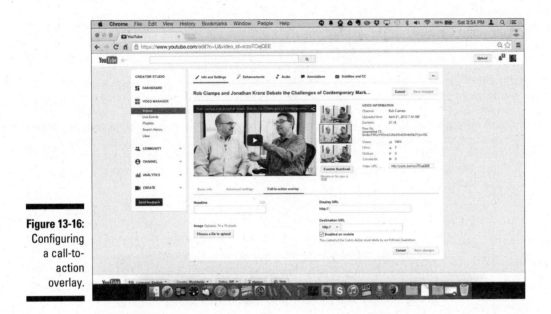

Figure 13-16:
Configuring
a call-to-
action
overlay.

9. **(Optional) Click the Choose a File to Upload button to upload a picture file from your computer.**

   The image has to be in a format of 74 x 74 pixels.

10. **Click the Save Changes button.**

    The overlay should become active almost immediately. Play your video to verify it.

Google Preferred

In 2014, YouTube announced the premium advertising platform Google Preferred, an in-stream advertising format that allows advertising to target the top 1 percent and the top 5 percent of the most popular content on YouTube. The figure below shows popular Google Preferred channels for technology. The lineup changes regularly.

Google Preferred is targeted at big-brand spenders and has a premium price that Google will discuss with you privately. As an advertiser, don't despair if you can't buy the top 1 percent or 5 percent of YouTube. The other 95 percent of content on YouTube may actually be better suited for your channel objectives — and your budget.

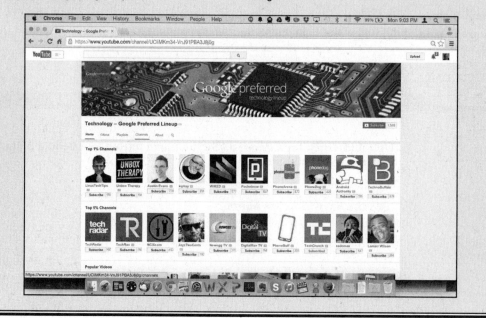

Chapter 14

Mining the YouTube Goldmine

. . . .

. . . .

*I*f you have a great channel with fabulous content and you excel at social media and community interaction, you have a good shot at making some money from your all your hard YouTube work. In YouTube and digital advertising lingo, this is *monetization*. If you've already read Chapter 13, you know all about how advertisers pay for YouTube advertising. You've probably figured out that the advertising money has to go somewhere. It does — into the hands of Google, your partners, and you: the channel manager/publisher/creator.

You can make money from your YouTube work in many ways, too:

✔ **Create a paid channel.** Charge users to view some or all of the content on your channel.

✔ **Monetize your video content.** Allow ads to be placed against your content.

✔ **Join a multichannel network.** Become part of a MCN. (For more on MCNs, see Bonus Chapter 2.)

✔ **Sell products.** Use your YouTube content to help your viewers make a decision about your products or services.

✔ **Get an endorsement deal.** Sponsorship deals work when they're made without too much over-the-top promotion.

You can read about monetization in this chapter, and you may already have the basic info about MCNs and selling products from previous chapters.

Completing the last item in the preceding list means that you've hit the big-time if you're getting six-figure deals to promote products.

Nothing prevents you from combining some of these various monetization approaches. MCNs are the exception, so you have to speak with your MCN managers and lawyers about the rules around monetization.

Be patient on your monetization journey, though. If you focus on the basics of building your channel with content, discoverability, subscribers, and engagement, the ad revenue you receive will grow in kind. Your YouTube earnings will come from multiple sources, including:

✔ The Google Display Network (GDN)

✔ AdSense auctions

✔ Reservation buys (those nonclickable ads)

✔ YouTube

Don't waste your time trying to conjure up a viral video that you hope to monetize. Instead, focus on slow and steady channel growth.

Your first step to income involves tying together all the AdSense and YouTube plumbing. You can find out more about these topics in the remainder of this chapter.

Integrating AdSense

AdWords for Video is *the* way for advertisers to target YouTube and the Google Display network for ad placements. (For more on AdWords for Video, check out Chapter 13.) Publishers and creators can control what types of ads are shown against their content.

Content owners often take a great deal of pride in the content they produce, so it only makes sense that the ads conform to their brands and ensure a good overall experience for their viewers.

Google AdSense is how web content creators and YouTube channel managers control ads and get paid by advertisers who place ads against their YouTube content and websites. Like AdWords for Video, AdSense is a huge topic — we don't have room to cover every nook and cranny in this chapter, but we can give you a sense of what's necessary to get you started with YouTube monetization. AdSense, like all Google products, evolves regularly. To stay current, check out https://support.google.com/adsense.

Setting up YouTube monetization

Before you start seeing any money in your bank account, you need to set up your channel for monetization. Here's how it's done:

1. **Log on to your YouTube account.**

2. **On your YouTube page, click your channel's icon and then choose Creator Studio from the menu that appears.**

   Doing so brings up the Creator Studio dashboard.

3. **Click the Channel section in the Navigation menu on the left.**

   If you see a Monetization link under the Status and Features link in the Channel section right under the Status and Features link, your channel is already set up for monetization and you can proceed to the next section, "Linking your channel with AdSense." If you don't see a Monetization link, continue with Step 4.

4. **Select Status and Features from the Channel section of Navigation menu on the left.**

   Doing so brings up a page similar to the one shown in Figure 14-1.

5. **In the Features section of the page, click the Enable button under the Status column.**

   A page about the YouTube partner program opens.

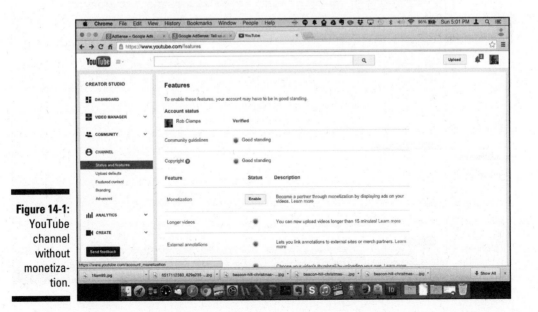

Figure 14-1: YouTube channel without monetization.

6. Click the Enable My Account button.

You see a dialog box with lots of legal info about terms and conditions, honesty, and rights.

7. If you (or your lawyer) agree with the terms, select all three agreement boxes and click the I Accept button.

You then see another dialog box that lets you select the ad formats you're willing to associate with your video content, such as overlay and TrueView in-stream. (For more on ad formats, check out Chapter 13.)

All display ad types are preconfigured, and none of them can be changed.

8. Select the ad formats to allow and then click Monetize.

You see the confirmation dialog box.

9. Click the Got It button.

You're brought to the Videos page of the Video Manager.

10. Select the video you want to monetize by clicking the $ button on the row with the video.

If you were to click on Channel in the Navigation menu, you'd see a new Monetization link on the Navigation menu. If you selected Status and Features from the Navigation menu, you see a green radio button next to Monetization, under Status. Your channel should now look like the one shown in Figure 14-2.

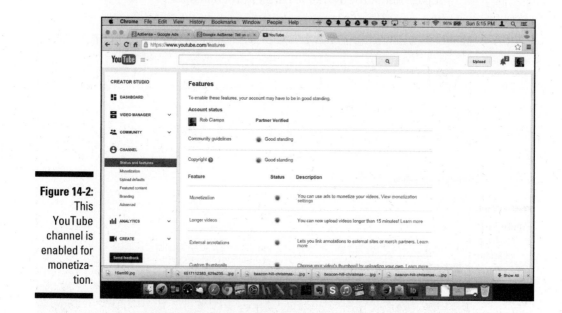

Figure 14-2:
This YouTube channel is enabled for monetization.

With monetization now in place, you can set specific ad controls for you videos. Details are shown in the section, "Making Monetization Adjustments." Before that, you'll have a few more housekeeping tasks that we discuss in the following sections.

Linking your channel with AdSense

To collect payment and control the types of ads shown on your YouTube channel, you need to link an AdSense account to that channel. If you already have an AdSense account, you can simply link that account. If don't already have an AdSense account, the following steps can help you do that. Either way, begin with the following steps:

1. **Log in to your YouTube account.**

2. **On your YouTube page, click the channel icon and then choose Creator Studio from the menu that appears.**

   Doing so brings up the Creator Studio dashboard.

3. **Click the Channel heading in the Navigation menu on the left.**

4. **Select Monetization under the Channel heading**

   You see the Monetization Account status page.

   You can also disable monetization at any point by clicking the Disable Monetization button.

5. **Click the How Will I Be Paid? link.**

   Doing so brings up more information about AdSense.

6. **Click the Associate an AdSense Account link.**

   You're brought to the Monetization screen.

7. **Click the Next button.**

   You're redirected to a YouTube and Google AdSense setup page. If you already have an AdSense account, log in to complete the association. If you need to set up an AdSense account, follow the directions in the next section.

Creating your AdSense account for YouTube

If you're in the process of linking your YouTube and Google AdSense accounts and you need to set up a brand-spanking new AdSense account, here's what you need to do. From the AdSense setup page, follow these steps:

1. **If you're coming here from the previous section, you should be on the AdSense setup page. If not, enter** `https://www.youtube.com/account_monetization?action_ adsense_connection` **into your web browser and click Next to go to AdSense setup.**

   You'll be presented with a page like the one shown in Figure 14-3.

   If you're creating an AdSense account for the first time and it's associated with your YouTube channel, then you need to sign up for AdSense through YouTube, not directly through AdSense. Notice both the YouTube and AdSense logos at the top of Figure 14-3 — that's the sign you're in the right place. If you only see the AdSense logo, then you'll be given a warning to sign up for AdSense through YouTube.

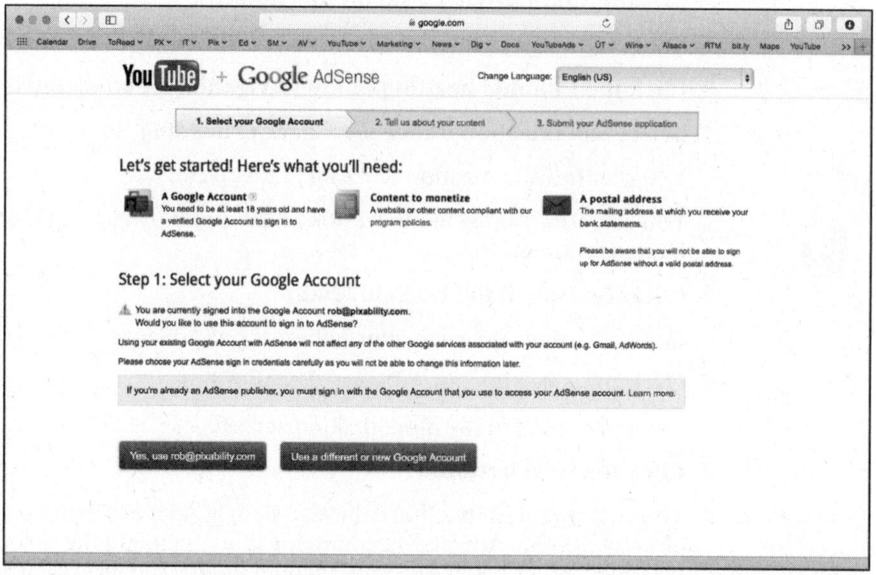

Figure 14-3:
Setting up
AdSense
through
YouTube.

2. **From the AdSense setup page, select the Google account that you want to associate with AdSense by clicking the blue button on the bottom left that either shows your account or asks you to sign in.**

   If you're just starting out, it's easier to use the same Google account for YouTube, AdSense, AdWords, Gmail, Google+, and other Google properties.

3. **Verify that your YouTube channel is listed and pick the content language using the Content language drop-down menu.**

   You should see your channel listed right next to the line that says "I will show ads on," as in Figure 14-4. The Content Language drop-down should be right below it.

4. **Click the Continue button.**

   You see the AdSense application screen.

5. **Fill out the AdSense application and click the Submit My Application button.**

You're redirected to your YouTube channel.

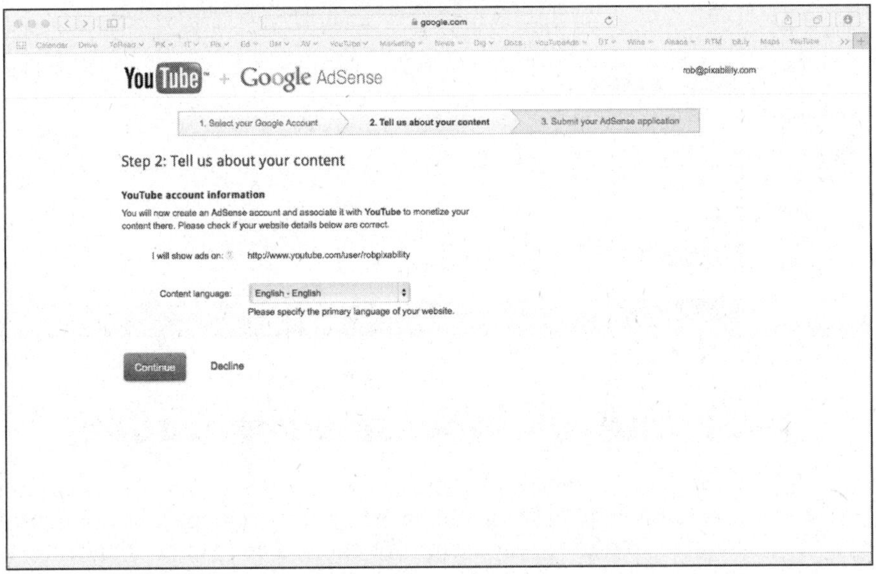

Figure 14-4:
Verifying your YouTube channel for AdSense.

Your application needs to be reviewed by Google; you should hear back about your approval within a week.

After being approved, you'll receive an email from Google directing you to accept its terms of service. (Whenever money is involved, so is lots of paperwork.) With your AdSense account approved, your Monetization page under Creator Studio should look like the one shown in Figure 14-5. If necessary, you can change or remove the direct association between your YouTube channel and your AdSense account.

When you set up your AdSense account through YouTube, it's known as an *AdSense-hosted* account. If you want to incorporate AdSense into your website, you have to upgrade the account, which is pretty straightforward. If you already have an AdSense account that predates your YouTube integration, no conversion or upgrade is necessary; you can just use the older account.

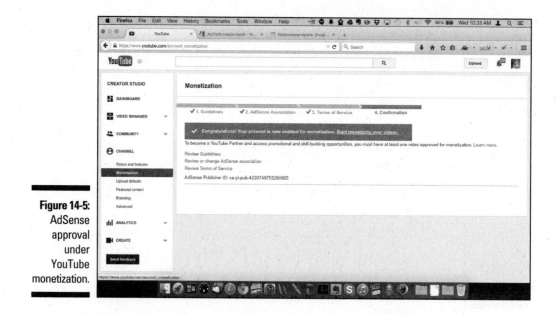

Figure 14-5:
AdSense
approval
under
YouTube
monetization.

Setting up AdSense monetization

Linking your (approved) AdSense account to your YouTube account is a great first step, but you still have to jump through some configuration hoops in order to begin monetizing your channel and your video content. Here's what you still need to do:

1. **Log on to your AdSense account at** `http://adsense.google.com`.

2. **Click the gear icon to the right of the Google account name.**

3. **Choose Settings from the menu that appears.**

   Doing so brings up the AdSense Personal Settings page, where you set up contact information, email preferences, and default language.

4. **After specifying your contact information, email preferences, and default language, click the Save button.**

5. **From the gear icon drop-down menu, select Status and verify that your account has no policy violations.**

   Many of the policy violations are centered on what are referred to as *artificial clicks*. Remember that the publisher gets paid whenever someone legitimately clicks on an ad. Clicking on your own ads or encouraging others to do so fraudulently doesn't result in legitimate clicks — they're fake (artificial) clicks. Artificial clicks are a no-no.

   Be sure to address policy violations promptly; if your channel is considered to be in violation of AdSense policy, all ads will be disabled and any monetization that you may have enabled will be stopped. Instructions and advice on AdSense policy violations can be found at `http://productforums.google.com/d/forum/adsense`.

6. **From the gear icon drop-down menu, select Payments.**

   Doing so brings up the Payments screen, which you use to handle all payment setup and reporting.

   The Payments screen is an important administration section for channel managers, creators, and publishers. It consists of three parts:

   - *Payment history:* This section shows your monthly transactions, which consist of costs, earnings, payments, adjustments, and taxes. You can pick the reporting period and export the data, if necessary.

   - *Payee profile:* This section includes a special billing ID, tax reporting details, and billing contacts.

   - *Payment settings:* Here's where you set up your payment schedule and configure your payment method, including banking information.

     You can easily change any of the payment information if you choose to do so later.

Not everything is monetizable

If you're at all familiar with the ways of YouTube, you probably have already figured out that you can't just grab a copy of Korean entertainment artist Psy's "Gangnam Style" video, modify it slightly, and put it on your channel. Sure, everyone would love a few billion monetized views, but in the end it all comes down to content ownership and copyright. To monetize anything, you need to own the rights to both the audio and visual components of the content. You also have to be careful about some of the visual elements, such as logos and other graphics, which may also be protected by the rights holders.

(continued)

(continued)

YouTube keeps tabs on copyrighted content with a feature it calls ContentID, a database of files that YouTube uses to compare copyrighted content against new content being uploaded to the site. ContentID can be used to make claims against your content, which may affect your ability to monetize. Note that with ContentID, the rights holder may choose to monetize *your* content

Copyright is a tricky topic, and you can read more about it in Chapter 16. You can also check out `https://support.google.com` to find out more about the partner program and monetization. When in doubt, consult with a lawyer or watch a YouTube video on the subject, assuming that it's not blocked by copyright, of course.

Analyzing Ad Performance with YouTube Analytics

You may have figured out already that Google rewards you with more interesting data when you link various accounts. You may have seen it with Google+ for YouTube channel management and with AdWords for YouTube advertising. Well, making money on YouTube is no different. When you link your AdSense account with your YouTube channel, you get more detailed information about your earnings. The good part is that you can get lots of this information directly from YouTube Analytics.

YouTube Analytics is your go-to resource when you want to find out how your channel is performing with your audience. Chapter 11 gives you the whole YouTube Analytics story; this chapter concentrates on how YouTube Analytics can help you figure out your ad and earnings performances.

Getting your YouTube ad information

In YouTube Analytics, you'll find a section called Earnings Reports, a vital resource for channel managers responsible for monetization. Within the Earning Reports section are two important reports:

- ✔ **Estimated Earnings:** Includes the details about your earnings and which of your video is making you the most money.

- ✔ **Ad Performance:** Shows which ad types are most effective for driving revenue on your channel.

To get to the reports for your channel:

1. **Log on to your YouTube account.**

2. **On your YouTube page, click your channel's icon and then choose Creator Studio from the menu that appears.**

    Doing so brings up the Creator Studio dashboard.

3. **Click the Analytics heading in the Navigation menu on the left.**

    By default, you should go directly to the Overview submenu.

4. **Under the Earnings Reports heading in the navigation menu on the left, click on either the Estimated Earnings link or the Ad Performance link.**

Seeing which metrics are offered

YouTube Analytics is a truly robust feature. Looking at only the Ad Performance report, check out all the attributes you can measure:

- ✔ **Impressions:** The number of times an ad is presented to a viewer.

    There can be multiple impressions per playback. If a viewer is served a TrueView instream pre-roll ad, a display ad, and an in-video overlay, it counts as three impressions, not one.

- ✔ **Estimated monetized playbacks:** A single playback occurs when your video is shown and one or more ads are presented. A playback also occurs whenever a viewer quits an in-stream ad.

- ✔ **Playback-based CPM:** This is the average gross revenue per thousand video playbacks (*cost per mille* in ad lingo) on which an ad was shown.

- ✔ **Playback-based gross revenue:** This is the *total* gross revenue for all ads that are placed against a video before any of the ad revenue is shared with YouTube and other partners. Remember that multiple ads may be shown against your video during a single viewing.

    Revenue is different from earnings. Earnings remain after YouTube and other partners take their cut.

From the Estimated Earnings report, you find the following metrics:

- ✔ **Total estimated earnings:** Net earnings remain after partner allocations for Google-sold advertising.

- ✔ **Ad earnings:** These earnings are from AdSense auction and DoubleClick reserved buys.

- ✔ **Transaction earnings:** These include paid content, YouTube rentals, and Fan Funding.

It used to be the case that earnings data and playback information in YouTube Analytics were always estimates because there was an information lag of as many as seven days. That's no longer the case: You'll have your information within 24 hours after the close of the business day. Your transaction history as reported in AdSense will therefore contain accurate information, not mere estimates; just keep in mind that this information is reported *after* all the data has been collected. YouTube Analytics will show information — within reason — as it's occurring. Actual earnings will be visible and available for download within 24 hours on YouTube or AdSense.

As a publisher or creator, you need to calculate one critical metric on your own: revenue per mille, or RPM. *RPM* tells you how much you earn for every 1,000 ad impressions. You calculate RPM this way:

$$RPM = (\text{total estimated earnings} / \text{impressions}) * 1000$$

The time period for total estimated earnings and impressions has to be the same.

Analyzing your ad performance

A YouTube Analytics ad performance report, as mentioned in the previous section, can highlight tons of different metrics regarding your channel's gross revenue and performance by ad type. Accessing that ad performance report is easy:

1. **Log on to your YouTube account.**

2. **On your YouTube page, click your channel's icon and then choose Creator Studio from the menu that appears.**

   Doing so brings up the Creator Studio dashboard.

3. **Click the Analytics heading in the Navigation menu on the left.**

   By default, you should go directly to the Overview submenu.

4. **In the analytics Navigation menu on the left, click the Ad Performance link under the Earnings Reports heading.**

   You see a line chart (see Figure 14-6) that highlights one of the three key ad-performance metrics (playback-based CPM, playback-based gross revenue, and estimated monetized playbacks) and graphs out the monetary performance of each ad type. (To switch between the three metrics, click the appropriate tab at the top of the chart area.)

   You can change the analysis period and specify particular videos that you want to examine. (We tell you more about that in Chapter 11.)

5. **Scroll down to the Details section under the chart to take a closer look at your channel's performance data.**

Figure 14-7 shows how the monetized ad types perform across key metrics. By checking the box next to each type, you can determine what shows up on the graph for a more precise picture of which ads are working best (or worst) against your content.

Figure 14-6: A YouTube Analytics Ad Performance report with metrics and graph.

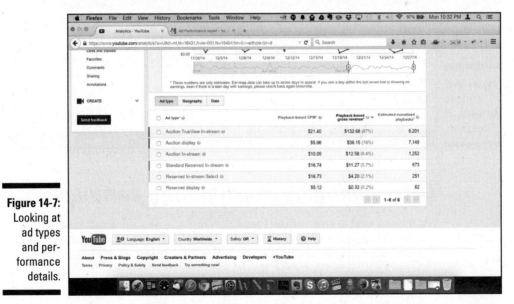

Figure 14-7: Looking at ad types and performance details.

By default, you're on the Ad Types tab in the Details section. You can also see where and when ads work best by clicking the Geography and Date tab.

If you're not seeing performance data for a specific ad type, go back and review the monetization setting you configured. You can find out more about configuring the monetization of existing videos a little later in this chapter.

6. **Look for things that stand out in the charts, such as spikes or valleys in the data to determine what's working well and what may need improvement.**

    Use the Chart Type toolbar — that line of icons running down the left side of the Chart area — to try out different models. Sometimes, simply changing the chart type from a line chart to a bar chart gives you a much better look at ad type performance. (Figure 14-8 shows what we mean.)

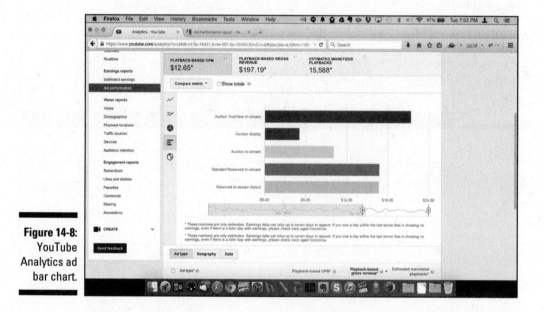

Figure 14-8:
YouTube
Analytics ad
bar chart.

Determining your estimating earnings

It's time to look at the bottom line. The YouTube Analytics estimated earnings report shows your earnings, which some call *net revenue*. It's what remains after Google and its partners take their share. To find out your channel's estimated earnings, do the following:

1. **Log on to your YouTube account.**

2. **On your YouTube page, click your channel's icon and then choose Creator Studio from the menu that appears.**

   Doing so brings up the Creator Studio dashboard.

3. **Click the Analytics heading in the Navigation menu on the left.**

   By default, you should go directly to the Overview submenu.

4. **On the Analytics Navigation menu on the left, click the Estimated Earnings link under the Earnings Reports heading.**

   You see a line chart (see Figure 14-9) that highlights one of three important earnings metrics (total estimated earnings, ad earnings, and transaction earnings) and graphs out the desired metric for the time period. Total estimated earnings is net revenue from all Google-sold ads. Ad earnings reflects net revenue from AdSense and DoubleClick, which is yet another Google property that can put ads against your content. Transaction earnings is paid content and fan funding. (To switch between the three metrics, click the appropriate tab at the top of the chart area.)

   Again, you can change the analysis period and specify particular videos that you want to analyze. (We tell you more about that topic in Chapter 11.)

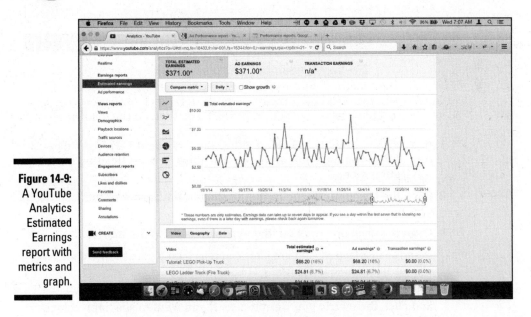

Figure 14-9:
A YouTube Analytics Estimated Earnings report with metrics and graph.

5. Scroll down to the Details section under the chart to take a closer look at your channel's performance data.

Figure 14-10 shows the earnings performance across monetized videos. You can click on an individual video entry to see earnings details by geography and date.

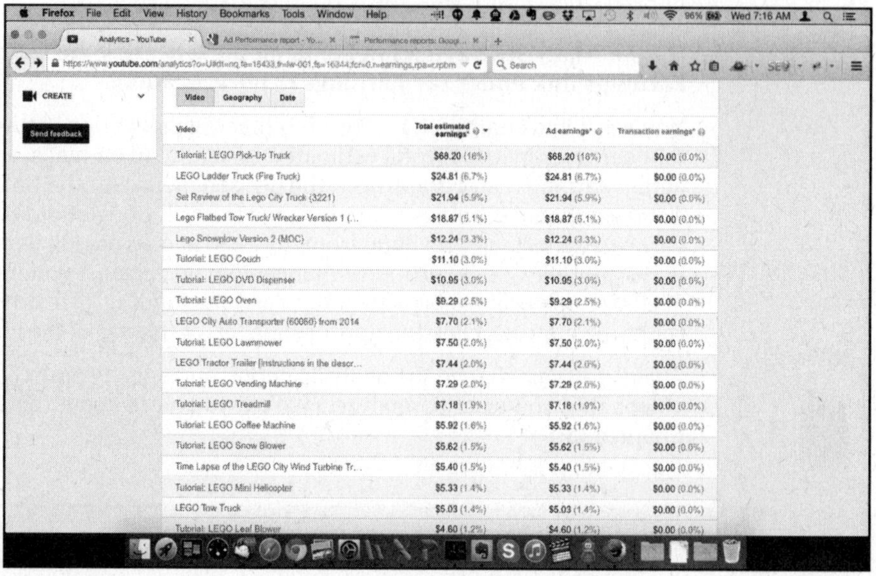

Figure 14-10:
YouTube
Analytics
estimated
earnings
with video
details.

Some important metrics, such as impressions, are not shown by default in estimated earnings or ad performance reports. If this is information you want to see, you need to customize your reports. To do that, do the following:

1. In YouTube Analytics, click on either the Estimated Earnings link or the Ad Performance link under the Earnings Reports heading on the Navigation menu.

2. Click the Compare Metric button in the top left corner of the Chart area.

3. From the drop-down menu that appears, select More Metrics.

Doing so displays a Compare Metric screen listing your metric choices, like the one shown in Figure 14-11.

4. Go to the Estimated Earnings section of the Compare Metric screen and click the metric you want to use. If you want to see impressions (always a good choice), then click the Impressions link.

The metric shows up on the graph and as a column header in the Details section under the graph.

Fan funding

If you're a YouTube partner in good standing and you have an integrated AdSense account, you can set up your channel so that your fans can make voluntary contributions to help finance your uploading of content to your channel. YouTube is quite strict about how you ask for funds, and it can't be used to fund future videos or outside activities. You can enable fan funding through your channel's status and features under Creative Studio. For detailed rules and information around fan funding, visit `https://support.google.com/youtube`.

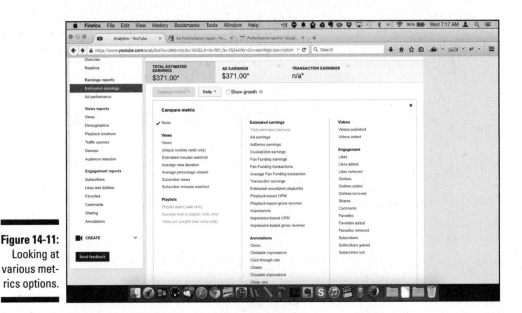

Figure 14-11:
Looking at various metrics options.

Managing AdSense for YouTube

If you have your AdSense account approved, set up, and linked with your YouTube channel, give yourself a pat on the back. You have accomplished much, but is it truly time to go shopping for that new car with your expected pot of gold? Not just yet. Yes, YouTube can be both personally and financially rewarding, but you have to give it time to grow.

AdSense offers its own set of analytics data, distinct from YouTube analytics. You have to understand both to derive the right insights to make effective content and ad placement decisions. It isn't a one-shot deal. You need review all the reports and take action on an ongoing basis. That's the key to maximizing your YouTube channel's monetization potential.

Reconciling AdSense earnings data with YouTube Analytics

Deciding when it's important to look at YouTube Analytics earnings data versus when you need to look at AdSense earnings data is one of the biggest sources of misunderstanding for YouTube channel managers, creators, and publishers. Candidly, Google made the decision rather confusing because there were different earnings data in both. Your YouTube earnings often include income from multiple places. Making matters worse was the time delay in earnings updates in YouTube Analytics over AdSense.

In March 2013, important changes were made to eliminate the confusion. You still need your AdSense account, but your earning information is now reported through YouTube Analytics, which looks at not only YouTube Ads but also display ads bought via Google AdSense. Even better, all the combined data will is available within 24 hours of the end of the business day.

Adding AdSense controls and reporting

Though your earnings information now comes from YouTube, you need to know that AdSense continues to supply the following critical information, which isn't available in YouTube Analytics:

- ✔ **Payments:** You're still paid via AdSense, so keep all your contact, banking, and tax information current.

- ✔ **Ad controls:** As a YouTube channel manager, you have control over which AdSense display ads are presented. (More on that in the next section.)

- ✔ **Ad performance:** You can see analytics for ads served against your content, including number of clicks, click-through rates, cost-per-click, and RPM.

Controlling ads

AdSense gives you a great deal of control over what ads are served (or not) against your YouTube channel and content. To see how controls work, do the following:

1. **Log on to your AdSense account.**

   You can also get there by accessing the Monetization section of Creator Studio and clicking on AdSense Settings.

2. **Click Allow & Block Ads in the top menu bar.**

3. **The Allow & Block Ads screen appears.**

4. **To block specific advertisers, click Advertiser URLs tab.**

   You're taken to a page where you can enter target links to block.

5. **Click Block URLs.**

6. **You can click on the other tabs on the Allow & Block Ads screen for additional ad control.**

   You can allow or restrict ads based on

   - General categories (restrict broad topics for ads)

   - Sensitive categories (block politics, magic, religion, and so on.)

   - Ad networks (manage placements from specific ad networks)

   - Ad serving (control new ad formats)

   - Ad reviews (see ads before blocking)

You can find more details on AdSense ad controls at `https://support.google.com/adsense`.

Measuring ad performance

AdSense also lets you see how well ads are performing against your content. The click-through-rate (CTR) is an important metric that gives you a sense of how well viewers are responding to the ads against your content.

CTRs are measured using percentages and are frequently in the single digits. If your CTRs are very low and trending downward, something is likely wrong, and you may want to modify your ad controls so that something more suitable is presented to your viewers.

The types of ads placed against your channel and content impact your brand. Google does a great deal of work to ensure that only ads that make sense are placed against your content, but ultimately you have control, so use it when necessary.

To check out your ad performance using AdSense:

1. **Log in to your AdSense account.**

   You can also get there by accessing the Monetization section of Creator Studio and clicking on AdSense Settings.

2. **Click Performance Reports in the top menu bar.**

3. **Select a time period filter in the top right by clicking the date and setting up a date range in the drop-down menu.**

4. **Click Apply.**

5. **Click on any of the tabbed items running along the top of the Graph area to add them to the graph.**

Figure 14-12 shows what happens when you select Clicks. In this example, you can see an overall CTR of 4.72 percent for the selected period. Pay attention to the spike around the beginning of July, which indicates some seasonal component for the channel and content.

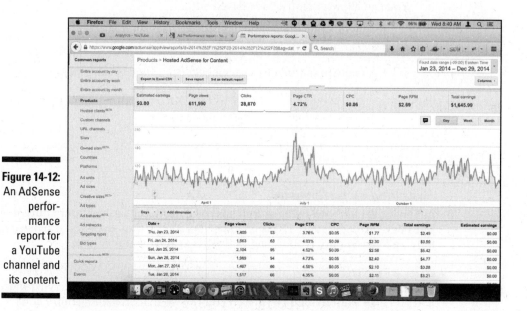

Figure 14-12: An AdSense performance report for a YouTube channel and its content.

Making Monetization Adjustments

A set-it-and-forget-it mentality doesn't fit into an effective YouTube channel-management strategy. If you want your channel to truly succeed, you need to commit to an ongoing series of adjustments to content, engagement, and advertising. How you manage ads served against your channel and content is no different from your other YouTube activities: You have to look at metrics and adjust accordingly.

Looking at key ad-serving metrics

In the earlier section "Analyzing Ad Performance with YouTube Analytics," you can read about using AdSense reports to analyze trends in CTRs and making adjustments to ads served. You should also measure RPM trending — that's the *revenue per mille*, or how much you earn for each 1,000 ad impressions. Figure 14-13 shows a YouTube Analytics Estimated Earnings report with impressions added as a comparison metric. Using that information, you can make use of this handy RPM formula:

$$RPM = (\text{total estimated earnings} / \text{impressions}) * 1000$$

Plugging in the numbers from Figure 14-13 produces this result:

$$RPM = (\$67.57 / 16,622) * 1000$$

If you do the math, you see that it gives you an RPM of $4.06. In other words, you make just over 4 dollars for each 1,000 ad impressions against this video. Is that good? Is that bad? The only way you can find it is by analyzing how this compares with your other videos.

Managing monetizable ad inventory

Keep in mind that you don't have to monetize all the content on your channel all the time. You can pull videos in and out of the monetization mix. To control which videos are monetized, follow these steps:

Figure 14-13:
Estimated earnings used for RPM calculation.

1. **Log on to your YouTube account.**

2. **On your YouTube page, click your channel's icon and then choose Creator Studio from the menu that appears.**

   Doing so brings up the Creator Studio dashboard.

3. **Click the Video Manager heading in the Navigation menu on the left.**

   By default, you should go directly to the Videos submenu.

   You should see a dollar sign ($) icon next to each video if your channel is enabled for monetization.

4. **Click the $ icon for the video whose monetization settings you want to change.**

   You see a monetization page, similar to the one shown in Figure 14-14.

5. **Select (or deselect) the Monetize with Ads check box to enable (or disable) monetization for that video.**

6. **If you're monetizing, pick your settings for ad formats, ad breaks, and product placements.**

Figure 14-14:
Monetizing
your content
and select-
ing ad and
placement
behavior.

Part V
The Part of Tens

 Enjoy an additional Part of Tens article about some YouTube channels worth checking out at www.dummies.com/extras/youtubechannels.

In this part . . .

✔ See how you can improve your YouTube search results.

✔ Explore the intricacies of copyright law.

Chapter 15

Ten Key Steps to Improving YouTube Search Results

In This Chapter

▶ Defining and optimizing video metadata

▶ Improving channel search results

▶ Avoiding misleading metadata

*Y*ouTube is about one thing: Getting people to watch your content. Before they watch it, though, they've got to find it. Simple, right? In theory, yes, but your challenge is to help viewers find your channel and your content. That's what search results are all about: Placing your content in front of the right viewers so that they can watch.

Unfortunately, YouTube doesn't share the secret sauce for getting found, but you can help improve the odds of your videos showing up in YouTube and Google Search as well as in Suggested Videos on the Watch page. To get that search engine to work for you, you need to optimize both your channel and your videos. It may come as a surprise to you, but YouTube cannot have a human watch all your videos to determine what topics they cover. To let YouTube understand what your videos are all about, then, you need to include metadata that describes the content for YouTube to index. (That's part of the optimization process.) In this chapter, we describe ten key steps for improving YouTube search results for your content.

Updating Video Metadata

Metadata are the words you use to describe your video — stuff like the video title, keyword tags, and video description. When uploading new content to your channel, YouTube walks you through the steps to add metadata. If you want to go back and tweak that metadata later, as part of your optimization strategy, do the following:

1. **Log in to your YouTube account.**

2. **On your YouTube page, click the channel icon and then choose Creator Studio from the menu that appears.**

3. **Click the Video Manager section of Creator Studio.**

   By default, it should go directly to the Videos submenu.

4. **Find the video and click the Edit button next to it.**

5. **Modify the thumbnail, title, description, and tags to better reflect your optimization goals.**

6. **When done, click the blue Save Changes button.**

The two search results right under the ads in Figure 15-1 show good metadata — compelling thumbnail images, great titles, and punchy description data. Metadata helps visitors make viewing decisions, and good metadata helps visitors make better viewing decisions.

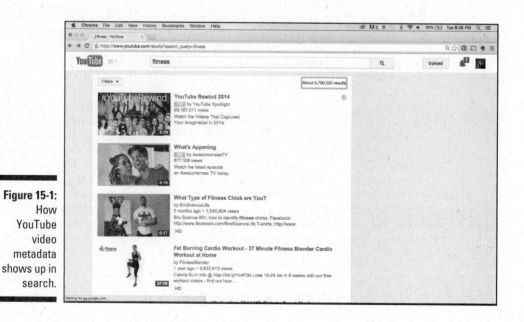

Figure 15-1: How YouTube video metadata shows up in search.

Managing Video Titles

Descriptive video titles are not only helpful for your viewers to identify content they may want to view but also important for YouTube's search engine. These titles are one key indicator used to index your videos. If you do nothing at all, at least be sure to use a keyword-rich title — a title full of descriptive words or adjectives, in other words. You always have the opportunity to rename your videos after you upload them to your channel. A good title tells the viewer what the content includes and who created the video, such as "Easy Stretches for Runners Led by Certified Yoga Instructor."

Good titles are 60 characters or fewer. Any longer and the title gets cut off in search results. Mobile devices often show even fewer characters before the title is cut off. If you have a large mobile audience, put the most important keywords at the beginning of the title so that they are visible to all users.

Understanding Working Titles

Editors — whether they're of the Hollywood variety or the YouTube variety — often use a working title for a film being edited. That's all fine and dandy in the privacy of your studio, but we're here to tell you that you should never upload an asset using a working title. Always upload your videos with a descriptive title — say, 2014 Napa Earth Quake Overview.mp4. Even if the descriptive title doesn't end up as the final title, it's important to have a descriptive title associated with the file. YouTube never loses this original upload title, so it always remains with your video file in YouTube's database. (This is simply another way to ensure that YouTube knows what your video is about, even if you forget to include any other metadata.)

Optimizing Thumbnails for Viewer Session Time

Thumbnails are visual snapshots of your video, similar to a poster for a movie. They have a tremendous impact on a video's view rate, so you should choose a good one. By default, YouTube chooses thumbnails from three optional frames taken at the beginning, middle, and end of your. You can, however, create a custom thumbnail for each video. If you do so, it's best to choose a thumbnail that is illustrative of the content in the video. Thumbnails show up in the following areas:

- ✔ Channel page
- ✔ Watch page
- ✔ Playlists
- ✔ Suggested videos
- ✔ Channel guide
- ✔ Subscriber feed
- ✔ YouTube search
- ✔ Web search
- ✔ Mobile display
- ✔ Mobile search

Although it's vital that the title of your video accurately reflects its content, it's even more important for a viewer's mobile viewing experience that you add a compelling video thumbnail. Users of mobile devices often base the decision of whether to watch your entire video on the appeal of the video thumbnail. The thumbnail should not confuse viewers; it should prepare them for the entire viewing experience. You can even create custom thumbnails for your playlists.

Playlists can show up in YouTube searches along with the video results, and they often lead to longer viewing sessions. The longer a viewer's session time, the better it is for your video and channel ranking. Viewer session time is the primary ranking factor on YouTube's search engine.

Managing Video Descriptions

The video description is a 5,000-character field that YouTube provides you to describe your video. It's a great place to add details about not only your video but also your channel, along with links for other videos, subscriptions, other channels, and web assets. In other words, it's a goldmine for both metadata and user guidance. The viewers who care about your video will read the description, so make it worth their while.

The first two lines of the first paragraph of the description (approximately 100 characters) comprise the only element that shows in YouTube search results; thus, it's the most important part of the description copy. Everything to follow is consumed by YouTube's algorithms, and passionate followers who click the Show More link below the description copy. The first line should describe the content of the video and grab viewers' attention with alluring copy to lead them into the viewing experience. If you don't have a lot of time, focus your creative energy on the first paragraph.

The first line should also include a conversion link. The best practice is to include a short link to save space — you can compress any link using a link shortener like bit.ly, a free link-shortening website. The link might lead to a playlist with the video, the landing page on or off the YouTube site, a product page, or a blog. Figure 15-2 shows a good description.

Figure 15-2: YouTube video description copy.

You can set up default metadata for your new uploads. Always remember to customize the title, tags and descriptions of every video. Your metadata should closely reflect each video's unique content.

Adding Closed Captioning

YouTube and certain other platforms let you upload text files that contain closed-captioning subtitles for your video. You can then reach people who have hearing impairments, and it pays off for your search engine ranking. The captions are used by YouTube search to determine the topic of your video. (See Chapter 10 for information about adding captions.)

You don't have to write captions yourself. Several affordable services can create these caption files for you. 3Play Media (www.3playmedia.com), for example, provides captions for only dollars per minute.

Handling Tags

A *tag* is a keyword that identifies your video's content within YouTube for discovery. These unique, descriptive keywords are limited to 30 characters per keyword. Try to apply at least 15 tags per video, with a maximum of 500 characters per video. Tags are applied through the Video Manager portion of Creator Studio. You can add tags when you upload or modify them later on. Make the tags extremely relevant to your video content, and scatter them throughout the description copy. Start with the most specific tags first, to help viewers find your videos more easily when they're looking for a particular topic.

Start off with specific keyword tags, but if you have space, then add some general purpose ones as well to identify the category of your video, such as beauty or DIY or entertainment.

Refreshing Metadata

Recently published videos typically rank higher in YouTube Search because they have newer content — though we're not saying that all old videos disappear. Older videos that have been watched frequently and are contextual matches for specific searches will rank well. It is important to revisit your older video content regularly and add in any new or trending metadata terms that are relevant.

Refresh your annotations to link to newer, more relevant videos and playlists on your channel. (See Chapter 10 for information about annotation optimizations.)

Understanding Channel SEO

Channels can show up in relevant YouTube searches along with video search results. You'll see a square channel icon and the first few lines of the channel description in the search results. To ensure that your channel appears in the search results, you have to let YouTube know what your channel is about. Your channel has a description field that you can use to communicate precisely what content viewers can find here. (See Chapter 9 for instructions on how to update and edit your channel description.)

A channel also has a field for keywords that you can use just like you use the Tags field for videos. To update your channel keywords:

1. **Log on to your YouTube account.**

2. **On your YouTube page, click the channel icon and then choose Creator Studio from the menu that appears.**

   Doing so brings up the Creator Studio dashboard.

3. **Click the Channel heading in the navigation menu on the left.**

4. **Click the Advanced button.**

   Doing so brings up a page dedicated to the advanced channel settings, as shown in Figure 15-3.

5. **Add relevant, descriptive keywords, separated by commas in the Channel Keyword field.**

6. **When done, click the Save button.**

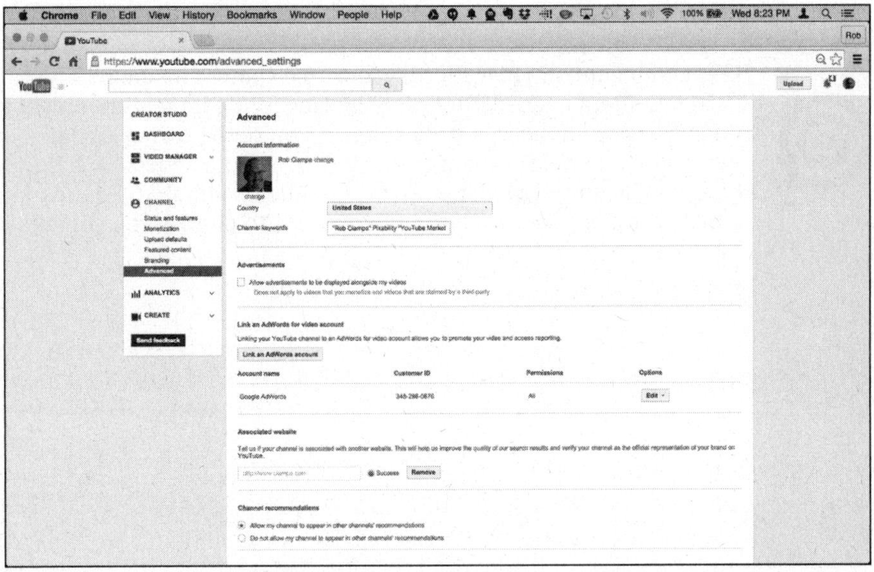

Figure 15-3:
YouTube channel metadata.

Create a keyword-rich channel description. Craft an engaging first few lines of the channel description, because those are the elements that are revealed across YouTube with your channel.

Add specific keywords first, and finish off with broader terms if space allows.

Avoiding Misleading Metadata

Using misleading or deceptive metadata is against YouTube policies. You cannot include metadata that isn't contextually relevant to your video content or that misrepresents the video's content. You cannot add a series of unrelated tags to your description copy to show up for additional search results. If Katy Perry isn't in your video, you shouldn't add her name to the title, tags, or description. Adding repetitive words in the description copy and tags indicates spam to YouTube and is disregarded.

The most important thing is to not try to trick viewers into watching your content with misleading titles, thumbnails, tags, or description copy. These resources are at your disposal to add more contextual value to your video asset — not to fool viewers into clicking. Misleading metadata is a futile exercise. When viewers click on your video and don't find what they were looking for, they will click to go elsewhere quickly. This hurts your watch-time statistics and definitely hurts your search rankings. YouTube excels at detecting spam and misleading metadata, so trying to game the system will never succeed in the long run.

Flag comments on videos if they look like spam. This helps YouTube improve its spam filters even further. Use the Flag for Spam feature only if you're confident that a comment is truly spam. If you're the owner of the content, you can remove or delete spam comments from your videos to help the viewer's engagement experience. Removing comments should be done only to create a better experience for your audience, not to control the conversation.

Chapter 16

Ten Things to Know About Copyright

*J*ohn Locke said "The end of law is not to abolish or restrain, but to preserve and enlarge freedom." In the same spirit, copyright law protects the creator from having her material used by someone who didn't create it without permission. The goal is to protect the creator's freedom to create without having to fear that others will profit unjustly. Create something, and the intellectual property belongs to you by way of copyright. If anyone palms off your intellectual property as their own, the law protects you and provides measures for legal action. And if your copyrighted content should appear in video form on YouTube without your permission, YouTube acts as the law on your behalf.

That's great if someone is trying to take advantage of you, but sometimes it's you who gets put on the hot seat. Thanks to multimedia, people often create things that use other people's work — say, adding a piece of music you didn't write to a video you've made — and they don't realize that they're doing anything wrong. Collaboration is a good thing, but you need to have the proper permission to use any music, artwork, photographs, excerpts, or whatever else was created by an individual other than yourself.

When someone infringes on copyright — whether it's someone doing it to you or you doing it to someone else — there *will* be consequences. YouTube takes the breach seriously and will take down the infringing video. It also penalizes the offender with a strike. And as in baseball, if you take three strikes, you're outta there! YouTube boots you and your channel if it gets to this point.

To ensure that it doesn't happen to you, follow the advice in this chapter.

Remember Who Owns the Copyright

It's fairly simple: If you created the video, the copyright belongs to you; if you upload content created by someone else, the copyright belongs to that person, and you had better have permission to do it.

As soon as the work is created, so is the copyright, and since 1992, there's no longer a renewal process. Copyright lives with the creator — and even lives on for a period after the death of the creator.

Basic stuff, right? But often it's the most basic rules that are not followed. People jaywalk all the time, and people don't honor copyright all the time on YouTube, either. That means YouTube is kept busy because, if another user uploads your content without your permission, or if you do the same, YouTube tracks down the offender, YouTube sends a take-down notification, YouTube blocks the video, and YouTube can potentially sanction the offender with a strike.

Attribution Does Not Absolve a Copyright Violation

Some people steal other people's work and claim it as their own, and that's blatant infringement. But it's no less of an offense when you use content and then add a line saying, "Created by so-and-so." It's still a breach that can earn a strike and a block the video.

If you use someone else's work in your video without that person's permission, it doesn't make it less of an offense just because you give the person credit. You're still in violation because attributing the creator doesn't absolve you if don't get permission. The only exception is fair use, but we will tell you more about that topic later in this chapter.

Here are some elements to watch out for in your videos:

✔ **Music:** If you didn't write it, didn't play it, didn't record it, and you didn't get permission to use it, you can't use it.

✔ **Someone else's pictures:** Pictures found on the Internet are not yours for the taking. Instead, try a practical solution, like purchasing inexpensive rights images on various stock photo sites, such as www.istockphoto.com/, www.shutterstock.com/, and http://us.fotolia.com/.

✔ **TV or movie clip:** Again, you simply can't do it, even if you provide an attribution. Some exceptions are afforded under the principle of fair use, which we describe later in this chapter. And though the studio may not track you down and ask you to remove it, YouTube eventually will, and it will throw you a fastball over the plate.

Know the Consequences

YouTube takes copyright issues seriously — and it blocks or takes down any video that infringes on copyright. Two things can happen, and though they sound similar, they're completely different:

✔ **Takedown notice:** If someone notices content they've created being used without their permission, they can send YouTube a complaint. If it's a breach, YouTube takes down the video.

If you feel compelled to lodge a complaint, just be extra sure that it's your content and that the breach is accurate, because you're initiating a legal process.

✔ **Content ID match:** Content ID is a system YouTube uses to automatically match content that violates copyright against the millions of videos uploaded every month to the site. For Content ID to work properly, copyright owners have to upload so-called reference files — original versions of their work that prove they own the rights. Normally, record labels, movie studios, or TV stations go through this process for all the work they publish, so individual artists don't have to worry about it. Every new video uploaded to YouTube is checked against this huge library of reference files, and if there is a match, YouTube automatically files a copyright claim for the owner of the work.

It is possible to have permission to use music, pictures, or video yet still have a Content ID claim filed against you. Content ID is an automated process, and the idea is that claims are triggered when the robots sense that the musical, photo, or video content belongs to a copyright holder other than yourself. But don't worry: If you had permission to use that content, you can file a dispute challenging the accuracy of the claim.

To find more information about Content ID and the processes behind it, go to www.youtube.com/yt/copyright/.

No matter how a copyright violation may have been discovered, if you breach another content creator's copyright, that creator is in a position to have YouTube take down your content. In the event of a mistake, you can send YouTube a notice saying that an error occurred, but you had better be darn sure about it. If the claim ends up being proven correct, or if you were untruthful in any way, you may find yourself in much bigger trouble, including legal action.

The Profit Motive Is Irrelevant

Some folks will say "Hey, it's all right if I use someone else's content, because I'm not looking to make any money." Say that before the judge and the verdict will still be "Guilty of copyright infringement!"

Whether you intend to make money from the video or you simply want to share your masterpiece with the world, it still doesn't mean that you can violate copyright law. You need to get permission from the copyright holder. Not thinking about profit doesn't absolve you if you used someone else's content without permission.

Rather than take any chances, reach out to the copyright holder, explain your intended use of the content — profit or otherwise — and see what the person says. Sometimes, the copyright holder will give you written permission with no stipulations, whereas at other times she may attach restrictions on the type of use, length of time of use, or content.

Getting Permission for Using Copyrighted Material

Getting permission to use someone else's copyrighted material is often well within the realm of the possible. A nicely written note explaining how you would use the content usually is enough for a rights holder to grant permission. Just remember that it can get dicey, because sometimes permission comes with the caveat that you cannot monetize the overall video. That restriction can hurt big-time if your intention is to quit your day job, but it may end up being a bittersweet solution if you're merely looking to add flavor to your video.

Fair Use Is Complicated

Albert Einstein never failed math, unicorns don't exist, and fair use is anything but easy — or fair — to understand. Debunking the first two of these myths is easy. All right, maybe the first is, but when it comes to fair use, that's a single-horned horse of a different color.

Many misconceptions exist surrounding fair use, among them the notion that you can use anything you want as long as you don't go beyond some arbitrary time constraint. But it's much more complicated. In some editorial situations, you can use copyrighted material without permission, but you must fully understand those situations to avoid future trouble.

If you feel the need to exercise fair use, and the use is for nonprofit and educational purpose, here a few acceptable uses to consider:

- **Criticism:** Reviewing a movie or some form of music makes it perfectly acceptable to use copyrighted material without permission, for example short clips on the work you critique.

- **Parody:** If you're poking fun at something, it's acceptable to use content without first gaining permission.

- **Commentary:** This one depends on how you use the material. If it's used just enough to illustrate your point, it's acceptable. For instance, gamers on YouTube often record themselves playing a new video game and offer funny observations. This is, within limits, fair use.

And now for the misconceptions:

- **You can use 40 seconds of anything:** It's completely untrue. You can't use even *4 seconds* if it doesn't comply with the circumstances in the preceding list.

- **The notion that you can decide fair use for yourself:** Fair use is complicated for many situations, so you may not be sure exactly what you're allowed to do. The thing is, if you stretch the limits of fair use too far, you can be sanctioned by YouTube. That's why a copyright attorney should decide any serious question over fair use.

Don't Let Copyright Issues on YouTube Lead to a Strikeout

Three strikes and you're out is a common understanding when playing baseball. But in baseball, you get another chance after another eight batters have had their try. YouTube doesn't share this benevolence, so if they give you strikes — especially for copyright issues — that means a lifetime ban. That's something you don't want on your record; worse yet, once that happens to you, you won't be able to recover any of your videos. So you want to avoid getting strikes at all costs.

There are two types of YouTube strikes:

- **Community Guideline Strikes:** These can result from a variety of reasons, ranging from uploading objectionable content to having a misleading thumbnail or caption.

- **Copyright Strike:** If some part of your video includes content from another creator and that creator did not grant you permission, you can get a strike. You can also get a ContentID claim lodged against you that can turn into a strike. You can appeal it in both cases or take down the video to avoid a possible strike.

Other things you should know:

- **Mandatory copyright school must be completed:** With every strike, YouTube requires that you take an online course and take a little quiz to be sure you're up to speed on copyright regulations.

- **Strikes come down, eventually:** As long as you haven't struck out, some strikes disappear after a while — usually six months. If you get another strike, the clock starts over.

- **Your fate usually lies with the copyright holder:** That person can decide whether the video you uploaded should be removed, flagged in certain regions, or even monetized. Yes, that's right: Even though the video may contain only a small portion of the person's material, he's entitled to all monetization proceeds. He can even put ads on your video, if you haven't added monetization.

Wipe the Slate Clean

When it comes to removing strikes from your account, these two contradictory idioms come to mind:

- The squeaky wheel gets the grease.

- Don't open a can of worms.

If you get a copyright strike from YouTube and you're positive that you're in the right, go ahead and appeal the strike. By not staying quiet, you can fulfill the prophecy of the first idiom by having that strike removed.

Yet there's that second idiom. If you're not sure whether you can win, maybe it's better to wait it out until the strike expires. You see, after you appeal the strike, your personal information goes to the copyright holder and that person can possibly sue you for copyright infringement. If the situation gets to this level, you still can work out an agreement directly with the copyright holder and see whether he will file an appeal with YouTube on your behalf if you both agree that you were within your rights to use the copyrighted material. It's worth a shot.

As for strikes related to the community guidelines, feel free to appeal those, because they're only between you and YouTube.

YouTube's Robots Are Good at Finding Copyright Infringements

Whether intentional or inadvertent, sometimes the content of other creators gets used in a YouTube video. Sometimes the breach is noticed, and at other times it goes undetected by the original creator. But as YouTube continues to refine its copyright detection system, it will find it more quickly than ever.

Part of those refinements to YouTube's copyright detection system include sophisticated algorithms that scan every uploaded video and compare it to similar uploaded content, looking for matches with music, video, or pictures. It seems music gets detected the most. Even if it's background music, you may get sanctioned. Usually, YouTube blocks the video, and you must submit a dispute form.

Copyright Is Not Forever, But It's Likely Forever Enough for YouTube

Copyright lasts for 75 years past the death of the author; after that point, the copyrighted content enters the public domain. When that happens, the content is no longer protected by intellectual property laws, and anyone can use it without permission. Of course, for many people on YouTube, that content isn't available to use without permission until we near the next century. Of course, if the creator (or heirs) files a copyright extension, she can hold on to the rights — then the video of your dog dressed as a spider can stay in the family for as long as possible.

Index

About the Authors

John Carucci has written about technology for more than 20 years. He has written several books on the subject, including *GoPro Cameras For Dummies*, *Webinars For Dummies,* and *Digital SLR Video and Filmmaking For Dummies*. John has also published more than 100 articles on photography, video, and technology. Currently, John works as an entertainment news producer for Associated Press Television, where he covers music and theater.

Rob Ciampa is chief marketing officer at Pixability, an ad buying and video marketing platform for YouTube. Rob works with brands, agencies, media companies, celebrities, and entertainment artists on YouTube strategy, marketing, advertising, and monetization. Rob is YouTube-certified, and is a frequent speaker and writer on digital video strategy for brands and content producers. He is co-author of Pixability's "Top 100 Global Brands On YouTube" study, one of the most comprehensive and data-intensive studies of YouTube. Prior to joining Pixability, Rob served in strategic marketing roles at both innovative startups and several Fortune 500 companies. Rob holds a BS and MS in computer science and engineering from the University of Massachusetts, and an MBA from Boston University, all with honors. He has multiple patents in data transmission, analytics, and visualization. Rob shares his views on marketing and other subjects at `http://www.ciampa.com`.

Theresa Moore is VP of Professional Services at Pixability, an ad buying and video marketing platform for YouTube. A seasoned video marketing strategist who received one of the first YouTube certifications available, Theresa leads the management of Pixability's wide portfolio of global brand and agency accounts. She has spent more than six years expanding Pixability's customer base and provides strategic consulting for customers in New York, Chicago, San Francisco, Boston, and the UK. Theresa holds a BA in cinematic arts and technology from California State University - Monterey Bay.

Rob, Theresa, and their teams manage the ever-engaging Pixability corporate YouTube channel: `http://youtube.com/pixability`.

Dedication

Rob Ciampa: I wish to dedicate this book to my wife, Laura, who tastefully balances being both an admiring fan and an impartial critic. I also dedicate this book to my sons Matt and Zach, who turned our attic into a YouTube studio, built a popular channel, and complained about cutting the grass because they were too occupied making videos instead.

Theresa Moore: This book is dedicated to my mother, Hope, for always pushing me to be the most creative version of myself and for showing me that hard work and dedication to one's passions is the only way to move forward in life.

Authors' Acknowledgments

Rob Ciampa and Theresa Moore: Keeping up with the YouTube world is not so different from minding a two-year-old in a toy store; it's fast moving and often feels as if everything is out of control. Fortunately, we had many helping hands to keep us up to date and help deliver the book you're now holding in your hands (or viewing on your tablet). We would like to thank the team at Wiley who came to us with a great idea and a system to make it so, including Steven Hayes, Paul Levesque, and Becky Whitney. A big thank you also goes out to collaborators Adam Wescott, John Carucci, and Stan Muller.

Sincere thanks to Andreas Goeldi, CTO of Pixability, for being the most efficient man on Earth, and Bettina Hein, founder and CEO of Pixability, for putting together a truly great ad tech company. We'd like to thank our professional services and marketing teams at Pixability who helped review our manuscript while simultaneously keeping our YouTube customers happy and the world informed about the virtues of video marketing. A big thank you to Michael Benson, Laura Ciampa, Bill Darmon, Alexandra English, Ellen Flaherty, Matt Jackson, Shaman Kothari, Jessica McCarthy, Merrily McGugan, Jackie Swansburg Paulino, Sam Sacks, Emily Waskevich, and Ryan Whitten.

A special thank you goes to Jeff Rozic of YouTube for helping us navigate the ever-changing YouTube user interface.

Publisher's Acknowledgments

Acquisitions Editor: Steve Hayes

Senior Project Editor: Paul Levesque

Copy Editor: Becky Whitney

Technical Editor: Curt Simmons

Editorial Assistant: Claire Brock

Sr. Editorial Assistant: Cherie Case

Project Coordinator: Kumar Chellapa

Cover Image: ©iStock.com/scyther5

Apple & Mac

iPad For Dummies,
6th Edition
978-1-118-72306-7

iPhone For Dummies,
7th Edition
978-1-118-69083-3

Macs All-in-One
For Dummies, 4th Edition
978-1-118-82210-4

OS X Mavericks
For Dummies
978-1-118-69188-5

Blogging & Social Media

Facebook For Dummies,
5th Edition
978-1-118-63312-0

Social Media Engagement
For Dummies
978-1-118-53019-1

WordPress For Dummies,
6th Edition
978-1-118-79161-5

Business

Stock Investing
For Dummies, 4th Edition
978-1-118-37678-2

Investing For Dummies,
6th Edition
978-0-470-90545-6

Personal Finance
For Dummies, 7th Edition
978-1-118-11785-9

QuickBooks 2014
For Dummies
978-1-118-72005-9

Small Business Marketing
Kit For Dummies,
3rd Edition
978-1-118-31183-7

Careers

Job Interviews
For Dummies, 4th Edition
978-1-118-11290-8

Job Searching with Social
Media For Dummies,
2nd Edition
978-1-118-67856-5

Personal Branding
For Dummies
978-1-118-11792-7

Resumes For Dummies,
6th Edition
978-0-470-87361-8

Starting an Etsy Business
For Dummies, 2nd Edition
978-1-118-59024-9

Diet & Nutrition

Belly Fat Diet For Dummies
978-1-118-34585-6

Mediterranean Diet
For Dummies
978-1-118-71525-3

Nutrition For Dummies,
5th Edition
978-0-470-93231-5

Digital Photography

Digital SLR Photography
All-in-One For Dummies,
2nd Edition
978-1-118-59082-9

Digital SLR Video &
Filmmaking For Dummies
978-1-118-36598-4

Photoshop Elements 12
For Dummies
978-1-118-72714-0

Gardening

Herb Gardening
For Dummies, 2nd Edition
978-0-470-61778-6

Gardening with Free-Range
Chickens For Dummies
978-1-118-54754-0

Health

Boosting Your Immunity
For Dummies
978-1-118-40200-9

Diabetes For Dummies,
4th Edition
978-1-118-29447-5

Living Paleo For Dummies
978-1-118-29405-5

Big Data

Big Data For Dummies
978-1-118-50422-2

Data Visualization
For Dummies
978-1-118-50289-1

Hadoop For Dummies
978-1-118-60755-8

Language &
Foreign Language

500 Spanish Verbs
For Dummies
978-1-118-02382-2

English Grammar
For Dummies, 2nd Edition
978-0-470-54664-2

French All-in-One
For Dummies
978-1-118-22815-9

German Essentials
For Dummies
978-1-118-18422-6

Italian For Dummies,
2nd Edition
978-1-118-00465-4

Available in print and e-book formats.

Available wherever books are sold. **For more information or to order direct visit www.dummies.com**

Math & Science

Algebra I For Dummies,
2nd Edition
978-0-470-55964-2

Anatomy and Physiology
For Dummies, 2nd Edition
978-0-470-92326-9

Astronomy For Dummies,
3rd Edition
978-1-118-37697-3

Biology For Dummies,
2nd Edition
978-0-470-59875-7

Chemistry For Dummies,
2nd Edition
978-1-118-00730-3

1001 Algebra II Practice
Problems For Dummies
978-1-118-44662-1

Microsoft Office

Excel 2013 For Dummies
978-1-118-51012-4

Office 2013 All-in-One
For Dummies
978-1-118-51636-2

PowerPoint 2013
For Dummies
978-1-118-50253-2

Word 2013 For Dummies
978-1-118-49123-2

Music

Blues Harmonica
For Dummies
978-1-118-25269-7

Guitar For Dummies,
3rd Edition
978-1-118-11554-1

iPod & iTunes
For Dummies, 10th Edition
978-1-118-50864-0

Programming

Beginning Programming
with C For Dummies
978-1-118-73763-7

Excel VBA Programming
For Dummies, 3rd Edition
978-1-118-49037-2

Java For Dummies,
6th Edition
978-1-118-40780-6

Religion & Inspiration

The Bible For Dummies
978-0-7645-5296-0

Buddhism For Dummies,
2nd Edition
978-1-118-02379-2

Catholicism For Dummies,
2nd Edition
978-1-118-07778-8

Self-Help & Relationships

Beating Sugar Addiction
For Dummies
978-1-118-54645-1

Meditation For Dummies,
3rd Edition
978-1-118-29144-3

Seniors

Laptops For Seniors
For Dummies, 3rd Edition
978-1-118-71105-7

Computers For Seniors
For Dummies, 3rd Edition
978-1-118-11553-4

iPad For Seniors
For Dummies, 6th Edition
978-1-118-72826-0

Social Security
For Dummies
978-1-118-20573-0

Smartphones & Tablets

Android Phones
For Dummies, 2nd Edition
978-1-118-72030-1

Nexus Tablets
For Dummies
978-1-118-77243-0

Samsung Galaxy S 4
For Dummies
978-1-118-64222-1

Samsung Galaxy Tabs
For Dummies
978-1-118-77294-2

Test Prep

ACT For Dummies,
5th Edition
978-1-118-01259-8

ASVAB For Dummies,
3rd Edition
978-0-470-63760-9

GRE For Dummies,
7th Edition
978-0-470-88921-3

Officer Candidate Tests
For Dummies
978-0-470-59876-4

Physician's Assistant Exam
For Dummies
978-1-118-11556-5

Series 7 Exam For Dummies
978-0-470-09932-2

Windows 8

Windows 8.1 All-in-One
For Dummies
978-1-118-82087-2

Windows 8.1 For Dummies
978-1-118-82121-3

Windows 8.1 For Dummies,
Book + DVD Bundle
978-1-118-82107-7

Available in print and e-book formats.

Available wherever books are sold. **For more information or to order direct visit www.dummies.com**

Take Dummies with you everywhere you go!

Whether you are excited about e-books, want more from the web, must have your mobile apps, or are swept up in social media, Dummies makes everything easier.

Leverage the Power

For Dummies is the global leader in the reference category and one of the most trusted and highly regarded brands in the world. No longer just focused on books, customers now have access to the For Dummies content they need in the format they want. Let us help you develop a solution that will fit your brand and help you connect with your customers.

Advertising & Sponsorships

Connect with an engaged audience on a powerful multimedia site, and position your message alongside expert how-to content.

Targeted ads • Video • Email marketing • Microsites • Sweepstakes sponsorship

21 Million Monthly Page Views & 13 Million Unique Visitors